One of the
Family

WENDY W. FAIREY

One of the Family

W · W · NORTON & COMPANY

NEW YORK · LONDON

Printed in the United States of America.

FIRST EDITION

The text of this book is composed in Galliard with the display set in Snell Roundhand and Centaur. Composition and manufacturing by The Haddon Craftsmen, Inc. Book design by Marjorie J. Flock.

Library of Congress Cataloging-in-Publication Data

Fairey, Wendy W.
One of the family
  Wendy W. Fairey.
    p. cm.
    Includes index.
    1. Fairey, Wendy W.—Family.   2. Graham, Sheilah—Family.
  3. Ayer, A. J. (Alfred Jules), 1910–   —Family.   4. English
teachers—United States—Biography. 5. Mothers and daughters—
United States—Biography. 6. Fathers and daughters—Biography.
I. Title.
PE64.F64A3   1992
070.4′4979143′092—dc20
[B]   91–27630

ISBN 0-393-03093-8

W.W. Norton & Company, Inc., 500 Fifth Avenue, New York, N.Y. 10110
W.W. Norton & Company Ltd., 10 Coptic Street, London WC1A 1PU

1 2 3 4 5 6 7 8 9 0

FOR EMILY AND SEAN

CONTENTS

ACKNOWLEDGMENTS

I BEGIN BY THANKING Dee Wells, Lady Ayer, who acted on her impulse to tell me the long-concealed secret of my paternity. This deed has had an incalculable influence on my life, and my memoir owes its existence to her intervention.

Dee was one of a small group of people—the others being Robert Westbrook, Donald Fairey, and Gully Wells—who knew both my parents and helped me to think about our family history. Thanks, too, to Gully's husband, Peter Foges, for his insights about Freddie and to my cousin, Ruby Rossiter, for sharing her memories of my mother and her knowledge of the Shiel family.

I am indebted to a number of old family friends who so kindly took the time to talk with me about my mother. Among them are Jean Dalrymple, Ted Berkman, Gerold Frank, Paul and Spoli Mills, Alan and Helen Hooker, Mike and Sis Kaplan, David Shipman and Felix Brenner, and Anna Bayer. Thanks to Ted Honderick for meeting with me to discuss Freddie and to Ann Westbrook Hochberg for clarifying points concerning Trevor.

I am grateful to the colleagues and friends who gave so generously of their time in reading and commenting on drafts of my manuscript. Two friends, Bonnie Anderson and Anna Lawson, read and reviewed with me every new chapter, consistently challenged my language and formulations, and proved invaluably supportive from the start to finish of my project. Other readers whose responses and suggestions were very helpful include Harriet Adams, Helene Aguilar, Lionel Bier, Rachel Brownstein, Anna Cancogni, Elizabeth Dalton, Madeleine Grumet, Rita Kashner, Patricia Mainardi, Roni Natov, Sally Steinberg, and William Wendroff.

I thank the City University of New York Research Foundation, which awarded me a grant to cover my research expenses, and Mr. Munk, archivist of the Mocatta Library, University College, London, for making available to me records of the Norwood orphanage. A special thanks goes to my friend and agent, Robert Lescher—we first met when I was thirteen and he the young editor assigned to work with my mother on *Beloved Infidel*—whose belief in my project has been a constant encouragement. I also am indebted to Betty Prashker, who encouraged me to start writing, and to my astute and helpful editor, Edwin Barber, who showed such unerring good judgment in noting the extraneous word or paragraph.

Above all, I am grateful to my parents for leading such vivid lives and, in a sense, giving me my story. I am sad, writing these acknowledgments, that they are not alive. I especially wish that I could thank my mother, who made me feel, from a very early age, part of a family of storytellers and later encouraged me as a writer. With her customary disregard for fainthearted excuses, she told me I ought to get on with writing a book. In my mind this is the book that she kept asking for. I hope I do not fool myself in imagining that she would have liked it.

And I am grateful to my children, Emily and Sean Fairey. They never met Freddie, but certainly they knew my mother.

Their understanding of her—and of me—their insights about this story, their astuteness as readers of my manuscript, and their love and support helped to give me the courage and belief in continuities that I needed to write this book.

One of the Family

One

"EASEFUL DEATH"

IT WAS THE SUGGESTION of my mother's old friend and admirer, Savington Crampton, that someone should read Swinburne at the memorial service. "The Garden of Proserpine," he said, phoning from Florida, where he and my mother had both ended up, Savy in St. Petersburg on the bay and my mother in Palm Beach in an oceanside condominium, the last of her many homes. Florida, she liked to tell me, was "God's waiting room." Her zestful humor about such matters was one of the most attractive things about her. At least until the heart attack, aging could be put in its place by a *bon mot*. "I was a has-been, but now I'm a relic," she declared at eighty, arthritic but touring the country to publicize her latest book, *Hollywood Revisited*. The final illness, though, could not be vanquished with a quip. It offered her no role she cared to play. It was completely discordant with the self that she had renamed Sheilah Graham and believed could do almost anything.

"Sheilah was ready to die," said Savy. "She didn't want to go on in that diminished condition." He told me how the lines in

the Swinburne poem were haunting her. She had recited them
to him over the telephone.

> I am tired of tears and laughter,
> > And men that laugh and weep;
> Of what may come hereafter
> > For men that sow and reap:
> I am weary of days and hours,
> Blown buds of barren flowers,
> Desires and dreams and powers
> > And everything but sleep.

I toyed with the idea of reading the Swinburne, but somehow the poem seemed wrong. Too world-weary. Too rejecting
of the assembled living. Too sensuous as well. I envisioned
myself intoning that languorous death wish to those old, old
people, the surviving friends. It seemed intrusive into the re-
gion of their own closeness to death, intrusive too into the
intimacy between death and my mother, that private, conspiratorial, almost sexual negotiation that excluded all survivors. Though I had rejected another old friend's more life-
affirming suggestion that the memorial be a lunch at "21" or
the Russian Tea Room, those show-business haunts where my
mother always had her special table right up front by the door,
still, I would not read Swinburne. Let Savington Crampton
come and read it himself or send it to be read as his personal
statement. I remembered our family story about him, the man
my mother had broken a brief engagement to in the 1930s
because, flying from the East to see her, he had arrived in California wearing a red cummerbund.

"How could I marry a man who wore a red cummerbund?"
she confided to us children. We laughed and agreed. I had
always, however, felt embarrassed to know about Savington
Crampton's red cummerbund. After my mother's death, he
asked for a picture of her, explaining that he had torn all his old

ones up in anger. Ah, the red cummerbund, I thought, glimpsing the pain of his side of the story.

"What era would you like it from?" I asked him. "There are lots of pictures. Why don't I send you two?"

He chose two eras—the thirties and the early fifties. I rummaged through my supply and sent off two eight-by-ten glossies—both very glamorous—to Florida. Savy could not attend the memorial because he was on the mend from his own hip-replacement operation, which had occurred a few months after my mother's at a point when she was already living out her final heart-damaged months, reciting Swinburne, playing Scrabble with her round-the-clock nurses, and waiting for death. She presented her mood as one of withdrawal and longing for oblivion. "I'm getting dim, Wendy. Very dim. I'm ready to sleep." I didn't quite believe her, but I sensed the underlying misery and anger and was frightened.

After years of coping with the pain and constriction of arthritis and months of vacillation about whether, as she put it, to "do the hip," my mother had entered the New York Hospital for Special Surgery on April 26, 1988, to undergo her second hip-replacement operation. The first operation, seven years earlier, replacing the left hip with a plastic part, had been an unqualified success. Now the right hip had deteriorated, but my mother had long held back from the surgery. She feared the vulnerability of her more advanced age; she feared the helplessness, albeit temporary if all went well, that the operation would impose; and I think she feared most of all not so much dying but the possibility of not properly recovering.

I myself had a terrible sense of dread. The operation seemed momentous, the more so because of all the advance fuss. My mother had at one point even checked into the hospital, the surgery scheduled for the next day, and then checked out again because she didn't like the disclaimer forms she was asked to sign and the way the orderlies treated her. Now, though ane-

mic and all in all at eighty-three not very well, she felt there was
no turning back. She could not cancel yet another date given
her by the busy specialist.

For me the night of April 26 was one of those almost vision-
ary moments—of which I had several before she died—when,
half discounting what I felt as anxious superstition, I nonetheless "knew" that something was about to happen. I felt very tied
to her gallant frail body, as linked with mine as the bodies of my
children, and I brooded on the notion of being cut to the
bone. Forgetting other connections to friends, children, other
loved ones, I seemed alone in the world with my mother and
about to lose her. To counter the pain of this loss—and to
mark it, I think, as well—I got out the photo albums of my
own childhood and sat with them open on my lap, grieving and
remembering. I wanted to reclaim the past, to fix in my mind
the person my mother had been, to reaffirm the intertwining of
our histories. Looking at the pictures—me, my mother, my
brother, our houses, our pets, our nursemaids—I mourned the
passing of my beautiful mother, the days, long gone really, of
her full energy and sway when it seemed that she could always
make things happen and always make them fun. I did not forget
that she had also been my adversary, an enemy, in her own
great childlike need, to my autonomy and fulfillment apart
from her. But the "bad mother" receded. I wanted to remember her beauty and our connection and to set the myth of our
golden past against the dreadful emptiness of a future from
which she would be missing.

On the afternoon of April 27, I contacted the hospital and
was told that Mrs. Westbrook, as my mother called herself, was
in satisfactory condition after surgery. Later I got to speak to a
nurse who reported that my mother had been nauseated and
disoriented—I remarked the professional emphasis on precision in the words of explanation—but that now she was sleeping. When I visited the next day, sitting quietly for a couple of
hours in a corner of her room, she continued to be plagued by

nausea and seemed miserable. The hip replacement, however, was deemed a success, and perhaps it should be seen as a consolation that her hip was not a bother in those final debilitated six months.

On the morning of April 29, Dr. Perrone, my mother's internist, phoned me at my home in Brooklyn to say that she had suffered a massive heart attack and that I should get to the hospital as soon as possible. I asked whether I should contact my brother, Robert, to come from California, and the doctor thought this advisable. When I reached the hospital, he met me to explain the progressively draconian measures that he would take to try to steady the heartbeat and to keep my mother alive. An electric shock had already been administered, and my mother, still conscious, was complaining of a band of hot iron around her chest. He spoke of medications to thin the blood and of a balloon to be inserted into the aorta that might cause hemorrhaging and so ruin the hip. Fortunately, this last wasn't necessary. By the time Robert arrived that evening after a cross-country flight that he described as the time of his own first realization that our mother really could die—even more beguiled by the myths, I think, than I, he had always considered her immortal—her heartbeat had steadied, more or less on its own, and she was in critical but stable condition.

We visited her the next day in the intensive care unit of New York Hospital, to which she had been moved, and she was very angry. Monitored and heavily medicated, she lay in her hospital bed, her upper body raised at a slight angle. The leg that had been operated on—still so very sore but hardly a concern when so much else had happened—was propped on a pillow. An oxygen tube was attached to her nose, an IV tube to her right arm.

"Hello, Rob," she said to my brother. "So you've come to see your poor old mother. They nearly killed me."

She had some trouble talking, but she could still give her sweet but also maddeningly all-knowing smile—certainly it implied knowing better than the inept fools in the hospital. Robert, who had rushed east on the premise that she was dying and then had had to readjust, said it was worth the price of his $1,000 nondiscounted ticket just to see the look of gratitude and pleasure on her face when she saw him enter her room and realized that he had come to see her. I registered my twinge of disappointment that *my* being there and caring seemed less noteworthy—after all, she had seen me just the day before; also she protected herself against expecting too much from me by her theory that I had little patience with illness. I don't think she was correct in this assessment. But we had no consistent openness between us, and it was often hard for me to express towards her the warmth I knew she hoped for. At the time of the first hip operation, she had wept in her anger and frustration to have "such a cold daughter," and I had sat there desperate and helpless and unmovable. Struggling against recurrence of this familiar paralysis, I asked how she was feeling.

"Look at my poor arm," she said, extending to us the arm with the IV, which was covered with scabs and bruises. "Those idiots. They don't know anything. If I ever get out of here, I'm going to write a story."

She paused and looked at us hard, about to deliver the punch line. "Can you guess what it will be called?"

We couldn't.

"Actually," she said, "I'm going to write two stories. One will be 'Hip, Hip, *Not* Hurray.' Isn't that good? And the other—can you guess?"

"No," we said.

"The other will be called . . ."—dramatic pause—"the other will be called 'Obituary'!" She pronounced this with the emphasis both of anger and of pleasure in her own wit. Her point was that the hospital with its maladroit doctors and nurses was out to kill her. Six months later, when her remarkable obituary appeared in the *New York Times,* I remembered this moment and the charm of her title took on a fresh poignancy.

We talked with her a bit more. Her greatest discomfort, she complained, involved her excretory functions, about which she had always been—to my more self-conscious taste—embarrassingly frank. She was having trouble urinating, and she made a reference—I wondered if I had caught it correctly, since she was generally very circumspect about sex—to being narrow "down there" and this being one reason for her great success with men. Robert heard it too, and, as we discussed afterwards, had been similarly taken aback.

It had been a long time, I realized, since Robert, my mother, and I had been together. I was aware, gathered there in the intensive care unit, that we reconstituted the family nucleus. We had dispersed. Robert lived in California, composing the mystery novels that were enabling him, after years of struggle, to make a living as a writer, and he had seen very little of my mother in the preceding twenty years. I in the same period had seen little of him, and for all my contact with my mother, I had been careful to keep my emotional distance. Robert and I had other families, families now of our own. But all this gave way to the bond of our peculiar past. Here, I thought, is the essential unit. We are the people who understand one another best in the world.

My mother, quoting Napoleon, used to like to say, *"Je suis mon ancêtre."* She had created herself—her history, her success—and was her only point of reference. My case was different. As far as ancestors go, she was mine. She was someone to resist, but I also admired her greatly. My overwhelming desire when she died (and I could allow my admiration less impeded sway) was to have people know who this mother was, to represent her adequately to the world. Through my agency now, I would extend the drama—not let it yet be over—of her lifelong act of self-generation. It was in this context that I found myself considering and rejecting Swinburne as a poet to read at her memorial, more willing to serve as the handmaiden of her legend than I had ever been while she was alive.

Savington Crampton's suggestion of the Swinburne served to remind me of my mother's great love of poetry. I had always suspected, perhaps uncharitably, that this was less pleasure in the poetry itself than in the fact that *she* was so attuned to it, so unable to forget the words, so appreciative of their sonority. Without the slightest encouragement—which certainly I never gave—she would launch into the jingoistic poems that she had learned during World War I in her orphanage in the East End of London, charmingly self-mocking, but nonetheless proud of her memory, proud of her love of language, proud of having been such a good pupil. She and F. Scott Fitzgerald were devoted to poetry in his famous College of One, in which she was the star and only pupil and from which she would have graduated but for his death. I knew the story so well: how he was reading the *Princeton Alumni Magazine,* stood up, clutched the mantel, then dropped dead of a fatal heart attack in the living room of her Hollywood apartment. It was December 21, 1940, four days before Christmas. The complete outfit of clothes that she had bought him arrived in a long box laid out like a corpse.

My mother's caution to me had been never to have an affair with a married man since, if the man dies, the family reclaims the body and you have no place in the story. People often asked if Scott Fitzgerald was my father, and I would have to explain that the dates made this impossible—I was not born until September 1942. My mother always said that she had married Trevor Westbrook, head of wartime aviation production for England and a self-made man who took pride in his claim never to have read a book, because she could not face the anniversary of F. Scott Fitzgerald's death. Two children were conceived before their union dissolved, with greater logic than it seemed to me had formed it, and Robert and I grew up, our mother's charge, an ocean away from our English father. Trevor had died in 1978.

If there was to be poetry at the memorial, the best selection might be Keats's "Ode to a Nightingale." The line "Already with thee! tender is the night" brings Fitzgerald to mind. And indeed, he had recorded the poem for my mother on an old 78 -rpm record that I had listened to before she gave all her Fitzgerald books and memorabilia to Princeton. Also better than Swinburne is that more vibrant expression of the death wish in the poet's confession to being "half in love with easeful death." My mother loved this line. She would repeat the syllables, drawing out the sound of "ease" in "easeful death." She also took pleasure in a rather pointed emendation directed to me, her daughter, of another line from "Ode to a Nightingale," "No hungry generations tread thee down." She would say, "No hungry generations tread *me* down." Challenge and defiance. Our struggle to the end.

At first when my mother died, it seemed extraordinary to me that I had survived her, and I thought about a strange conversation that had occurred six days before her death. The months since the heart attack had been dreary. Over a month in the hospital in New York was followed by removal to Florida. Here she could sit on her balcony and look at the ocean, but walking meant using two canes, and then as she grew weaker came confinement to a wheelchair. There had been several hospitalizations, several near-dyings, and now we were come to what really seemed the final crisis. Her plasma count was down. The doctor wanted to rehospitalize her. But she refused. She phoned me from Florida, urgent and anxious.

"Wendy, do you know a good mortuary in Palm Beach? I've got to find one."

I was taken aback but refrained from any expression of incredulity that I—a person in the prime of life and living, moreover, in New York—would be expected to have this information.

"Gee, Mom, I don't," I carefully replied. "Would you like me to look into it? Or I'm sure you could find out the name of one from your doctors or your nurses."

"It's got to be the best," she insisted.

"I'm sure you can find the best," I said. "You always do."
Suddenly, though, the subject had shifted.

"I couldn't bear it," she said, "if you were to die before I
did. I just couldn't bear it."

I couldn't see how she had jumped to this thought. Wasn't
it she who was dying? I tried to stay matter-of-fact and to answer her concern. Perhaps she was just consoling herself that
she would not have to live in a world without me.

"Well, Mom, I can understand that. But under the circumstances I don't think you have too much to worry about. Of
course, one never knows what will happen."

We returned to the subject of the mortuary and to plans for
her death.

"You'll come right away, Wendy, won't you? Right away,"
she said with great emotion.

"Yes, Mom," I reassured her. And then, responding to
what I sensed as the underlying issue: "Don't worry. I'll know
where you are. I won't lose you."

My mother died on November 17, 1988, two months after
her eighty-fourth birthday. She woke up unable to breathe, was
rushed to the hospital, and—this last crisis mercifully brief—
died "without discomfort" at 8:17 P.M. This is what Dr. Moskowitz, the Florida heart doctor, explained to me in his brief call.
I was on another line, talking with my daughter, Emily, who
had phoned from college, and the doctor's news intruded on
"call waiting." "This is Dr. Moskowitz. Your mother died at
eight-seventeen this evening. She was heavily sedated and did
not feel any pain."

"Thank you for telling me," I said, but in my mind was that
anxiety that one feels about getting back to the other caller. I
asked no questions and pushed the button to be back with
Emily. Later this seemed a strange failure of curiosity at a moment that deserved more attention. But what was the point of
knowing more?

"My mommy's dead, my mommy's dead." I felt so bereft and kept wailing the same phrase into the phone. Sean, my sixteen-year-old son, came from his room into mine and lay down next to me on my bed. I had the whimsical notion that my two children were around me like earmuffs, one at the end of the phone and the other, his face next to mine, on my bed.

Beginning that night and continuing over the next few days, my two responsibilities—the things I felt I must do and do well—were to see to the disposition of the body and to talk to the people who needed to be talked to, the family members and friends and, important as well, the inquiring reporters. The talking was generally a relief, a refuge from more private pain, but the involvement with the body I found very difficult. It had always been easier for me—and why should this be different in death?—to talk about my mother with other people than to deal with her actual presence and person.

The way that body and spirit remained for me so strangely disconnected had to do at least in part with my mother's dislike of religious practice and ceremony. Her will specified a simple cremation without a funeral. Thus, as far as the body was concerned, it needed to be moved from the hospital to the mortuary that my mother, wasting no time, had already identified as the best in Palm Beach—I learned from Richard, her night nurse (it was with him that she liked best to play Scrabble), that an appointment had been set for the following week to work out arrangements with the E. Earl Smith and Son Funeral Home. This was where I had the body sent. Then the next day by telegram I arranged for its cremation.

I still have the piece of paper on which I scribbled my message: "I, Wendy Fairey, hereby give permission to the E. Earl Smith and Son Funeral Home to cremate the body of my mother, Sheilah G. Westbrook." Only when it came to it, I didn't feel up to dictating this to a Western Union stranger. Contacting a friend of mine who had always been devoted to my mother, I asked her, although I felt guilty to be sparing myself in this way, to do me the favor of reading my message to the operator.

Nor did I, as my mother had asked of me, go right away to Florida. Robert and I went together three weeks later when he returned from Greece, where he had been spending the fall, and it was a hard, sad business sorting through all her things. Had I gone right away, it would have been me, just me, alone with the body. No gathering of mourners. No assurances of ritual to orient me back among the living. I was afraid, though even now I'm not quite sure of what. I had never seen a dead body, and oddly enough, through a conspiracy of circumstances—our nonparticipation in religious rites, our lack of family and lack of contact with the little family we had—I was forty-six and had never attended a funeral. I think a funeral would have offered the structure and protection that I needed. Without it, the idea of journeying to see my mother's corpse in cold storage at the E. Earl Smith and Son Funeral Home seemed the loneliest trip I could ever make. I knew she had asked me to come. I hoped, imagining her ongoing consciousness, that she would understand why I hadn't.

The crematorium asked me what should be done with the ashes, and thinking of my mother's passionate love of the ocean, I said they should be scattered over the Atlantic. This seemed what she would have wanted, and at last I felt at peace with my task when I knew it had been done. Later among my mother's papers I found her own thoughts on the matter in a brief reflection entitled "What Is Death?"—one of the fifty or so short pieces that make up her last unpublished compilation of autobiographical snippets. My mother had pulled these together into a manuscript alternately called "Scrapbook" or, after the 1927 Noel Coward hit in which as the chorus girl understudy she had gone on for the star and been a smash success, "One Damn Thing After Another." "What is Death?" ends with her concern about the disposition of her body:

When I saw my lawyer to make my will, and stated that when I die, I wished to be cremated, he asked me, "How do you want your ashes disposed of?" He knew that I loved living by the ocean and thought I would like to have my ashes sprinkled over the water. "Oh no," I said. "I'm always afraid of drowning."

"How about *burying* the ashes?" "No, I'd suffocate." We decided to leave the problem to my children.

Reading this unsettled me but did not make me think I had done the wrong thing. It was just that my mother had left me no choice that I might know or imagine would have pleased her. My son had once suggested as a seven-year-old worrier about death that my mother should be buried in the graveyard near our house of that time in Maine. And if we should ever move, he said, we could dig her up and take her with us. This seemed a wonderful proposal to my mother, because, as she said, it expressed such love for her. I think it was being neglected by the living that she feared, the anxiety that out of sight might be out of mind. So in water or in earth, it made sense that she would have imagined herself equally lonely. But if of necessity death meant in some way being left behind, she had insufficient confidence—or so I argued with her ghost—in the strength of our abiding connection.

I did not keep my promise to "come right away." But I think I kept the more important promise not to lose her. The way I chose—and it seemed fully consistent with her way of living—was to devote myself in the hours and days following her death to the ongoing telling of her story. This, after all, had been what kept her going through the years that I had known her. "Wendy says I'm the only person she knows who has written nine autobiographies," she would joke to friends. "Working on the book," and the book was always one variant or another of her life story, assuaged fear and loneliness, restored belief in self, and, I think it's not too much to claim, made her feel immortal.

Within an hour of Dr. Moskowitz's call, I was dialing the number of Larry Van Gelder, our old friend at the *New York Times*. Larry had started off as my friend, a cross between boyfriend and mentor, when I had a summer job as a nineteen-year-old copy girl on the *New York Mirror* and he, a twenty-nine-year-old reporter on the paper, took me under his wing. The *Mirror* was then also my mother's paper, carrying her syndicated column. Through me the two of them became friends, and their camaraderie as journalists had proved a durable connection. Larry was now an entertainment editor at the *Times* and in recent years often asked my mother to movie previews as his guest. She liked this and she liked him. "What a pity you didn't marry Larry Van Gelder," she would muse sometimes, though adding in response to my expression of impatience, "But I guess you weren't in love with him." Her categories always perplexed me. They seemed so absolute. I also inwardly protested her assumption that men were so at one's disposal—to be seduced, married, "kept," "kicked out," whatever the exigencies of the moment.

Larry, I knew, would help me to arrange for the obituary. He was out when I phoned, and I left a message with his teenage daughter. "Ask him to call Wendy and tell him that my mother died tonight."

"Yes, I will," said the girl, a teenager's matter-of-fact reply. I recognized that my reference to the death was a way of testing its reality.

Larry called back. He thought the obituary had been prewritten the previous June after my mother's heart attack, and he assured me that Albin Krebs, the *Times* obit editor, would be calling me the next day to confirm a few final facts.

Among the pieces in the "One Damn Thing After Another" manuscript is a vignette in which Larry is mentioned. It is called "The Wrong Party. And How I Received My Come-Uppance," and it is a wonderful example of my mother's verve in approaching life—and death. My mother liked to make fun of what might have seemed her own self-involvement but became in her stories her "vagueness"—that recurrent failure on her part to notice what other people were doing or even who they were. She would be sailing along, happy and oblivious. Then would come the shock of some actual situation, a momentary deflation or put-down, to be followed, almost always, by her resilient triumph. Such is the format—with a surprise twist in its ending—of "The Wrong Party":

"Where is the party?" I asked on arriving at the building on Broadway in the mid-forties. I was directed to the sixth floor. Wine and cheese were to be served before the preview of a movie. This often happens in New York to put the critics in a mellow mood.

I was the guest of Larry Van Gelder, whom I would meet later in the small theater a couple of floors higher. Larry usually works late at the *New York Times,* rushing in a minute before the movie starts. Knowing I am always early, he suggested I should join the group at the party hosted by the producers.

Usually I recognize most of the people attending these affairs. But the men and women in this group were all strangers and were very much dressed up. Seeing that I was looking somewhat embarrassed with no one talking to me, an attractive, tall, slender, eightyish white-haired man sauntered over and introduced himself.

"I'm Jimmy Van Allen, and what is your name?" I tried to remember where I had heard or read his name, and what newspaper he worked for. But he was just as blank as I was when I said, "Sheilah Graham."

He attempted to jog my memory. "Most of us here," he said, "are from Newport, Rhode Island." I could not imagine what a group of Newport socialites were doing at a preview party in New York. He explained, "The film we are going to see downstairs was made in Newport, and all the people here worked in it as extras." I was in the wrong party.

"Do you play tennis?" he suddenly asked me. "I used to play every day when I worked in Hollywood." "Oh," vaguely. But now he became more confidential. "Does my name mean anything to you?" I tried to look polite. "Well," he said, leaning closer so that only I could hear what he would say, "I'm the man who invented the tie-breaker in tennis. The matches used to go on forever. Now, as you must know, when two players are at six-six, they go into the tie-breaker. It makes the game more exciting and shorter."

Now that I knew who *he* was, it was time for him to know who *I* was, and that I was as well known as he. "When I die," I told him, "my obituary will be in the *New York Times.*" "And I will read it," he replied. I left for my own party, one flight up.

The lead obituary in the November 19 *New York Times* was three columns long and accompanied by an excellent picture that I recognized as one of the publicity shots taken in connection with the 1959 movie version of *Beloved Infidel.* The fact that the *Times* had made a mistake and given the date as 1969 served to reinforce the magic of my mother's abiding beauty. Could she really be sixty-five and look like that? Even at fifty-five it was remarkable. I noted this much as I stood outside my corner newspaper shop at six-thirty on Saturday morning, the paper opened in haste to the page where I knew I would find the story. Robert, whom I had tracked down in Crete the day before, was scheduled to phone me back at seven, but I had slipped out before his call to get the paper. It was a cool, sunny fall morning, and standing there scanning the article, I felt immensely pleased and excited that my mother should receive this recognition. The obituary joined me to a vast collective of people who would now understand my loss, the readers of the *New York Times.* It seemed such a help to have my mother's importance thus confirmed and to have so many people know about her life and death. I went back into the store and bought three more copies of the paper, explaining to the young Pakistani who took my money, "My mother died, and there's a piece about her." I think I even showed him the picture. Then I took home my newspapers, sat with one spread open on my bed, and, making an effort to moderate my excitement, at least enough to make sense of the words, read the following:

Sheilah Graham Is Dead at 84; Wrote Hollywood Gossip Column

By ALBIN KREBS

Sheilah Graham, who for some 35 years was part of what she called "the unholy trio" of powerful Hollywood gossip columnists—the others were Louella O. Parsons and Hedda Hopper—died Thursday of congestive heart failure at Good Samaritan Hospital in Palm Beach, Fla. She was 84 years old.

Miss Graham, who also served as a war correspondent in Europe in World War II and who at various times had her own Hollywood-based radio and television shows, is probably best remembered for her love affair with F. Scott Fitzgerald, whose last unhappy years she described in her first book, *Beloved Infidel*, published in 1958.

That book concentrated on the Pygmalion and Galatea aspect of the relationship between the novelist and Miss Graham, in which he created a "college of one" for her, drawing up lists of books she read to complete "the education of a woman," as her book was subtitled.

'The Very Best Portrait'

Beloved Infidel, which Miss Graham wrote in collaboration with Gerold Frank, became an international best seller, received critical approval for its warmth and authenticity, and was hailed by Edmund Wilson in a long review in the *New Yorker* as "the very best portrait of Fitzgerald that has yet been put into print."

Born into poverty in an East London slum, Miss Graham parlayed a native intelligence and her great good looks, under the guidance of several worldly and cultivated men, into a reputation as a bright, brittle and often witty sophisticate.

She labored under no illusions, however, and late in life characterized herself as "a fascinating fake who pulled the wool over Hollywood's eyes." She was also not above turning her talent for abrasive criticism of "the lightweight pinheads of Hollywood" upon herself.

For example, in *The Rest of the Story,* published in 1964, she wrote: "Sitting at my typewriter, banging out the items, I sometimes laugh as I stir my witch's brew, putting in the onions and the herbs to give indigestion to people I don't like or to those I think have slighted me, the great me. And it's true that I sometimes mistake my typewriter for my teeth, because the more I bite the more my column will be read."

A Hard Childhood

Miss Graham's real name was Lily Shiel, which "to this day horrifies me to a degree impossible to explain," she wrote in *Beloved Infidel.* When she was an infant, she said, her father died of tuberculosis, and her childhood was characterized by a string of Dickensian hardships. For six years she lived with her mother, a domestic, in a rented basement room, then wound up in an orphanage. As a young woman, she put in a brief stint as a domestic, which she hated, and then went to work in Gamage's department store as a toothbrush demonstrator. Miss Graham said she got the job because she was pretty and had a dazzling smile and perfect teeth, "thanks to a sweets-deprived childhood in the orphanage."

At Gamage's she met her first Pygmalion, Maj. John Graham Gillam, who employed her in the iron and steel company in which he was an executive, taught her table manners and coached her to free herself of her Cockney accent. After their marriage, she adopted the name of Sheilah Graham, studied briefly at the Royal Academy of Dramatic Art and finally was hired as a chorus girl by C. B. Cochran, the British equivalent of Florenz Ziegfeld, who put her in a 1927 musical revue called *One Dam Thing After Another*. When the star fell ill, Miss Graham went on in her place, and, of course, was a smashing success, she said.

Cochran signed her to a contract for other shows and she soon began selling articles about show business to the penny press. She recognized that as a writer she possessed a quality of "salable mediocrity," she said, and decided to carve out a career in journalism.

At Home in Hollywood

In 1933, Miss Graham said, she moved to New York and for two years wrote for the *New York Mirror* and the *Evening Journal*. In 1935 she was offered North American Newpaper Alliance's syndicated Hollywood column, and she moved to Los Angeles. She divorced Major Gillam in 1937.

She felt at home in Hollywood, more so than she had in New York, she said, because "Hollywood was notorious even in London for the ignorance of the people who made the films—no one could embarrass me with erudite conversation."

It was in July 1937, at a party given for her by Robert Benchley to celebrate her engagement to the Marquess of Donegall, that she met Fitzgerald. It was love at first sight for both of them, she said. She broke off her engagement and entered into an affair with Fitzgerald that was to last more than three years, until Dec. 21, 1940, when he died in her arms.

The years with Fitzgerald were, for Miss Graham,

both idyllic and harrowing. The famed novelist was in failing health, fighting an epic and losing battle with alcoholism. He looked upon himself as a burned-out case, and he was having trouble turning out movie scripts to pay for his daughter's education and his wife Zelda's mental asylum bills.

But they were devoted to one another and Miss Graham gave him not only her love and patience but also a measure of peace of mind. She served as the model for Kathleen, the heroine in *The Last Tycoon*, the Fitzgerald novel that was unfinished at his death.

"I was never a mistress," Miss Graham said. "I was a woman who loved Scott Fitzgerald for better or worse until he died."

War Correspondent in England

After his death Miss Graham returned to England as a war correspondent. It was there that she met, and married in 1941, Trevor Cresswell Lawrence Westbrook, an executive of the company that manufactured the Spitfire fighter plane. Before the marriage ended in divorce in 1946, they had two children, Wendy and Robert. A brief third marriage, in 1953, to a man she identified only as "an American of Polish ancestry with an unpronounceable name," also ended in divorce.

Miss Graham resumed her Hollywood column after the war and, to earn as much money as she could, also wrote for magazines and conducted a radio show and a television show, *Hollywood Today,* in the mid-'50s. By 1964 *Time* magazine could report that Miss Graham had "deposed Hopper and Parsons as doyenne of the Hollywood columnists," appearing in 178 newspapers, compared to about 100 for Miss Hopper and 69 for Miss Parsons.

Miss Graham also produced several more books,

three of them centering on Fitzgerald—*The Real Scott Fitzgerald, The Rest of the Story* and *College of One.* That volume, published in 1967, after Miss Graham found the handwritten Fitzgerald "curriculum" he created for her, listed his favorite books and musical works that he insisted she become familiar with. Other Graham books included *The Garden of Allah, Confessions of a Gossip Columnist* and the steamy autobiographical novel *A State of Heat* (1972). She also published *Hollywood Revisited* in 1985.

Miss Graham is survived by her daughter, Wendy Fairey, who is dean of the College of Liberal Arts and Sciences at Brooklyn College; her son, Robert Westbrook, now living in Khania, Crete; and by three grandchildren. A memorial service will be held in New York next month.

How pleased my mother would have been to read her *New York Times* obituary. That was my thought as I finished it. It would have seemed to her a great triumph and vindication, stressing as it did, right in the lead paragraphs, so much that she was proud of: her stint as a war correspondent, the emphasis in her relation with Fitzgerald on education, the fact that Edmund Wilson had praised *Beloved Infidel*—my mother could practically recite the 1958 *New Yorker* review in which Wilson had called her portrayal of Fitzgerald the best yet in print and made clear her contribution to the writer's last years. She would have liked as well the recognition of her beauty, her wit, her courage, her lack of illusions about herself, and, all in all, her striking accomplishment of self-creation.

The fact that the obituary ended with such a specific mention of my job as dean of Brooklyn College at first puzzled me, but then seemed to fit with Mr. Krebs's emphasis on the theme of education. He had understood the importance to my mother of education, and I believe he saw the relevance to her aspirations of having a daughter who became an academic dean. I was later to find among the photographs stashed away in my mother's Florida apartment a picture of me from my wedding that is labeled "Dean Wendy Fairey." At the time of my wedding, however, I was a good decade away from bearing this title. To me the young woman in the photograph—a graduate student with her first part-time college teaching job and on that day a bride—is not Dean Wendy Fairey. Is that so centrally who I was to my mother? It's like the joke about the Jewish mother who runs along the beach shouting, "Help, help! My son the doctor is drowning!" I know that my mother was very proud—and also a little frightened, for might I not look down on her?—of my academic success. She too might have been a teacher, she always used to say, had she been allowed to stay on at school past the age of fourteen. Instead, she had become an adventuress, but Mr. Krebs had glimpsed the restless hunger, not just for distinction but for learning and knowledge, that impelled her throughout her life.

The obituary seemed my mother's accomplishment—I was proud that her life could generate such a story. In a smaller way it seemed mine too in my new role as her posthumous press agent. I had spent a good part of November 18, the day after my mother's death, in telephone conversations with journalists, who began calling in the early hours of the morning. In addition to Albin Krebs, a courteous man who expressed his condolences, then posed his few questions for factual confirmation—date of birth, date and cause of death, names of survivors—I was contacted by several Palm Beach and Miami papers and by the Associated Press. The Florida papers were so quick to know of the death that I realized they must keep a reporter on a hospital or mortuary beat. Awareness of my loss came and went, the waves of grief swelling within body and consciousness, but then, like the pains of childbirth, subsiding. It helped to have things to do, and by talking to the press, I hoped I might set straight some facts and influence the tone of the stories that would be written. One reporter asked me how I had

felt growing up as the daughter of a Hollywood gossip columnist, with the suggestion that this must have been hard. I answered rather brusquely that his question was not to the point
and guided the focus back to my mother. As Hollywood gossip
columnist and misperceived "mistress"—the label she so
hated—of F. Scott Fitzgerald, as a woman, moreover, whose
zestful self-deprecation sometimes backfired, my mother had
had her share while living of derisive press coverage. Though
death is not the occasion for mockery, more than one of the
articles that now appeared would quote her lament "I won't be
remembered for my writing. I'll be remembered as Scott's mistress."

The *Times* piece made all this inconsequential. Above all, I
appreciated, as would have my mother, that it conferred on her
such dignity. My mother had a lot of dignity—in particular the
dignity of taking absolute responsibility for herself. Not everyone understood this, given her knockabout life and irrepressi-
bly indiscreet tongue. But Albin Krebs did. His article had
captured, in large part through her words, the dignity of her
aspirations as well as the valor and gaiety of her spirit. I was
grateful and deeply moved.

So November 19 was the day of my mother's obituary in the
New York Times, this elegant, kindly shaping of her story. People who had read it kept phoning me, and I kept telling those
who hadn't read it to get hold of the paper. Finally the day
drew to an end, and I noticed as I walked down the street that
the next day's paper, Sunday's *Times,* was on the newsstands for
sale. Normally, I would have picked up my copy to have at my
bedside the next morning. But that day I didn't. I hurried on
without stopping. It hurt to realize that my mother's death
would soon be yesterday's news. I did not want to yield to this
reality. The Sunday paper would have new obituaries, and day
by day hers would recede further into the past. I cried out for
time to stand still and for there never to be a new day's distrac-
tions.

An odd thing, though, began to happen. In the succeeding days as I talked with more and more people who had seen the obituary, as people kept exclaiming about my mother's extraordinary life and telling me I was the one who ought to write about it, I was beset by a familiar sense of dread. My mother's obituary, which had at first been such a comfort to me—it showed the world who she was, and I was somehow a sharer in her greatness—took on a life of its own and grew into something a little monstrous. *No hungry generations tread me down.* There she was, still larger than life, and I still persuaded that somehow this made me smaller.

I had decided, in consultation with Robert and some of my mother's good friends, that there should be a memorial in New York—a modest gathering of family and friends, no religious trappings, no reporters—where people who had known and cared about her could speak. I didn't think this through at the time, but I believe I looked to the memorial as an occasion where she and I could stand together as equals. There, surrounded by friends who loved us both, I could express my love for her and, as her daughter and survivor, give her the offering of this gathering of people in her honor and memory.

The date of the memorial had been set for January 8. Robert would be back then from Europe, and I, meanwhile, turned with great focus and energy to the planning of this event. It was a way, above all, of lingering with my mother, not yet moving on to life without her and all the loneliness and liberation that this might bring.

Two

ENTER FREDDIE

T WAS FIVE WEEKS after my mother's death, in the course of planning her memorial, that I came to hear the secret.

My informant was Dee Wells, one of the people whom I had contacted to ask if they would say a few words about my mother as part of the memorial program. We knew Dee from her marriage to our family friend, the philosopher A. J. Ayer, a man whose acquaintance with my mother went back to World War II and who in fact had been dining with my very pregnant mother in New York—he was there on assignment with British intelligence—the evening I showed signs of readiness to be born. So Freddie, as the future Sir Alfred was always known to his friends, had taken her to the hospital, and in this sense was closer to my birth than Trevor Westbrook, who was off in England and learned about it only by telegram.

I was introduced to Freddie on my first trip to London, when I was eleven. He took me to a bookstore and bought me *Tess of the D'Urbervilles.* I was charmed by this engaging professor of logic, clearly my mother's most intellectual friend, though only later did I come more fully to understand his reputation. As author at twenty-five of the seminal *Language, Truth, and Logic,* he had written the basic English-language work on logical positivism and established his importance in the empiricist tradition. Intellectual heir to Bertrand Russell, though he modestly said it would be glory enough if he could be thought "to have even played Horatio to Russell's Hamlet," he was celebrated for the incisiveness of his arguments and the lucidity of his thought. Teaching when I first knew him at University College, London, then later back at Oxford, where his career had started, he was impressively eminent, yet never the least bit stuffy. I took pride in our special relationship and enjoyed telling people of his connection with my birth.

Our family tie with Dee Wells had its history too. Dee had entered our lives unpropitiously when as an American journalist working in England in the 1950s she wrote a scathing review of *Beloved Infidel* that appeared in the *Sunday Express.* Its closing words were legendary in our family: "And I suppose in a way you have to hand it to this ex-East End orphan, once named Lily Shiel. Just *what* to hand her, I'd be hard put to say. But I do know it's nothing I'd touch with a ten–foot pole. With gloves on."

It turned out that Freddie, not yet married to Dee but living with her at the time, had actually seen the review before it went to press and done nothing to try to stop its publication. "I did say," he conceded to my mother, " 'Don't you think that's a bit strong?' " Freddie, my mother, and I were lunching together in a London restaurant—it must have been the summer of 1959 on one of our European trips. My mother walked out in the middle of the lunch, leaving Freddie and me rather sheepishly behind at the table. Soon afterwards, Freddie and Dee married, and somehow the breach was healed—at least more or less. "I'll never *completely* forgive that woman," my mother would say. But in fact she and Dee grew quite friendly, particularly when Dee, by then divorced from Freddie, moved with her lover to New York and would invite my mother to lunch or dinner at her apartment in Chelsea. This was one of the places that my raconteuse mother—"She was either getting or telling stories," a friend once said about her—liked to go and talk.

Because of the old review in the *Sunday Express,* I hesitated before asking Dee to speak at the memorial. On the other hand, I was looking for articulate people who knew my mother as a friend rather than a celebrity, and Dee seemed to me to fit the bill.

One result of my getting in touch with her was to find myself at a small dinner party at the home of Gully Wells Foges, Dee's daughter and Freddie's stepdaughter. Eight years younger than I, so then in her late thirties, Gully lived in New York on Bank Street with her British writer husband and small daughter and worked as an editor for a travel magazine. I had most recently seen her when we ran into one another in the restaurant where she was lunching with Freddie—this was my first encounter with either of them in years—and she afterwards invited me to Freddie's seventy-seventh-birthday party. That had been the previous October, a year before my mother's death.

I phoned Gully after speaking with her mother to make sure she would feel welcome to come with Dee to the memorial. It was December 23, and she invited me to dinner that night. "My mother will be there, and some old friends," she said. These turned out to be Gully's uncle and aunt and Dee's roommate from Paris right after the war. At the dinner table we sang songs to entertain four-year-old Rebecca Foges, who sat with us in her black velvet party dress and clapped her hands with glee at the antics of Old McDonald's farm. I felt grateful to be included in this family occasion. It helped to ease my sadness at facing my first Christmas without my mother.

I was placed next to Dee at the table and learned more about her plan, which she had broached over the phone, to move back to Europe to live again with Freddie. Both were, as

the French say, *disponible,* her lover gone and his next wife after
Dee having died. Freddie had been ill over the past year with
emphysema and needed someone to take care of him. Currently
their twenty-six-year-old son, Nicholas, was looking out for his
father in the South of France, where Freddie and Dee still
shared the house they had bought during their marriage. Dee's
plan was to join them there. "And we'll probably even get married again," she said, clearly pleased. She made a passing wry
reference to the Oxford widow's pension. But I felt the heart of
the matter was something else.

"Freddie could have so many beautiful women—even now.
And it's *me* he wants," she told me. There was an intensity in
this expression of triumph that made me feel I had seen something too intimate—a wound, a desire; I wondered if she knew
she had shown it to me. I thought back to this moment when I
heard some weeks later from Gully that, notwithstanding the
reunion with Dee, Freddie had thoughts of a springtime tryst
with a new girlfriend.

"How can he?" I asked. "Isn't he sick?"

"Well, that's Freddie," said Gully.

Around ten o'clock, Dee looked ready to leave, and I asked
if I could give her a lift home in my car. She accepted, and as we
went along the short distance from Greenwich Village to Chelsea, she spoke of Freddie and of his particular affection for me.

"You must come and visit us in France," she said. "There
aren't many people whom Freddie cares about, but he does care
about you."

"Yes, yes," I replied. "I'm very fond of Freddie too. After
all, it was he who took my mother to the hospital when I was
born. Our relationship goes way back."

I was pleased at Dee's insistence on my specialness but at the
same time hesitant to take what she said too seriously. I had
seen a lot of Freddie when I was a child and into my twenties,
but aside from going to his seventy-seventh-birthday party, I
had not been in touch with him in the last thirteen years. He

had married the third wife (Dee was his second), I had heard they were happy together, and then came her death. It was proof of how thoroughly he and I had lost contact that I had never even met her.

We were now in front of Dee's house on West Twenty-second Street, and she was about to get out of the car. She looked at me hard and spoke slowly. "Has it never occurred to you that Freddie is your father?"

I felt the reflex calm of a person who has just had an accident but doesn't yet know its severity. "No," I replied. "It hasn't. I look like my own father."

"Well, you also look like Freddie. And like Freddie's mother. There is a picture of her in his book. Not when she got older and sadder. But when she was young. The same smile. The same expression around the eyes."

Dee had already packed her books for the move but thought that Gully might have a copy of Freddie's autobiography, in which these pictures could be found.

"Anyway," she said, "get hold of Freddie's book."

"How do you know this?" I asked. "Is it from Freddie?"

"Yes," she said.

"And is it a speculation or a certainty?"

"Freddie thinks it's a certainty."

"Well," I said with deliberation, "I guess I did know that Freddie and my mother had an affair."

I presented this to Dee as a statement, but really it was a question. I realized as I spoke that this was the first time I had directly entertained the possibility that Freddie and my mother had been lovers. My mother had never discussed her sexual adventures, past or current, with her children. And my concern to have her be, above all things, my mother had made me, I now understood, concertedly obtuse about many "family friends."

"You bet," said Dee in response to my statement of the obvious. Was my mother, I wondered, one of those beautiful women, Freddie's women, against whom Dee had matched herself? Suddenly I felt overwhelmed and wanted only to conceal my agitation. "Well, in any case," I said, "I'll be very happy to visit you both in France."

Driving home to Brooklyn, I felt the stir of my thoughts like an electrical charge, coursing through all the nerves and muscles of my face, down through neck and shoulders and arms, to fingers tightly gripping the wheel. Freddie Ayer, my father. I had an instant flash of recognition of the resemblance. As Dee had said, it lay in the eyes and the smile. But more than that, I felt it from the inside out, a focusing of the same eyes, a forming of the same smile, preparing one's face with eyes and smile to meet the faces that one meets.

As soon as I got home, I went to the chest in which I keep my photographs. I had no photos of Freddie, but there was a picture of myself, in profile, smiling, aged forty, that had come to mind in my moment of sensing the resemblance. I sat looking at it, puzzling over the features, studying the expression, sure and yet not sure of its evocation of Freddie. I did, of course, have pictures of my mother, and I reviewed the ways I did and did not look like her. People had always said I resembled my mother. The idea was that I looked like her but had Trevor's dark coloring. Also my mother's face was round, and his and mine were more oval.

The few pictures that I had of Trevor were not particularly clear ones, but I got them out: pictures of him in his forties on his two or three visits to us in California, dark-haired and dressed in a dark suit as he did his best to romp with his little children; a family snapshot taken on that 1959 trip to Europe, all four of us—my father, my mother, Robert, myself—lined up in front of Warwick Castle on what I remember as a very dogged excursion; pictures from my wedding album that show him among the family members present—he came from England to attend my college graduation and my wedding; and then finally a picture taken in Biarritz in 1971—he had joined my mother, my husband, Donald, one-year-old Emily, and me for a few

days of that particular holiday. Trevor and I are standing together in a street of the town, unsmiling but not unhappy-
looking. This had been the only picture of us together as father
and grown-up daughter. I had liked having it, and I had always
thought it showed our Westbrook affinity—a matter-of-fact,
feet-on-the-ground approach to life in contrast to my mother's
theatricality.

The case is open, I thought. Really, it is still quite possible
that I am Trevor Westbrook's daughter and not Freddie Ayer's.

But I didn't want to be, whatever the accepted realities of
the past. Trevor was ten years dead and Freddie was alive. Trevor was a man in whose company I had never been at ease; I had
always felt the stress of trying to be his daughter. Freddie was
the blithe sparkling hero of my childhood, who had bought me
Tess of the D'Urbervilles, walked with me through the Tate looking at the Turners, introduced me to London buses and to
small French restaurants in Mayfair and Soho. As I got into bed
late that night, I allowed Dee's revelation a final moment of
unreserved magic. "Freddie Ayer is my father." The sentence
reverberated in my head—a question, an exclamation, and
something close to a prayer.

The dates, though, were on Trevor's side as the next day
I rehearsed my mother's story of their marriage and my conception. Grief-stricken at the death of F. Scott Fitzgerald and
haunted by a recurrent nightmare in which Hitler was personally
gunning her down from a bomber, she had gone back to England as a war correspondent in the summer of 1941, her assignment to cover women's work in the munitions factories and
to describe the London bombings. The nightmares ceased.
She met Trevor Westbrook—dour, self-educated, the man who
did not read books but who responded to her glamour and her
smile and, like so many others, fell in love with her. She was drawn
to him, she said, because he seemed to offer protection and he
was so utterly different from Fitzgerald. Semi-engaged to Trevor
—his diamond was on her finger—but not at all sure what to
do, she returned to New York. The December anniversary of

Fitzgerald's death approached. My mother was distraught. She couldn't bear it. She cried out for help. Then, as she put it in *The Rest of the Story,* her sequel to *Beloved Infidel,* "God heard my despair and immediately took care of the matter."

Trevor had come to Washington—he was on a secret mission along with Winston Churchill and Lord Beaverbrook—and my mother was sent by her syndicate to interview the visitors. She traveled to Washington, she and Trevor decided to marry at once because they didn't know how long he would be staying, and I was conceived. It was as miraculous and as simple as that. She was saved from the despair of the anniversary—by Trevor and me.

The problem I now faced was that if Trevor's visit, as I believed, occurred in early or mid-December 1941 and I was born exactly nine months later on September 11, 1942, what room did this leave for Freddie Ayer? Could my mother have been sleeping with him within days of Trevor's arrival? This was not impossible; yet it seemed to me that I was having to work awfully hard to get Freddie into the picture. Perhaps Freddie just surmised that he was my father. Perhaps even my mother did not know for sure.

It was after the New Year that I found in the Brooklyn College library a copy of *Part of My Life* by A. J. Ayer, the first of Freddie's two autobiographical volumes. Its photographs were inconclusive. But this, if anything, only intensified my obsessive scrutiny. There was Freddie's young mother, dark-haired and smiling. I thought I detected a resemblance around the mouth and chin less to me than to my daughter, Emily. The painting that e.e. cummings had done of Freddie in his early thirties, with the long nose, the curling, full upper lip, the shape and gentleness of the face, seemed to me to look a great deal like my son, Sean. But then I had also thought that Sean resembled Trevor. I saw myself reflected in a picture of "the author in his forties"—Freddie in profile, seated at his desk—and I worked out what to me was an entirely persuasive analysis of my own nose as a genetic cross between Freddie's and my mother's. When, however, I showed these pictures to the friends whom I was beginning to involve in my drama, their response was to see a slight but not overwhelming resemblance. Moreover, they were hardpressed to choose between Freddie and Trevor.

It disturbed me how much I wanted Freddie Ayer to be my father. The desire upset my old accommodation with the fact of having had essentially one parent. Trevor had been a very occasional figure in our lives, though to be fair to him, which I tried to be, my mother hadn't encouraged his involvement. She used to say that she had had to be for us both father and mother, and as I think of the stories she told about Trevor, they served generally to reinforce that we couldn't count on him and we could always count on her. I tried to get to know him on my own when I got older. But he was a closed-off man, a difficult man, and my efforts were never very sustained ones. When Trevor died in 1978, I wrote and published a story about him and our relationship, the title taken from *King Lear,* "Nothing Can Come of Nothing." His death had made me feel sad and somewhat bitter, but the success of the story cheered me up and somehow settled things between us. I rarely thought of him after that.

If as a child I had any secret longings for a father's presence, they were for a different kind of father, a gracious, intellectual father—someone, in fact, like Freddie Ayer, though I don't think I had him in mind when I used sometimes to imagine the figure of the desired father in our midst. I had a recurrent fantasy in which I would seat this figment at the foot of our oval mahogany dinner table, and there, dignified and subdued, he would lead the family in discussions of politics and culture. My mother was cast in the role of a listener, but even in fantasy she remained at the head of the table—or at least the end that I considered the head because that is where she sat, the end at which the housekeeper would set the dinner platter and which

I associate with my mother's presence and absolute predomi-
nance.

My consolation to myself for not having had much of a
father, intellectual or otherwise, was to have had my spectacu-
lar mother. But I must have longed sometimes to be rescued
from her, and now the notion of my relation to Freddie re-
leased a wellspring of new fantasies. We would sit together in a
sunlit garden in the South of France and talk and laugh together and express our love. He would embrace me as his long-
lost daughter, come back to him at the end of his life. Perdita.
Lear and Cordelia in the scenes they never had. He would make
everything clear to me that had happened in the past, and I
would be there to cheer and care for him. But if it wasn't true
that he was my father or there was no way of knowing for sure
or he refused to acknowledge me, I would be worse off than
before Dee spoke to me. My mother still dead and all my new
tender hope of a father cruelly dashed. I would be doubly bereft. Doubly orphaned. I had called myself an orphan in a conversation with Sean shortly after my mother's death. "No
you're not," he said. "An orphan is a child whose mother and
father are dead and who needs them to take care of her. You're
just a person whose parents are dead. You've taken care of yourself and other people for years."

"I guess you're right," I admitted, though I had often felt
like an orphan even with both my parents alive.

I phoned Dee Wells a few days before her departure for
Europe to ask what she thought of my writing Freddie a letter.
"Oh dear," she said. "I hope what I said didn't upset you. It just
seemed so stupid your not knowing the truth."

"No," I replied, and it occurred to me that I was lying. I
was willing to admit that the revelation did interest me and that
what I hoped for was an acknowledgment.

"Well, let me see," she said. "You could write, but you
mustn't say you learned it from me. And you've got to leave
him an out." She outlined an alternative story in which I would
speak of my longtime suspicions based on the physical resem-

blance and then make up something about evidence found in my mother's papers. I could say that I also knew Trevor had been on the scene and that it was still quite possible that Trevor was my father—this was the out I would be leaving. But now with both Trevor and my mother dead, I was turning to Freddie in the hope that he could enlighten me.

Dee's suggested approach felt awkward. I didn't want to have to lie, and I wasn't sure I could make the lie persuasive. Still, I felt obliged to do as she asked. Suddenly she seemed an impediment, someone standing between me and Freddie. "Do you think he'll write back?" I asked anxiously. "Is he up to writing back?"

"I tell you what I think is best," she said, and I wondered afterwards how what I had said prompted her next thought. "I'm going back to Freddie. I'll be with him in three days. Why don't I first get a sense of things? You never know with these English what they consider proper to say and do. My guess is that he made a long-ago promise to your mother not to say anything. And then I'll get in touch with you. I'll write or call. You won't have to wait very long."

"All right," I said. But I was not pleased. Here I was on the brink of action, of taking charge of the course of my own story after it had been in other people's hands for so long, and I was being told, really ordered, oh so nicely, to wait. Perhaps Dee was right, and certainly she had been nothing but helpful to this point. But it was hard. I did not know if she would keep her promise.

After Dee's departure a string of discoveries built the case ever more strongly for Freddie as my father. I felt like a cross between Oliver Twist and Esther Summerson—robbed of my birthright and regaining it through the gradual unearthing of an old sexual secret. I was also Isabel Archer in *The Portrait of a Lady,* struggling in a drama of perception to understand what had always been right before my eyes. Perhaps I exaggerate the significance of my own agency, but by the time I got Dee's letter and then Freddie's letter two weeks later, it would not have been altogether mistaken to say, as Freddie put it, that I had been "feeling [my] way toward the truth."

First of all, there was the silver porringer. I was looking through my baby book, that pink-plastic-covered *Little Me— Baby's First Years,* in which in response to the sentimental promptings to note baby's first step, first tooth, first words, my mother had recorded my development and her devotion. Under the heading "Wonderful Christmas Days" there was an entry I had never read carefully before:

Christmas 1942—Wendy's first in Los Angeles. We had a silver Christmas tree with silver, blue, and red balls. With a white angel with silver halo on top. The angel seemed a little cock-eyed & we had to tie her with wire to the top of the tree. Wendy had some nice presents:

silver mug	*from Mrs. Val Bell*
silver spoon	*" Eddie Mayer*
silver porringer	*" Freddie Ayer*
silver rattle	*" J & M Ruddy*
play pen	*" John Wheeler*
dress and saving stamp	

[A line here is crossed out in heavy black pen, though one can half make out the words "her father."]

bibs	*from Scottie Frances Fitzgerald*
sweater	*" Miss Haines (her nurse)*
rattle	*" Ann (our maid)*
sun bonnet	*" Aunt Adrienne*

Adrienne was Trevor's sister, soon with her three children to sit out part of the war with us in California. John Wheeler was my mother's boss. Scottie was Fitzgerald's daughter. The other present-givers were either servants or California friends— with the one exception: Freddie Ayer. I had never noticed his name on this list before; now it jumped off the page. I knew that Freddie was then still in New York, which we had left in October, my mother, the baby nurse, and I, so that my mother might resume her Hollywood column. At Christmas I was three months old. We have a photo of me propped in an arm-chair, decked out in my frilly dress and little booties, staring with wide-open round baby eyes at the baubles on that silver tree. The silver mug shows in the picture, one of the presents around the tree, but not the porringer. But why would Freddie Ayer be sending this little baby a silver porringer? My mother had never spoken of him as more than a casual friend. And he at this time, deep in multiple sexual adventures as well as espio-nage—so I gleaned from his autobiography—seemed to have little reason to remember a baby out in California. The gift loomed significant, a portentous, quite thrilling new clue. I knew that I had had it in my possession along with the silver mug and silver spoon and baby rattle. It was engraved either "Wendy" or "Wendy Westbrook." But when I searched for it to check, I couldn't find it. The loss deflated me—it stood for a moment as a commentary on my hopes—and the connection with Freddie seemed depressingly precarious.

Following hard upon the porringer, though, was my dis-covery of the correct marriage date to Trevor, and all the exhila-ration of my uncertainty returned. I had a January 17 appoint-ment to enter my mother's safe deposit box at the Chase Manhattan Bank, which in keeping with New York tax regula-tions had been sealed at the time of her death. It contained her stocks and bonds, her small amount of jewelry, including the gold-and-emerald brooch given to her one Christmas by How-ard Hughes in thanks for her discretion in not publishing ru-mors about his romances, and various documents such as her citizenship papers and marriage and divorce certificates. To enter the box, I was joined by a tax inspector and a jewelry appraiser, my visit part of the complicated process to get the box unsealed. While the appraiser looked over the jewelry and the inspector inventoried the stocks and bonds, I went through the documents to copy key dates that I needed for a New York State Tax Bureau affidavit. The form asked about marriages, and having decided I needn't bother with my mother's first husband, Johnny Gillam, I was looking for dates to go with the names of the second and third. Papers for the marriage to Trevor were missing, but the divorce papers were there, and they cited the marriage date.

January 9, 1942. I wonder how striking this would have been without my recently stirred suspicions. My mother had never mentioned the date of this marriage, never celebrated or even noted an anniversary. But January 9 was after and not before the anniversary of the death of F. Scott Fitzgerald; even more to the point, it was only eight months and two days before my birth. I knew that Trevor was not around many days before the marriage—his arrival in Washington could probably be checked, but there seemed no reason to doubt this part of the story. If, then, the marriage occurred, as the papers declared, on January 9, there was no way I could be his child as a full-term baby.

There remained, of course, the possibility of premature birth. I had been a small baby—my birth weight only six pounds three ounces. But my mother had never said that I was early. Surely had I been, this interesting twist would not have been omitted from the details of her oft-recounted stories, among her favorites to tell and ours as children to listen to, of our births. With me her labor had started when she was dining with Freddie, a few days, not weeks, before the baby was due (she had hoped I would be born on *her* birthday, September 15). Freddie left her off at the hospital. She checked in, all set to be a mother. But then the labor pains ceased. It seemed a false alarm. The doctor said she could get dressed and go home.

My birth occurred because rather than do this and face the ridicule of her friends, my mother had persuaded the doctor to perform a cesarean section. This act of influence became all the more prescient and dramatic when I was delivered with the umbilical cord wrapped around my neck. In a few more unborn hours, my mother always stressed, I would have died of suffocation.

Robert, too, was a close call, but in this instance for her.

She had traveled east, a last-minute decision, to have the baby in New York because her California doctor was a fool and she trusted only her accommodating Dr. Rubin, who had shown such good judgment in my delivery three years earlier. "Geniuses," she insisted, "know the rules and then know when to throw the book away." And Dr. Rubin was enshrined in her galaxy of geniuses. She got off the train with double pneumonia. "You are going to have a gigantic baby," said Dr. Rubin. And on Christmas Eve 1945, almost a month early—my mother had had a brief get-together with Trevor the previous spring—Robert weighed in at eight pounds four ounces. Had he gone full-term, Dr. Rubin told her, he might have been a twelve-pounder. My mother nearly died from the pneumonia, but recovered apace when her overbearing boss, John Wheeler, offered to adopt me if anything should happen to her. Two weeks later she walked a mile to lunch at the Algonquin.

So I was on time and Robert was early, and each birth was a story that confirmed our mother's spirited dauntlessness and her unchallenged centrality in our lives. Trevor was our father, but when I was born, he responded in his congratulatory cable with mention of a friend who had been lucky enough to have a boy, and five months before Robert was born, he had canceled his life insurance because my mother would not agree to have the baby in England. I knew that Trevor had expressed doubts about Robert as his son. "What nonsense," said my mother. "Such a suspicious man."

The doubts about Robert had always served to reinforce that there had never been any doubts about me. I was Trevor's legitimate daughter and as such preferred by him to my brother. This was always so, and even in Trevor's will, where we were both essentially disinherited, I got first choice of a memento while Robert got second choice. Robert settled for a pair of silver cufflinks after I had chosen the "canteen" of silver, each piece embossed with the adopted Westbrook coat of arms, a mail boot. The canteen was a wedding present to Trevor from his company, and there is a small brass plate on the mahogany box that bears the inscription:

Presented to
T.C.L. WESTBROOK
ON THE OCCASION OF HIS
WEDDING
BY THE DIRECTORS OF THE
HESTON AIRCRAFT CO. LTD.
JANUARY 9th, 1942

I had noticed this date when the box came to me, was startled for a moment, and then reconciled the discrepancy with the facts as I knew them. January 9, 1942, was surely the date not of the marriage but of the presentation of the gift—after Trevor had returned by boat to England and conveyed his happy news to the directors of his company.

Faced with my accumulating evidence—the photos, the porringer, the fact of the January wedding that now left December as a time when my mother could undivertedly have been involved with Freddie in New York, the obscuring of the wedding date not only to us in conversation but in her books as well—I turned and turned again to my pivotal question: Could she have lied to me? For the strongest point against the case for Freddie's paternity was the total lack of evidence for it in my mother's words or behavior during all the years I had known her. "Your father, Trevor Westbrook." She had talked about him, complained about him, joked about him, had some compassion for him. And there had never been the slightest slip to suggest that he was not my father or that Freddie was.

My mother was a woman who lied all her life. Nevertheless, by the time we were grown-up, we thought that she had shared with us all the important earlier concealments and reshapings. As children we did not know her real name or background. It was only in 1957 when she was working on her first book, *Beloved Infidel,* with her collaborator, Gerold Frank, that Robert and I learned about Lily Shiel, and about Scott Fitzgerald as well. Before that there were vague stories of a genteel past, and she told us that her middle name was the name of a flower. Rose? Daisy? Petunia? We tried to guess what it was, but we never guessed Lily.

My mother's autobiographies were confessional, but they also served the interests of concealment, what was said masking the not said, the divulging of secrets serving to hide other more deeply buried ones. *Beloved Infidel* revealed my mother's impoverished childhood in an East End orphanage, but it suppressed her family, except for her mother, and also her Jewishness. In truth, my mother was the youngest of six children of Russian Jewish immigrant parents. Her father, a tailor, had died when she was a baby, and she, along with her brother Morris, had been placed in an orphanage because their widowed mother lacked the means to care for them. We learned about the brothers and sisters and about the Jewishness only after the publication of *Beloved Infidel* when one of her brothers gave the story of her "real" background to a London paper. Threatened with exposure—I can't remember if the story actually ran or the paper simply threatened to run it—she felt she had to tell us the truth.

I was sixteen, and to learn that I was half Jewish was a shock. After all, I had been one of the few children at the Hawthorne Elementary School in Beverly Hills to attend school on Jewish holidays, and for years my mother had packed me off—my protests unavailing—to the Sunday-school classes that I hated at All Saints Episcopal Church. We were in London, staying at the Dorchester Hotel (this was the same summer that my mother walked out on Freddie and me in the restaurant), and I remember her calling my brother and me into the bedroom of our suite, saying that she had something to tell us. After her revelation, I turned to the mirror on the wall behind me. I'm not sure what I expected to see, but surely some change to mark my new identity, and it jarred as much as it soothed me that I looked the same as before. Facing back towards my mother, I reproached her for her concealments, and for years to come I went around resolutely telling people that I was half Jewish. This irritated my mother no end, for as she so aptly put it, "They're going to know that it isn't Trevor Westbrook."

It was a shock as well to meet my mother's sisters (I never did meet the brothers), whom she took us shortly afterwards to visit. The fat sister and the thin sister, she called them. Sally and Iris, though they had started life as Sara and Esther. Iris, the thin sister and the elder of the two, nearly twenty years older than my mother, lived in Hove. Sally, the fat sister, a few years younger than Iris, lived in Brighton. The sisters had feuded years earlier and not spoken to one another since, though their homes were only a few miles apart. Iris was genteel and owned a building. Sally lived in a basement flat with her son Len, the unemployed barber, and was the gentler and nicer of the two, though my mother said one had to have the most respect for Iris. I was surprised when I met the sisters how much they looked like my mother. We divided our day between them, taking lunch with one and tea with the other. They had been hurt by my mother's omission of them from the book and by the years since my birth that she had not been in touch. It had been her decision, she explained to us, not to mix up her past with the privileged lives of her children. Now they forgave her, and contact resumed. Despite the years of disavowal, she was attached to them. She never again failed to visit them on her trips to England, and she liked to talk about them: their foibles, their illnesses, her memories of them from childhood. They were the only link to her early life, and she would express a childlike delight at the prospect of Sally's good Jewish cooking.

To the question whether this was a woman who could lie about the fathering of her children, the answer had to be yes. Of course she could—and easily. After all, she had suppressed her name, her background, her religion, her family. What, compared to these ties, was a mere father of children? The marvel was not the initial lie or its maintenance through the years of our childhood, but its being sustained so unassailably, so persuasively, to the very end. Then too, it was hard for me to grasp how she could still be lying to *us*. With the other lies, we had become her confidants, her conspirators in knowing the truth. But here was a case in which we, above all other people, were never to know the truth if she could help it. This is what astonished and confused me and put all the reality of our relationship in question.

What led me to know that Freddie was my father, even before I heard from him, was seeing the photographs in the second volume of his autobiography, *More of My Life*. I was having trouble getting hold of the book, but my good friend Anna Lawson, who lives in Virginia and whom I was planning shortly to visit, phoned me in great excitement to say that she had found a copy in the University of Virginia library.

"Do the pictures look like me?" I asked.

"Well, there's one," she said. "If you turn to page 163. I've seen the exact expression on your face a thousand times."

I asked if she thought Freddie was really my father, and she gave a guarded assent. "But you must see for yourself," she added. And that is what I proceeded to do.

I journeyed on the train to Charlottesville to the encounter with the Volume 2 photographs of Freddie Ayer. Arriving at Anna's house, I sat outside with her on the front stoop—I remember that it was an unusually balmy day for early February—and we looked at the pictures. There was one of Freddie seated between Raymond Carr and Hugh Trevor-Roper, his eyes crinkled up and smiling his genial smile. "I think that looks a bit like you," said Anna. "But look at this one. This is the one I was talking about."

She pointed to a picture of yet again a smiling Freddie Ayer. It shows him seated at a table, probably in a restaurant or a café, looking at a slight upward angle towards the camera, clearly pleased with himself and having a good time. At his side is a woman of obvious sophistication. They are leaning together, arms touching from shoulders to elbows, his jacket sleeve in contact with her white fur stole. The caption reads, "With Elizabeth von Hofmannsthal at Zell-am-See, 1957."

Freddie's age in this picture would have been forty-six, my exact age at this moment of discovery. The resemblance leaped out from the page, overwhelming and irrefutable. I think that until this moment I had hung on, not always even at the forefront of my mind, to a reserve of doubt. I had been playing with the idea of Freddie as my father, staging the drama and suspending disbelief but ever set to return to less dizzying reality. Now the doubt was gone. This *was* reality, however inexplicable. "My God," I said to Anna. "It's really true, isn't it? Absolutely really true. Freddie Ayer is my father."

And simultaneous with this realization came a great swell of fury at my mother, who, how could one construe otherwise, had kept this attractive father from me. "She can rot in hell, as far as I'm concerned," I heard myself saying later at dinner. This seemed an oddly melodramatic denunciation even as I pronounced it. For one thing, I cherish no belief whatsoever—and never have—in either hell or heaven. But what could I have said that would have been more precise? I felt hardened against my mother and implacably unforgiving. She had committed a great crime against me, whatever her reasons. For robbing me of Freddie was in an important way robbing me of myself. The question now was to what extent I could recoup the loss, redress the wrong. And peace with my mother seemed tied to my ability not just to understand her but to redress what she had done.

Quite soon, and not really as an act of will, the rage abated and I felt again the old connection with my mother, larger than her lie, the old embattled but powerful love. Much was to happen with Freddie as my new father. And something did change—I was other than I had been before. But beneath it all—the profound undercurrent always pulling me back in—there was the abiding bond, my mother and me, ours, after all, the important reckoning.

Three

ORPHAN AND DAUGHTER

MALIBU BEACH, 1951. My mother and I have our special driftwood log that in my nine-year-old's memory has always been there at the far end of the beach. We make the log our destination on our beach walks, and then, sitting astride it, face to face, we pretend it is a train to Timbuktu. My mother sits with her back to the ocean, which sparkles behind her in the afternoon light—whitecaps topping the iridescent blue. Her eyes are an iridescent green, "the softest gentlest eyes," someone was to describe them many years later, in awed remembrance of her beauty. The sun, also behind her, angles from the west and casts around her an aureole of light. Her hair is golden, and she laughs in pleasure at the game. All aboard. All aboard for Timbuktu.

I also remember sitting on the log—the time must be some years later—and my mother says that her great mistake has been to consider herself her children's friend rather than their parent.

"Why is that a mistake?" I ask.

"Because," she says, "we must lead more separate lives." She recurs to her favorite exemplary tale, from the Walt Disney movie about the bears. The mother bear sends her cubs up a tree and orders them to stay there—they mustn't come down, whatever the temptation; they mustn't come down until her return. She departs, and they do as ordered. They are good little bears, and obedience is a connection with the mother. She, though, does not come back. The movie shows time passing: it is day, then night, then day again. Finally, the cubs climb down from the tree and begin to fend for themselves. This is what the mother wanted. She left to make them independent.

My mother's relish for this story has always disconcerted me. I don't quite know what it augurs or why the options must be so extreme. Whenever she is angry with me, my mother announces her intention to go off and lead her own life. She wishes me well, but we must be more separate. Separateness is her fantasy and also her fear. I have my own difficulties with separateness. At twenty, I write to my mother that but for my knowledge that she will grow old and die, I would stay with her always and never marry.

New York, 1967. Another memory. I am twenty-five and for the time being living at home again after sharing an apartment with my now-discarded first serious boyfriend. My mother and I are at the dinner table, eating the Irish stew cooked and left for us by the maid. My mother chatters on about her work and her worries, and I am sullen, tense, withdrawn. I wish I were not with her. She loses patience and starts to shout at me. Her plan is to go out after dinner, but there is time for a harangue that continues up to the point of her leaving. As we stand together by the door of the apartment, she slaps my arm hard in her frustration.

When she was a girl and her own mother hit her—I know the story well—she hit her mother right back. I don't feel I can do this, and the inhibition enrages me. "I'm warning you," I say. "Don't you ever hit me again,"

"What will you do?" she asks.

"I'll leave," I reply.

My mother goes out. I feel relieved that she is gone. But only a minute later, there is a ring at the door.

"Who is it?" I ask.

"Your mother."

"What do you want?"

"To hit you."

Hearing laughter in her voice, I think she must be joking. Smiling, I open the door. She steps in, slaps my arm, and says to me, "Now leave!"

"That's a telling story," said a friend of mine. "Your mother was humiliating you with your dependence." I think, rather, that my mother couldn't stand the specter of rejection. My proclaiming my power to leave, even as an act of self-defense, was intolerable. She preferred issuing her challenge to living under my threat.

I didn't leave because it was eight o'clock at night and it seemed stupid to be wandering around in the streets with no-where to go. I said that I would leave in the morning, but by then we had patched things up.

It was not long after this incident—I was still in my twen-ties—that I went with my mother on an excursion to the East End of London, our project to revisit the neighborhood of her childhood. Whether the idea to go was hers or mine I don't recall. Somehow we formed our plan to travel by bus to Step-ney Green, where my mother could show me her home after leaving the orphanage. Lily Shiel had come home at age four-teen to live in a two-room tenement apartment with her mother, dying of cancer of the colon, and her eldest brother, Henry, until the mother's death, three years later, freed her to leave the East End and its dingy poverty behind her. Our excursion was, in a sense, my guided tour of the poverty from which she had escaped. It occurred to me that it was losing her mother that had given my mother so much freedom. After her mother's death she had no one to answer to. What would her life have been with the mother still alive?

I was staying with my mother in the house she then owned at 7 Lancelot Place, just off the Brompton Road. These were the years in which she kept multiple homes in New York and London and sometimes California, but the little two-story row house in Knightsbridge was her special treasure. She loved de-scribing its location as "a whisper from Harrods and a shout from Hyde Park."

We set off gaily on the number 14 bus that stops on the Brompton Road opposite Harrods, my mother at times like these so much fun, a wonderful conspirator in adventure. Our route lay through Piccadilly and the City, and then for me it grew unfamiliar. Twice we had to change buses. I was im-pressed at how vast London was—much bigger than my West End vantage point had ever led me to imagine—and I was also impressed at how well my mother remembered the way. Per-haps this should not have seemed so astonishing. She had told me of her restlessness after leaving the orphanage and the lure for her of the West End. On her day off from her job in an addressograph factory (from which she was soon fired for danc-ing in the washroom), she would travel by bus to the West End simply to use the toilet at the Savoy Hotel or, a longer escape, to queue for hours for a gallery seat to one of the shows: the Beatrice Lillie revue at the Vaudeville or *Chu Chin Chow* at His Majesty's Theatre in the Haymarket. I remember her teaching us as children the singsong line from *Chu Chin Chow* that she had found so memorable—"I am Chu Chin Chow from China"—the drawn-out words then followed by a crash of a hundred cymbals that we reproduced simply by shouting "CRASH!" at the top of our lungs. Coincidentally, *Chu Chin Chow* was the first show Freddie ever went to when his mother started taking him to West End musical comedies. Freddie writes of this in his autobiography, and reading his account, I imagined a first crossing of my parents' lives: the year 1919, fifteen-year-old Lily, the East End interloper, in her hard-won seat in the gallery and Freddie, six years her junior, a child with his mother in the stalls.

I have a very imprecise memory of my visit with my mother to Stepney Green. I remember our bus going down a long dismal street and our getting off in a shabby, visibly Jewish neighborhood where men in the streets wore black hats and yarmulkes. My mother found her way unerringly to the building that had been her home. It was still there, and we stood in front of it, wondering whether we should try to go inside. I think we did look into someone's apartment, and I was duly impressed by how stark and poor it was, but this memory has the quality of a dream; the incident may nor actually have happened.

We then found a little restaurant and ordered some blini. My mother talked about her horror of poverty and her drive to escape from living in a ghetto. She also retold the story of hitting her mother. Her mother had asked her to do a job she hated, to pumice the yard. When she sullenly refused, her mother had smacked her face, and Lily smacked right back. She was immediately contrite—to have hit her poor ill mother was a terrible thing—but as she explained to me many times, "Whenever I am attacked, I attack back without thinking." Her brother had beaten her senseless when he came home and heard what had happened.

It was after this that Lily felt she needed to leave—"Whenever I find a situation I cannot resolve, I go away from it. I

don't wait to see how it's going to come out"—and she found a
job as a live-in skivvy in a house at Brighton. She returned home
when her mother was actually dying, but then left for good,
landing her job as the toothbrush demonstrator at Gamage's—
it was a special toothbrush to clean the back of the teeth—and
moving on to her own little West End apartment. She felt that
she had never really known her mother and had not been a
good daughter. The mother comes alive for me only in odd
little flashes—I know so little about her. I do know that she
loved the ocean, and somehow this seems poignant, because
we—my mother and I—have also loved it. My mother described how her mother would stand facing the sea, inhale the
air, and sigh, *"Ah, die Luft, die Luft."* Also I know that my
grandmother used to call my mother by her Jewish name—was
it a middle name or an alternative name to Lily?—"Ah Chana-
leah." It's odd to me that I don't know—did I never ask?—
what my grandmother's name was, nor that of my mother's
father, the dignified-looking tailor from the one picture we
have of him, whose death when she was a baby left his family so
impoverished. He died on a trip to Berlin and is buried there in
the Jewish cemetery. My mother visited his grave in the early
1930s and told us about the German children who came around
throwing stones and shouting, *"Juden, Juden."*

My mother wanted to give us a childhood that had no poverty in it, no hardship, no Jewishness. Nor was the simple contrast of our privilege with her deprivation enough to satisfy her.
I'm not sure how systematically she thought this out, but our
total ignorance of her past must have seemed a measure of her
successful escape from it. My mother was a great believer that
the past could be left behind. When a situation was wrong, she
said, she would try to better it, and if that was impossible, she
would obliterate it from her mind. I'm not sure this worked as
well as she claimed. From her later obsession with her childhood, it's hard to imagine her forgetting for a week or even a
day the memories of her early poverty and her shame at being

Jewish. But at least these roots could be erased from the consciousness of her children.

And they effectively were. Whatever my later awareness and curiosity, my mother's origins remain quite apart from my basic sense of self. I try to feel Jewish, all the more so since acquiring Freddie, who had a Jewish mother, as my second parent. But I really don't. The Jewishness has always seemed a kind of optional overlay. I try to think of Sally and Iris as my aunts, but although I visited them several times with my mother, they are hardly more real to me as "relatives" than my mother's alleged "dead brother David," the blond little boy in a sailor suit whose portrait—a colored-pencil drawing—was paired with one of my mother as an ethereal-looking child in a sweet little blue dress, a daffodil held in her soft baby hand. These were in fact fakes. The boy was no brother but my mother's first husband, John Graham Gillam, and the portrait of my mother, taken from a snapshot of her as a baby, had been "renovated" so that it matched Johnny's.

We accepted our mother as she presented herself to us—the genteel little girl holding the daffodil or the beautiful working mother who inspired such confidence in her sufficiency that we never thought to wonder how she came by it. In any case, Beverly Hills was not a place where one dwelt much on the past, this film-world town where even the palm trees were *arrivistes* in an artfully transformed desert. Sheltered in our mother's house, the beneficiaries of her successful recreation, what need did we have to wonder about the life that had gone before?

When I think of my origins, I think of my mother, and I think of 607 North Maple Drive. In 1947, drawing on all her savings, my mother mustered a down payment on an old but elegant Beverly Hills Spanish-style house, and there we lived for close to twelve years with the assurance, particularly in the beginning, of utter order and solidity. It wasn't simply that the white stucco walls had a fortresslike thickness or that we were accommodated with pets and bicycles and a ping-pong table on the back veranda. It was the orderly life of the house, the reassuring points of reference in the people who worked there: my mother, whom I would always seek out after school, never afraid to interrupt her on my way out to play in the high wall-enclosed backyard; the housekeeper in the kitchen, making pastry dough or cooking or ironing laundry; the secretary tapping out my mother's column on her typewriter in the bookcase-lined den; the Filipino gardener working shirtless out of doors, adjusting the sprinkler system or trimming the edges of the manicured front lawn. It was a house full of industry, in which my part was to take everything for granted and to go my own way within its enclosure. This was *my* early life and all the past I ever knew. Beverly Hills with its streets tree-lined and hushed. Our house. A peach tree in the backyard. Friends. A series of cherished dogs. Then Malibu Beach in the summers for children, dogs, and servants. And our mother, our beautiful mother, unique parent, our only relative, the prime mover of it all. Our mother at the center of our lives. What did it mean to her to bear and raise children? What did it mean to her, since this is her story and mine, to have and be attached to a daughter, this mother whose own mother put her six-year-old child in an orphanage and then completed the lesson in self-sufficiency by dying before that child quite grew up?

When Sheilah Graham, accompanied by six-week-old Wendy Frances Westbrook, arrived in California in late October 1942, the woman who had been the most beautiful chorus girl of 1927, the fiancée of the Marquis of Donegall, and F. Scott Fitzgerald's "beloved infidel" was a very anxious thirty-eight-year-old new mother. A baby nurse brought from New York completed our little band, joining with my mother to safeguard the baby's precious new life. Looking at this triad another way, I see baby and nurse in the role that they combined to play for my mother: her entourage, her household, the substantiation, for herself and the world, of her new maternal identity.

It had taken my mother a couple of days after my birth to warm to me. She had hoped, I gather, for a daughter who would be tall and blond, and her plan was to name this person Penelope, since "Mrs. Ulysses," as she put it, had all those suitors. Tiny and brunette and with what she always described as a Japanese-style hairdo, I did not look like a Penelope, so she switched to Wendy. The Vanderbilts had just named a new daughter Wendy, and she said, "What was good enough for the Vanderbilts seemed good enough for me." She also had always loved the story of Peter Pan because Wendy was a mother to the lost boys. Once in a class in the orphanage the children had been asked what they wanted to be when they grew up. Other girls had answered nurse or teacher; my mother had said, "A mother." The fact that she herself still had a living mother distinguished her from most of the other "orphans," and she valued the superiority this distinction conferred.

On the second day that I was brought to her in the hospital, I still had my "Japanese" appearance, but in a moment of surrender she came to accept that I was her baby. As she told the story, I emitted a little grunt and got all red in the face. And that was it. Mother love struck. She fell passionately in love with me, and from that instant on, she said, would have killed to protect me.

Whether I was ever in need of such zealous protection is another matter. It strikes me that my mother lacked confidence in her baby as a creature with some inherent resources for survival. I was hers. My life depended on her. And she, in turn, with no prior experience of babies, depended on the seasoned wisdom of Miss Edna Haines, the grizzled professional baby nurse who augmented the importance of her own role by stressing the baby's complex, unnegotiable needs and consequent requirement of care that no mere first-time mother could provide.

Miss Haines had three passions: small babies, New York City, and cake and candy (according to my mother, she had had all her natural teeth removed and replaced by false ones so that she could indulge her sweet tooth without worry of tooth decay). My mother plied her with her favorite chocolates and got her to agree to leave New York, at least temporarily, to ensure through her vigilance my survival in inhospitable California. She stayed six months and by all accounts quite terrorized both my mother and me, though my mother had such faith in her skill that she brought her back from New York three years later to care for Robert. It was Miss Haines who egged my mother on to such acts of extremity as getting the Good Humor man to turn off his bells when he came down our street so as not to disturb my nap, and persuading the landlord of the little house my mother had rented on South Palm Drive to water the garden in the middle of the night so that the moisture, pernicious to the baby, would evaporate by morning.

As children we loved the stories of our mother's crazed obsessiveness over her babies, particularly me, the first one. The point was that she doted on us, was dotty about us. But how can it have been that simple? Doting is a strain. And how could a person who herself as a child had had so little not have resented being called upon to give so much? From journal entries that have survived among her papers, I get a glimpse of her difficulties, unacknowledged but expressed, beneath the effusive statements of devotion. I see her confinement; I see her strategies, absorbed as she was in the baby, to reclaim her separateness; I see her bafflement, painful beneath humor and self-mockery, in relating to this strange new creature in her life. "At three months," she writes of me,

> *there is a big change in the baby. She gurgles and coos and seems to recognize people or rather her nurse and me. I'm sorry to have to record that at this date she is fonder of the nurse than of me! The nurse can make her smile more than I can, and of course she handles*

her more expertly. She lies on her tummy and coos at the duck painted on her crib (Wendy, not the nurse). She drools quite a bit and anything she can stick into her mouth she does, this includes her hand, my finger, her rattle, and the nurse's face. Wendy's nurse loves her, but my heavens what a conversationalist! (the nurse, not the baby). Why don't I tell her that I am only interested in my baby and other babies that I know—not all the dozens of babies she has met and nursed in the past 20 years. I'm a coward, that's why. And she has the saving grace of loving the baby but oh dear oh dear. Wendy has an admirer—1 year old Peter Bell. To date he has given Wendy a tiny pair of shoes, a fluffy chicken, some little shirts, a dress, and a silver mug with Wendy Westbrook, September 11, 1942 engraved on it. Being a match-making mama, I can already see Wendy married to Peter Bell.

A couple months later I am crawling, Peter Bell is still my beau, and my mother, describing the travails of babyhood, continues also to communicate her own:

Friday, February 26, 1943   *Wendy has been really crawling for a few days now. We put a toy at one end of the crib, Wendy at the other. In her excitement at getting to the toy she sometimes crosses her legs and then of course can't move!!*

   She has been awfully slow on the milk again today. But oh how I love her. Mrs. Bell and Peter came to visit her as she lay in her pram in the patio. A tooth looks as though it might soon come through—there is a little blister on the gum. Everything is so hard and must be worked at, my poor Wendy. She is biting everything she can get hold of.

   Tonight the stars are hard and white and there is a strange perfume everywhere. I love these nights in California.

It disheartens me that my mother's emphasis falls on my difficulties rather than achievements, the getting stuck rather than the crawling, the blister rather than the tooth. All my life I sought her admiration, but I think admiration was something she basically needed to reserve for herself. For others she had sympathy, loyalty, pity, and an acute eye for the ways that, engaged in the struggle of their lives, they were foolish or weak. She wasn't contemptuous. It's just that she could care for people more if she could focus on their vulnerabilities, and I think she needed to feel the contrast of her own exceptional courage and panache. Often I have worried that she lacked respect for me. But I wonder if "poor Wendy" was not also at heart "poor Lily," and my little teething blister an emblem of our common pain and struggle.

Sometimes my mother envied people, not so much for what they were as for what they had—an education, ancestors who gave them a comfortable niche in the world, money that gave them possessions and assumptions, husbands and parents who loved them. As far as lay in her power, she bestowed such advantages on me, exuberant in her ability to do so. I was her product, her retort to society, she something like Magwitch creating his "gentleman" in *Great Expectations.* Yet unlike the example of Pip's criminal benefactor, my mother's foremost creation remained herself. Having fashioned me, she was then in competition with her handiwork. Separateness stubbornly reintruded. We were separate, rival forces, and again and again in her descriptions of me her pity or her wit or both were called upon to put me in my place. Thus, an account of my first birthday, beginning with the inventory of all the good things I ate and beautiful presents I received while my "doting mother *knitted!!*" and Walter Pidgeon paid his respects, concludes with the notation of my collapse. "The day's excitement was too much for Wendy and she ended the day by stabbing her cheek with a clothespin. (I'm certainly glad that birthdays come only once a year.)"

It was a month after my first birthday that my mother went away from me for a period of five months. She traveled to England to be with Trevor, while I remained behind in California in the care of her friend Valerie Bell, the mother of my "admirer" Peter.

Mrs. Bell, as we always formally referred to her, was a

wealthy woman whose family, as my mother put it, "owned" General Foods. She and my mother had met when both were spending the 1942 summer in Easthampton, my mother in the last months of her pregnancy. Mrs. Bell was planning to move the subsequent fall to California and welcomed a Hollywood-connected new friend. They went together to the movies and spent time, I imagine, talking about babies and men. My mother liked Mrs. Bell's elegance, and Mrs. Bell surely must have felt the charm of my mother's zest and energy. The friendship then continued in California and, while it lasted, seems to have been a close one. Mrs. Bell, living in a large rented house in Bel Air, came to visit us often, gave munificent presents, and all in all took a great interest in my mother's baby as well as in my mother. In addition to Peter, Mrs. Bell had an older child who was in some way mentally defective and had been placed in an institution. My mother always said that Mrs. Bell sought me as a normalizing companion for Peter so that he would not turn out like his brother.

In my mother's book *The Rest of the Story,* it is Mrs. Bell, thinly disguised as "rich fashionable Mrs. Richardson, the wife of an Eastern industrialist," who is credited with making possible my mother's return to England by offering to take care of me in California for however long the visit with Trevor lasted. My mother had not seen Trevor since the few days they spent together in Washington in January 1942. "It must be hard to think of Wendy as having a father," Scottie Fitzgerald wrote to her—an arresting comment—in an August 1942 letter. "And after a year and a half you must hardly remember what Trevor looks like." Out of fear of losing the baby, my mother had not wanted leave New York during her pregnancy; then she opted to return to California and resume her column rather than take me as an infant back to wartime London.

Trevor, as far as I know and can confirm, did not suspect, then or ever, that I was another man's baby. I recently learned from his niece, my cousin Ann Westbrook, who lives in New

York, that to get Trevor to marry her, my mother had pretended that she was pregnant with his child—I guess from the
previous September in England. "And then," said Ann, "she
said she wasn't pregnant. And then she was again, for real, with
you." To feign pregnancy to get a man to marry you is a time-
honored and conventional strategy, and probably to a man like
Trevor was quite forgivable in a beautiful woman. It must have
flattered him that she had been so intent on entrapping him.
And then too she got pregnant again so immediately after the
marriage, thus making good on the earlier fiction. What I am
struck by is the audacious layers of lies. Trevor thought she had
been lying when she wasn't (or at least she was only half lying—
she *was* pregnant, but not by him) and not lying when she was.
She had gulled Trevor so ruthlessly, so easily. It's frightening to
imagine what she can have thought of him.

My guess, though, is that she thought about him very little.
Her focus was on meeting her own needs, moving on from a
crisis, and Trevor was a solution to her problem. She lied to
him because she was used to lying—that was the way she knew
to maintain herself in the world. Nor do I think that the lying
puts in doubt her sincerity in then wanting to make the best of
circumstances and give this marriage a chance. Trevor kept urg-
ing her to join him, and she kept putting him off. I think she
realized, however, that if she wanted to stay married, she had to
go to England. The tenuous link between them needed substantiation.

Knowing this, I also know that Trevor meant little to her
and I meant a lot, and it does seem strange that she could leave
me, thirteen months old, with Mrs. Bell. It was the war, I tell
myself, and the war created unusual separations. She needed to
go; it would have been irresponsible to take a small baby with
her to air-raid-battered London—people were sending children
out of England, not bringing them in; and she had assured
herself that I would be well taken care of. Because of the connection with General Foods, Mrs. Bell's larder, as described by
my mother, bulged with canned foods, sides of bacon, and

cereal—everything for the well-nourished child. No need here to worry about rationing. And proper nourishment to my mother, the hunger of her childhood never behind her, loomed always as a powerful fixation.

My mother herself does not help much in the illumination of her motives. As recounted in *The Rest of the Story,* this particular tale, the story of the departure for England, featured a classic conflict between duty (to Trevor) and devotion (to me): "No one believed . . . I would actually go. They knew how my entire life revolved around Wendy, and they thought I would not have the courage to leave her. But Trevor had been so patient. I had to give our marriage a chance. . . ." I wince at my mother's clichés and suspect they are served up to hide things or at least shade the truth. Certainly, Trevor awaited. But what in California was pushing her to leave? Perhaps she was fleeing some sexual entanglement. Probably there was a fulfillment of fantasy in her "lending" me to a fabulously wealthy and elegant woman like Mrs. Bell. Great wealth intrigued her, and now I would be cared for in a way that cannot have failed to offer vicarious pleasure. I think too that there was relief for her in escaping from her baby. She said as much once shortly before her death, acknowledging in a passing comment that one of her motives for going had indeed been to get away. England, she said, was exciting, and confinement in California with a small baby and the nurses had been hard. I don't mind this, but I do resent the rhetoric of maternal devotion that obscured one whole side of the truth. My mother confused me to the end of her life by the equal intensity of her connectedness with me and her underlying ruthless separateness. She couldn't live without me, yet on a number of occasions she more or less ran away. She loved me, yet she could leave me behind. She was devoted to me, yet always wary. She was obsessed by the connection but could never quite trust in it—connection with me or for that matter with anyone in her life. And I was always stunned by her shifts.

I have found in my mother's papers the instructions that

she left with Mrs. Bell for my care when she departed for England in October 1943. Focusing mainly on food, bowels, and sleep, they reveal a woman both obsessed with and I think terrified by the burden of a young child. More than any other document I have come upon, they bring to light her equivocal feelings towards me, her daughter, this dependent creature who yet found an infant's ways to evince her own stubborn individuality.

The instructions begin without introductory ado on the topic of how to fool me into eating and drinking the things I didn't like: how to disguise potato by mixing it in with spinach or asparagus or peas, or to put any food that I might "turn against" in another type of dish. This applies to milk, explains my mother,

which we sometimes give her in a plain cup instead of her silver (Big) cup. And her cereal which we sometimes put in a plain plate instead of the porringer. It is usually advisable to give her milk (lukewarmish) in the big cup because usually she takes it in one go and when there is a pause she may not take much more. . . .

A matter-of-fact paragraph on diarrhea comes next, after which is the commentary on my cough:

She has the phoniest cough in existence. Use your own judgment in, ignoring it, or telling her with authority to stop it. She has been known to spend an hour at night starting off with this phoney cough and it usually ends with a real coughing spell. When I told this to Doctor Berkeley he told us to give her half a teaspoon of Cherycl. PLEASE DO NOT DO THIS ON ANY ACCOUNT UNLESS SHE HAS AN HONEST TO GOODNESS SERIOUS COUGH. Cherycl contains a strong dope and makes Wendy spit up her food.

The plans that follow for my toilet training seem humane—a program for gradual progress. But it is the need for restraint more than freedom that is stressed in the next few notations. I must be "strapped" into my chair because I "rock to and fro and try to stand up in it all the time." "THE BED STRAPS" (capitalized and underlined) are said to "have proved extremely successful," though my mother prefers that Mrs. Bell not use "the cuffs" unless I suck my thumb too much in the daytime, which my mother does not think I will do as I am "too much interested in everything else." But even my responsiveness is a cause for concern:

Wendy is extremely high strung. IT'S VERY IMPORTANT THAT SHE DOES NOT SEE STRANGERS IMMEDIATELY PRIOR TO HER SUPPER AND NEVER AFTERWARDS, or she will stay awake for hours. And too many visitors at any hour make her very excited and off her food. I'll be grateful Val if you remember this always. I want her to get used to people, but it must be VERY GRADUALLY. She has not yet had a toy or doll in bed with her and in her case it might be a mistake because it would distract instead of soothe her (we even have to hide the blanket clips because when she sees them she just plays with them for hours).

Other concerns include my appearance—which she worries about in some blurring with her own; she asks Mrs. Bell to "PLEASE ALWAYS BRUSH HAIR AWAY FROM . . . FACE AND EARS AND NECK," since my hairline, like hers, is "very low"—and my character, which she summarizes as follows:

The chief thing to remember about Wendy is that she is absolutely unpredictable. Miss Haines used to call her "The Unpredictable Wendy." One week she will loathe cereal. The next she will love it. If she dislikes anything, never assume that she won't like it tomorrow. For instance, she hated sweet custards. Now she loves them. She started by hating Jello. Now she adores it. . . .

The document ends with a description of WENDY'S DAILY ROUTINE that emphasizes timetable precision (oranges at 10:00 A.M., bath at 11:45, lunch at 12:00, etc.), long naps ("keep in bed for two hours regardless of how long her sleep"), and a short day (dinner at 5:30 and sleep for the night by 6:15).

As I can evoke her in conscious memory of childhood, my mother was not the grim, rigidly controlling person that emerges in these rather sinister instructions. I think that her comments reflect the prevailing wisdom of the era about babies: schedules were rigid, and I have friends of my generation who were also strapped into their beds. They reflect her deference to the nurses who preferred sleeping babies to more bothersome awake ones and were the most zealous enforcers of routine. And they reflect her guilt at leaving me, which must have been great.

Nonetheless, when all this is said and given due weight, I am still quite struck by my mother's lack of ease with me. I had been around, after all, for over a year, and it doesn't seem that she had settled down with me yet very comfortably, though granted I sound like a difficult baby. I feel a bit silly to mind this, but there it is, I do, however much I tell myself that her lack of ease was clearly with herself.

The day finally came that my mother left for England, giving up her column and committing herself to the unfamiliar role of dependent wife, in which, predictably, she was miserable. She found life with Trevor oppressive and above all hated having to ask him for money. Then too, she missed me and felt very far from me. An entry in my baby book describes how she used to walk around the Serpentine in Hyde Park with a desperate feeling that she would never see me again. And looking at the big map on the wall in their flat at 49 Hill Street, Berkeley Square, she despaired that the distance to New York, then to California, could again be bridged. Depressed and irritable, she took refuge in her knitting and spent much of her time making me booties and sweaters.

Trevor urged her to return to California in order to bring me back with her to England. This was the plan they agreed upon, but as she left him, getting out right before the first dropping of the buzz bomb, she wasn't at all sure that she could ever be happy in England with Trevor or would ever be back.

While she was waiting for the visa that would permit her to

reenter the States, my mother wrote a letter to Mrs. Bell that is full of her eagerness to be back in California. The letter explains that her syndicate, the North American Newspaper Alliance, was arranging her return—the syndicate had to vouch that she was needed to resume her job and thus should be granted a visa, though, in fact, someone else had taken over the column and she had no guarantee of getting it back. Undaunted, my mother's immediate concern was just to be reunited with her baby and to work out with Mrs. Bell the best scheme for a transition in child care:

What would you like me to do—take over Wendy immediately or leave her with Mary [Mrs. Bell's nursemaid] for a couple of weeks until she gets used to me again, and until I learn to cook her food from Mary? I'll be a good pupil now because I cook Trevor's dinner nearly every night and have a fair knowledge of cooking [my mother always hated cooking and was bad at it] but I would be grateful if Mary could show me how to cook Wendy's food. I thought if this was all right with you, I could assist Mary with the children, act as a sort of under-nursemaid for a few weeks so that poor old Wendy wouldn't have another abrupt changeover. . . .

The letter continues with discussion of other plans for her return and effusive thanks to Mrs. Bell—"it was marvelously sweet of you to take care of my baby . . . Dr. Berkeley described you as a 'wonderful woman'—I think he's got something there."

My mother was soon to lose such breezy confidence in her onetime friend. Taking passage on the *Queen Elizabeth,* which as a transport for troops (my mother, one of the few women on board, was given the honorary rank of captain) made its way across rough seas with eleven submarines lurking to sink it, she kissed the ground upon disembarking in New York, vowed never to leave this country again, and eagerly phoned Mrs. Bell. To her shock and dismay, the reception was cool. The friend seemed angry that she was back, and then when my mother got to California, made her take me away at once.

My mother struggled then and long afterwards to understand what had happened. It was her theory that Mrs. Bell had hoped she would simply not return—be killed in the war, I guess—and Mrs. Bell, the surrogate mother, would then get to keep me. When my mother did come back, Mrs. Bell couldn't adjust and simply wanted the both of us out of her life.

My reunion with my mother was not a happy one. I yelled at the first sight of her ("not with love," she noted) and struggled to escape when the nurse tried to hand me into her arms. Later when Mrs. Bell met with my mother for their one brief interview and we were all, mothers and children, together in the same room, Mrs. Bell called, "Come to Mama, Wendy," my mother rose expectantly, and I ran into Mrs. Bell's outstretched arms.

Mrs. Bell rejected my mother's scheme for gradual transition. She said she was against two mothers in the same house and in any case was shortly leaving for Mexico. Her plan would have been to take me with her, but she was sure my mother would now want to resume my care. My mother had to find a house quickly—she rented a small one in North Hollywood—and to buy a car. Still without a job, she could not afford any help. So for a while it was she alone who took care of me—doing, as she recorded, "all the cooking, etc. and what a time I'm having feeding Wendy who is a voluntary vomiter—throws up her food when she wants to." She was pleased, though, with what fast disloyalty to Mrs. Bell I learned to call her Mama again.

The baby-book entry for eighteen months also reveals that we were expecting Trevor's sister, Adrienne, "and her 3 (count 'em) children" to "come and stay until we can all go to England." I guess the marriage had not yet been explicitly acknowledged as a failure, though the five-month visit of my aunt and her three daughters, ages sixteen to ten, all of them hating California and Adrienne writing letters back to Trevor complaining about my mother, can have done little to help it. As my mother concluded after they had left us to go back East, "It didn't work out so well after all." But she was pleased to find life easier with me. "We have a happier time now, Wendy and I." Though still difficult about eating, I was more outgoing, she deemed me "very bright," and I gather we did a lot of playing and talking together.

At last she was relaxing and having some fun with me. The baby book, full of my quaint sayings and responses, shows how important it was to my mother that I could now express *my* devotion as well as be the object of hers. Her entries focus on the attention that I was giving her: I loved to take the combs out of her hair; I loved to feed her; I sat on the bench beside the court while she played tennis; together we came down with intestinal flu, and as we were vomiting together, I put my "dear little hand" on her face and said, "Poor Mummy." She also noted with pleasure my pleasure in myself. Holding her hand mirror, I kissed my face ecstatically, saying "Babee." I spoke of myself in the third person: "Wendy singing," "Wendy having a bath," "Wendy getting up." I was no longer shy and hailed children in the street. "Hi nice girl." Or "Hi boys," to soldiers and sailors.

Basically our life was settling down. My mother parlayed an offer from a rival syndicate into getting back her column with NANA; she hired our cook and housekeeper Stella, whom I loved as a second mother and who stayed with us until I was nine; we moved into a bigger house at 522 North Palm Drive, Beverly Hills, which is the first home I remember. It was to this house that my brother, Robert, was brought as a newborn baby; I played in the backyard that had a swing and a fig tree; and there we stayed for three quiet years until moving one block over to the house on North Maple. Though not without its shadows—sibling rivalry certainly among them—the stretch of childhood that I look back to as idyllic was under way.

As for Mrs. Bell and my strange interlude as "her little English refugee"—my mother's description of how I was trotted out to strangers—I knew of this only as one of the tales of our adventure-packed infancies, a peril from which I had escaped, though perhaps not unscathed, a brush with a kind of mildly wicked fairy-tale enchantress. Years later—I was thirteen and shopping with my mother at Bonwit Teller in New York—we encountered a tall, elegantly dressed woman in the elevator, one of those women of impeccable taste who you know are very rich. And that was Mrs. Bell. I was introduced to her, and she, friendly though basically haughty in style, observed to my mother, "I can't believe that this is Mousie." That had been the nickname conferred on me in my first few weeks of life, and I guess it had stuck for a while.

I don't know if my sojourn with Mrs. Bell affected me in any permanent way, but I confess that I have had a lifelong fear of being abandoned, and it does seem plausible to link this, at least in part, with the ordeal of changing "mamas" at thirteen months and then again five months later. Of course, I can only imagine what this must have felt like. I don't remember anything directly, since it all happened before I had much language to help in shaping memory and understanding.

My connection with the experience is therefore through my mother's story. I listened to her tale of poor Wendy and Mrs. Bell; it linked, perhaps even before we knew about my mother in the orphanage, with so much other family lore that stressed the *theme* of orphanage; and somehow I became a kind of orphan too: the child whose mother had gone away; who had not known her true mother's identity; who experienced the loss of *two* mothers, though one of these, the real one, did come back to her.

Four

607 NORTH MAPLE DRIVE

MY BROTHER AND I spent a day together a few years ago walking up and down the hills of San Francisco and talking about our childhood. We both, it turns out, have recurrent dreams about our old house at 607 North Maple Drive, emblem and talisman of a past from which we now feel severed. "We were raised in such glamour and then thrust out into such a different world," said Robert as we rested from our walking in a little health food restaurant—certainly a far cry from the Beverly Brown Derby or Romanoff's, the typical restaurants of our childhood.

I would not have used the word "glamour"—glamour for me was always problematic, the Hollywood aura, veneer, and commodity that my mother's column helped to purvey and that I insisted didn't really touch me. Still, I share my brother's sense of loss and disjunction. For me, it's not so much that we live less glamorously or less grandly. Indeed we do, though we each have had our moments of more conspicuous material success: Robert when he sold a book to the movies at age twenty-three and spent all the money within a year, mostly on dining out and travel, and I in my two years as the dean of a college in Virginia, where as a perquisite of the job I got to live in a three-story house that came with elegant furniture and a maid named Buttercup. My mother visited and said that the house reminded her of Tara in *Gone with the Wind*. To me, though, the house seemed insubstantial. It wasn't mine, and it felt like a stage set, a disguise masking some secret self who, whatever her achievements, has felt rootless and nomadic since leaving North Maple Drive.

That home was so precious to us, yet we cannot go back there. It seems a telling gesture that I chose the number 607 as part of my code for my current bank card. Thus, every time I deposit my paycheck or get cash for groceries, I reaffirm that I am Wendy Westbrook of 607 North Maple Drive. And I am also the person no longer of that address who has been struggling ever since to build a self, a life, a place that seems as persuasive and reassuring.

In my dreams about the house I am always back in it and always reunited with my mother and brother. Robert and I appear as our current grown-up selves, and our mother is old, but we are immensely happy and relieved to be back home. Sometimes we are guests, sometimes tenants or owners, and a recurring question is how long we are going to be allowed to stay. Sometimes the house is in disrepair—the backyard overgrown, the curtains framing the four French doors of the large oak-beam-ceilinged living room are frayed, and the anxiety of the dream is how to fix things up again, or how to pay the taxes or the mortgage so that we don't ever again have to leave. Sometimes our dog, Tony, the Dalmation, is back with us too—sick and old and requiring special treatment to be nursed back to health, but not dead. With meticulous dream logic I take note of the passage of time and find it surprising that there he is after all those years, restored to us, wagging his tail as he patters across the backyard.

People often ask me what it was like growing up in Hollywood in the heyday of the studios and the stars, and what I want to describe to them, if I care to make myself understood, is a world that I alone endowed with value: my personal world of childhood. I loved playing in the backyard with my dog. Stella, our Czechoslovakian housekeeper, was more important to me than any movie star neighbors, and we made no distinction among the guests at my fifth birthday party between Stella's nephew Irwin and Claire Trevor's son Charlie, both of whom—towheaded successors to Peter Bell—there was talk of me marrying. Hollywood was simply the business everyone was in—either as stars or agents or screenwriters or columnists or as lawyers, doctors, and accountants to the movie people. Or if I felt that we were special—and I did—it was because we set ourselves apart from Hollywood glitter. We preferred family weekends at the beach to gaudy Hollywood parties; our close friends were not stars or moguls; we had an unwaveringly clear sense of Hollywood phoniness.

I realize that my superior attitude was in part the bookish child's defense against a milieu that did not accord her much significance. But I was not alone within my family in emphasizing the distance from Hollywood. It was one of my mother's key claims about herself that although she wrote a Hollywood column for almost forty years, she was always an outsider. "I was never really involved with Hollywood," she explained in a 1985 newspaper interview. "Hedda and Louella thought they were part of it. I thought I was an onlooker." She believed this; her children believed it; and even one of our housekeepers, a successor to Stella, whom I visited recently in my search for witnesses of my past life with my mother, has confirmed this sense of my mother as someone who stood apart from the glamour and pretense. "You know, Wendy," said Anna Bayer, the baker's daughter whom in 1955 we had brought to Southern California from Switzerland, "she may have been a Hollywood columnist when she went out in the evenings. But really she was a plain girl at home."

And yet buying the house at 607 North Maple Drive was a move on my mother's part not to have a refuge from Hollywood but to beat the place on its own terms. She had determined when Robert was born, "as deliberately," she explained, "as deciding to cross a street," that she was going to be a success. This she defined, surveying what she called "the statistics of success," as earning $5,000 a week, the salary at that time commanded in their studio contracts by such top stars as Lana Turner, Van Johnson, and Robert Taylor. It is a part of my mother's myth of herself, as much as her regarding herself as an outsider, that she reached this goal. The budget for her 1954 daily television program, *The Sheilah Graham Show,* was $5,000 a week. And though out of this came the costs of paying two writers and of filming weekly features on the stars, there was a lot left over to count as income at a time when $5,000 a year could keep a family.

Buying the house came years earlier, in 1947, but it was explicitly a part of her campaign. She had carefully studied where you had to live if you were to be considered important. Beverly Hills was a good choice, provided you were north of Santa Monica Boulevard, where the houses begin to reach mansionlike size. Among the recommendations for 607 North Maple were its location midway between Santa Monica and Sunset (the multimillionaires were north of Sunset) and also some of its neighbors. My mother liked that it was only five doors away from Louella Parson's house. Then too, Danny Thomas lived around the corner and Dorothy Lamour one block over. Once settled in the neighborhood, we swam sometimes in the Thomas pool and used the Lamour tennis court, and I remember these and others stars' pools and courts as almost an extension of our personal domain. The stars were never at home, or at least not visible; we saw only the servants and the dogs. I was particularly drawn to Anne Baxter's shaggy black Newfoundland, wistfully observing us from behind a wire enclosure as if he too wouldn't mind a dip to cool off from the

California heat, yet with too much dignity to make a fuss, un-like Dorothy Lamour's yapping little poodles. But their barks dissolve in memories of the overriding stillness. It was the still-ness of affluence and of the unperturbed California air. Man-sion exteriors veiled the life within them while children played under the supervision of servants in walled-off back gardens. Out on the street an occasional passing car would ripple through the silence and be gone; and the only person I remem-ber ever seeing on the sidewalk was our mother's unctious, powerful archrival, Louella Parsons, walking her dachshund to the end of the block. This was the world that buying 607 North Maple Drive enabled my mother—and her children—to be part of.

Investing every penny of her $15,000 savings as down pay-ment on the $40,000 house, my mother was scared but exuber-ant. Her friend, the millionaire George Delacorte, came to inspect and declared, as my mother put it, "with the unsmiling face of the very rich" that she had made a big mistake putting all her eggs in one basket. My mother, however, had been willing to venture her all in a down payment on success and stability. The Spanish-style house with its good address and solid exterior of thick white stucco walls and red tile roof was the setting that she needed to reaffirm herself in her interlocking roles of columnist and mother. It gave her a facade that asserted her substance to the world, and it gave her the prospect of roots for her family. My mother said she wanted to have roots here as strong as those of the magnolia tree on the front lawn, though I doubt that in saying this she remembered that magnolias are as much transplants to Southern California as she was. It was her fantasy that we would stay in the house forever—or at least until I came down the beautiful curving staircase with its black wrought-iron banister in my wedding dress.

That was the same banister I clung to in protest against having to go to Sunday school, the same staircase where I would sit utterly forlorn whenever my mother would leave on a

trip to New York. The trips were to see her NANA boss, or a
television or radio sponsor, or perhaps just to get away for a bit,
though this could never be acknowledged as a motive. Because
I always got upset, she would usually wait until the last minute
to tell me she was going. Despite promises of presents from
F.A.O. Schwarz and Best & Co., I would cry and protest.
Then she would be gone. I would sit on the stairs feeling miserable. Finally, with some twinges of guilt that my grief was not
as enduring as I had dramatized it, I would think to myself,
"Well, it's really not so bad. There are other things to do." And
off I would wander to play with Robbie, as my brother was
known in those days, or to talk with Stella or Anna in the
kitchen or with the secretary working on my mother's column
in the den, or simply to read in my room.

As things turned out, we left 607 North Maple Drive ten
years before I got married, so I never got to come down the
staircase as a bride. I don't think living in the house, even when
we were there, ever gave us a sense of being truly rooted. But if
it was not a feeling of permanence that we developed—how can
one talk about being rooted in Hollywood?—it was something
perhaps as good. This was the sense that my mother's house
was a safe and sustaining place to be. Built as it was on her
fantasies, it nonetheless had the substance of her energy. She
supported it, earning more and more money every year; she
animated it with her presence, overseeing the complex life, the
complex of lives within it. It was both proof and illustration of
her status as a successful person. And to me, always unconsciously worried about holding my mother's attention, about
her constancy, it offered an important reassurance. I counted
on the house—both shelter and symbol—to reassure me that
our lives were stably linked together.

I loved our house, beginning with my own sunny room
with its windows to the south and west, the twin beds, the desk
where I did my homework, the small frilly dressing table where
with no sense of incongruity I would look in the Venetian

mirror and see myself reflected in the cowboy outfits that I wore until I was eleven or twelve, the large walk-in closet where the housekeeper kept my clothes so neat and well organized. For hours at a stretch I would lie on my bed and read, or sometimes I would take all my pennies out of my piggy bank and organize them by year and count them. Robbie, whose room was next door, was allowed in occasionally on sufferance. My mother, when she was home, came at bedtime. It was our ritual that she would sit on my bed and sing me the songs she had learned in her childhood, "O Rosemarie I love you," "Where the bee sucks, there suck I," "Brahms Lullaby," to which her words were "Night of love and night of stars, shine gently o'er the waters . . ." I would always ask for this song because it was the longest, ending after the last rising crescendo of "night of love and of sta-aars" with a protracted coda of la-la-la's. I wanted her to stay with me as long as possible.

Aside from my room and my brother's and our shared bathroom, the upstairs had my mother's master suite—a large bedroom with separate dressing room and bathroom, in which I remember the design of black swans set into the tiles above the tub. In the mornings, especially on weekends, Robbie and I would scamper into our mother's room, climb into bed with her, one child on each side, and we would make our plans. "She was such fun," my brother recollected, this standing out for him above all else at the time of her heart attack. "Do you remember how we would get in bed with her and she would say, 'What shall we do today? Shall we go to Ojai? Shall we go to Palm Springs? Shall we go to Malibu and ride horses?'" And then off we would go in our little Studebaker, my mother and Robbie and I, cohorts in adventure. We were enveloped in the magic circle of her charm and energy.

I have vivid memories of time spent just watching my mother—watching her dress, watching her take a bath beneath the tile swans, watching her eat her breakfast in bed, which was always the start to her day, a habit that made her seem a very

special person and that I understood not as a mark of spoiled-
ness or indulgence but as a way of conserving the energy that
would be called upon later. She was prodigiously productive
even before rising from bed: talking with her children, scrib-
bling ideas on spiral notepads, making phone calls, and generally planning the day's activities. There was one phone extension on the bedside table and a second on the enormous desk
that occupied a part of the room more officially given over to
work. I was always aware that I shared my beautiful mother
with her work, but then the work, we were told, was to support
us—and she made such a point of being available to us children. After school, if I hadn't encountered her downstairs with
her secretary, I might find her taking a little rest in her room.
She had a reclining chair in which she would often sit, at its full
backwards tilt, in the late afternoons. Other times she would
rest by stretching out flat on her back on the floor. And I
would sit or lie down next to her, on my back too, and we
would have our chats.

The downstairs of our house had the large sunken living
room that extended as a rectangular wing off the two-story
main structure. This was our most elegant room, with its high
French doors, two on each length of the rectangle, the massive
oak ceiling, and an imposing stucco fireplace. The room was
comfortably furnished with plush upholstered sofas and chairs
and reproduction-antique chests and tables. Two Degas balle-
rina prints, which later I learned had been a gift from Fitzgerald, hung in one corner above the baby grand piano at
which I would make a desultory show of practicing. Tired of
this, I might look into the nearby den, which doubled as the
secretary's office and our library. Here, between the facing walls
of books from the College of One curriculum, was the green
leather armchair where I liked to sit and read while the work of
producing the daily column went on around me. My mother
talked on the phone to people who seemed either irate or con-
ciliatory. The secretary tapped out items about Tyrone Power's

latest romance or Marlon Brando's most recent Academy Award–quality performance or Marilyn Monroe arriving late again on the set. And I read on, shifting between Victorian novels—precocious reader of *Bleak House* and *Vanity Fair*—and fan-magazine stories about the six husbands of Lana Turner or Dean Stockwell dyeing his hair for *The Boy with the Green Hair*.

The den and the living room were both off a spacious hallway that also opened into our dining room, and this in turn led through a swinging door into the back part of the house, which contained the kitchen, breakfast room, and maid's room. As I describe our house, I am struck by its integrations. It was a house of great intimacy and private gaiety, and it was also a house where people worked—my mother, the secretary, the cook, the *Sheilah Graham Show* writers (for whom the breakfast room got turned into an office), even Robbie and I doing our homework. I found the steady stir of industry reassuring, and I learned from my mother to value work well done above almost anything else in life. Yet much of the work that went on was the very thing we all said we had no respect for. The personages of Hollywood, its myths, its legends, were created in our den with the literary classics bought by F. Scott Fitzgerald looking on in witness. My mother was a Hollywood gossip columnist—that's how she earned her living—using her wit to inflate and deflate the stars: "Errol Flynn says he doesn't worry about money—as long as he can reconcile his gross habits with his net income"; or "Kirk Douglas is now starring in *Young Man with a Horn*. It should be a cinch. He never stops blowing it"; or (a disingenuous retraction on her radio show) "I'm delighted to tell you that Jane Wyman is not antisocial; she *does* have some friends. Jane Wyman does not break out in a rash when she is nervous. That is *not* the reason she wears high-necked gowns."

Of course, my mother also used her column to help people. And she cared about professionalism, priding herself on the accuracy of her items and also on being, beneath the gossip, a dedicated and scrupulous "hard news" reporter. She loved to outscoop Parsons and Hopper, though having got the scoop on Ingrid Bergman's extramarital baby with Robert Rossellini, her scruples held her back from using it, and it was Louella who ran the story so damaging to Bergman's career.

What we as children believed about our mother's work was that she was a professional and that Hollywood was a job and a game. If in its day-to-day gossip the column was sharp, this was because it had to be. No one would read a column that was too sweet, and what harm could the items do anyway, since Hollywood was a chimera. "My paragraphs," my mother would call the stars and moguls, thus mocking both them and her enterprise. Not all the stars were like Zsa Zsa Gabor, who sat in our living room advising against animation of the face because it caused wrinkles, yet managing to emit great gushes of insincerity—"Dahling, vat lovely cheeldren." Yet Zsa Zsa, a great fake, became a convenient image for us of generic Hollywood phoniness. Hollywood was phony, the column just a job, and we were real. It was this private knowledge that bolstered our sense of superiority and at the same time intensified our family gusto in taking advantage of what the movie world had to offer us. We exploited Hollywood as it suited us, yet in our minds stood aloof from its cant. Meanwhile, twenty million Americans read the column, that daily ten-inch strip of rapid-fire gossip and news:

Lana and Lamas holding hands at Yucca and Vine. Lana, wearing white pants and baby blue page boy jacket, holding the hand not in the cast . . . D'ya remember way back when Lana kicked because Lamas and not Montalban was paired with her in "The Merry Widow"? Now she's squawking because Ricardo and not Fernando teams with her in "Letter from the President" . . . Today Paul Henreid will acquire a new partner—L. B. Mayer, for Paul's pic-

ture, "Stubborn Wood." This is positively not a re-
make of "Petrified Forest" . . . Reason Rita is still in
touch with Aly—she's determined to give the Aga
Khan a new grandson . . . Georgie Jessel, now on a
$3,250 a week contract at 20th, can move to CBS at
$4,000 a week . . . We hear that Betty Hutton is
changing her religion—for love of Charles O'Cur-
ran . . . Frank Sinatra is out of "The Farmer Takes a
Wife." Frankie wanted all his salary in advance . . .
Judy Garland, due here next week, will present the
Music Award at the Oscar Derby . . . At the Holly-
wood Foreign Correspondents Dinner: Stanley
Kramer, her host at the table—"What I like about
Barbara (Stanwyck) is her hair." Gilbert Roland, her
escort—"What I like about Barbara is her legs" . . .
But what *I* liked about Barbara were her jewels . . .

That is a sample three inches, from the column of February 25,
1952.

It was at Christmas that both our putting down of Hollywood and our privileged status within it intersected most dramatically. Christmas was the time when, perhaps to compen-
sate for its unseasonable weather, Beverly Hills went berserk
with ostentatious decorations. We contented ourselves with a
modest string of lights around the front door, but nonetheless,
ours was a busy house, the doorbell constantly ringing with the
delivery of presents from the studios, stars, and agencies, all in
the forties and fifties still spending money on gifts to columnists. My mother was given enough liquor to supply all her
own entertaining for the coming year. And there were so many
radios, handbags, vases, and cigarette lighters that we would
wrap most of them up again to give the next Christmas to our
own family friends. Robbie and I were full participants in the
drama of the presents. We would receive them at the front door
and carry them in to their place under the tall tree in the living

room. Then on Christmas morning, after we had explored the contents of the stockings that our mother left on the doors of our rooms—always wonderful stockings with items both expected (pencils, erasers, paper clips) and unexpected (a watch, perhaps a wallet)—we would wake her up and race downstairs. Our own presents soon unwrapped, we would gleefully join in unwrapping hers, awed and amused at the opulence and excess. The living room was soon piled high with empty boxes and crumpled paper. Our mother would laugh and stress to us that none of this would be happening but for the power of her column. She urged us to keep in mind what was and wasn't "real." Yet I confess: Christmas, as I have experienced it since, more modestly and realistically, has never seemed to me as convincing.

Even more wonderful to me than Christmas morning was our annual party the night before, our December 24 party that was also a celebration of Robert's birthday. This was our party for "real" family friends, who included only a few movie celebrities. Shirley Temple Black, in retirement between "The Good Ship Lollipop" and Republican politics, always came with her naval officer husband, and I liked them both because they were down-to-earth and friendly. Another regular was Maureen O'Hara, a quiet presence in one of our quilted armchairs, beautiful to me with her red hair, pale complexion, and Irish accent. She and my mother had met on the set of *How Green Was My Valley* and become friends. One time Maureen brought along her daughter Bronwyn, a rather plain, overweight child whom her mother seemed to love devotedly, which I found reassuring. I knew that there had been a custody battle over Bronwyn, and also that Maureen was involved in a lawsuit against the scurrilous magazine *Confidential,* which had printed a story about her having sex in the back row of Grauman's Chinese Theatre.

As I listened to such stories, they seemed interesting but remote. For all the sophistication and sexual innuendo around me, I was not a sophisticated child. The party's highlight for me was the carol singing. It was my task to play the piano while the assembled guests sang, my wrong notes drowned out by the vibrato of Teddy Getty, John Paul Getty's third ex-wife, who had given up her aspirations to a career in opera for whatever the gains of that marriage. I also used to read out loud the rough little poems that I wrote each year to commemorate my brother's birthday. One, I remember, began:

> Seven years ago today
> When snow was coming down,
> There lay a little baby
> In the middle of New York town. . . .

Hollywood was manageable for me if I retained some sense of my own place and worth in the face of it. I felt just fine when we laughed at Zsa Zsa Gabor or befriended Maureen O'Hara. Hollywood had entered my house, but I had a secure place within that house. Also I was a zestful participant in the family game of fringe benefits—the Christmas presents, the free lunches and dinners in restaurants (we would ask for the bill, then wait conspiratorially with our mother for the maître d' to approach—"Oh no, Miss Graham. *Of course* it's with the compliments of the house"), the weekends in resorts with swimming pools and stables and croquet lawns, and even the trips to Europe. My mother liked to say that we weren't millionaires but we lived like millionaires, and it was fun to be her assistant in the magic of this sleight of hand.

Yet Hollywood was also oppressive. Even events supposedly for children could turn into Hollywood occasions for publicity and display, the professional photographer always present. We still have the pictures from my fifth birthday party, at which Bozo the clown, the painted smile on his face asserting radiant happiness that was not apparent in any of the children, managed to keep Robbie in a state of terrified howling the whole afternoon. And from my seventh at the Disney studio, where the whole party saw a special screening of *Bambi*. Of course, I didn't think of *these* parties as "Hollywood" ones, since they were my own; I was the birthday girl, the guests were my playmates and schoolmates. It was other movie children's birthdays that so often seemed competitive and confining. We went to Liza Minnelli's third at Judy Garland's Santa Monica beach house. The main attraction was a donkey ride, but photographers kept putting more important people's children on the donkey. In my mother's version of this story, she eventually seized the donkey, put me on it, and walked me around, did the same for Robbie, and then we left. Whatever her self-definition as an onlooker, my mother could never bear to be slighted. I also remember an awful party for Tommy Rettig, the child star of *Lassie,* where we weren't allowed to pat the numerous Lassie dogs that did tricks. The discovery that there was more than one Lassie was itself a great disillusionment.

Worse still sometimes, as far as I was concerned, were the affairs for grown-ups—the movie screenings, the studio lunches, the interviews with stars at the Brown Derby or Chasen's. My mother often took us, especially me, along with her. She wanted to be with us, thought we would be amused or get a good meal, and I also think she liked people to see that she was a mother. My role tagging along on the interviews was to sit quietly, as out of the way as possible, and eat my filet mignon. On the whole I was ignored, and frankly, attention was even worse than the lack of it. If the press agent eating with us turned to me and asked me how I liked school, I would answer tersely, needing to show that I knew my liking or not liking school had nothing to do with the business at hand: the stars promoting themselves and my mother getting the items for her column. Sometimes stars eating in the restaurant would come over to my mother's table with their "Dahling, how are you? So lovely to see you." Again I always felt mortified, though by exactly what I wasn't sure—perhaps being witness to the phoniness *and* to my own insignificance. My mother, however, I always excused as simply playing her part in an expedient masquerade.

It's odd to me, remembering how bad I felt on these outings, that they continued to include me. It got decided that I was shy and a bit willful, not that being an appendage at Hollywood functions was difficult for a child. My mother took me with her to attend the premiere of *The Robe*. We arrived at the theater—Grauman's Chinese—in a limousine provided by the studio. Looking out the window, I saw the fans straining behind the police lines to get a good look at the arriving stars. From our limousine, I realized, would emerge this small, unimportant, unfashionable little girl, and to this day I remember my dread in anticipating the fans' disappointment.

Perturbed by glamour, I rejected it as an option for myself and took my stance against frills. Skirts were required at school, but as soon as I got home, I would rush to change into my uniform of blue jeans, white T-shirt, checked flannel shirt, and brown cowboy boots. For special occasions Robbie and I had complete Roy Rogers, Gene Autry, and Hopalong Cassidy outfits, but these too could have their snares. I remember my chagrin when, attending a visiting Barnum & Bailey circus, I was called over to meet Gene Autry and realized that I was wearing my Roy Rogers hat. I was better prepared when my mother got Hopalong Cassidy to stop at our house before going up the street to a children's party at Louella's to which we had not been invited. Robbie and I had our picture taken with him beside our Christmas tree, all three of us dressed in our Hoppy clothes, six-shooters drawn, by the professional photographer brought in by my mother for the occasion.

My hair at this period of my life was coarse and straight, and I liked it cut square and short. Gone were the golden curls that had made me briefly a blonde when I was three years old. Gone too were the bows and ribbons that Stella had arranged in my hair up to the time I was six. I did not feel ugly, but what I hated was the notion of being fancy. My style was plain, and it was part of the order of my world that this distinguished me from my mother. One of my favorite pictures from my childhood shows our family trio beside a hotel swimming pool in Palm Springs. My mother, blond and smiling, has on a shiny cotton sundress and sequined sweater with polish on her fingernails and toenails. Flanking her are Robbie and I, ages six and nine, identically clad in our rumpled jeans, flannel shirts, and scuffed-up oxfords. Robbie has his rabbit foot on his beaded belt. The picture captures for me what it felt like to be my mother's daughter—the security of the connection, the security of the contrast.

When I was in sixth grade my mother took me to the Beverly Hills branch of Saks Fifth Avenue to buy me some better clothes. We got two outfits, a straight-skirted yellow outfit and a flared-skirted red one with a floral blouse. I remember coming home from the store and eagerly trying each on again in the privacy of my room. These were meant to be school clothes, but when I ventured to school, in the red clothes first, my classmates asked if I was dressed for something special. I felt intensely embarrassed to say I wasn't, as if caught in the act of trying too hard. Nonetheless, I liked my new clothes, and I liked it too when my mother sent me to the hairdresser to have my hair done. I still wished to avoid any show of ostentation, but I was finding ways to begin at least to think of myself as an attractive girl. All this, however, was powerfully complicated by an event that for years afterwards I found hard to talk about—it seemed such an unfortunate, such a devastating thing to have happened. This was the intrusion into our lives and our house of my mother's third husband, the would-be father whose rejection of me was something I hardly worried about because mine of him was so complete.

There is never any father in my dreams about 607 North Maple Drive. Certainly not Trevor, who visited so infrequently, though I do remember the pleasure of his being with us once when I was about six and then the awkwardness of his

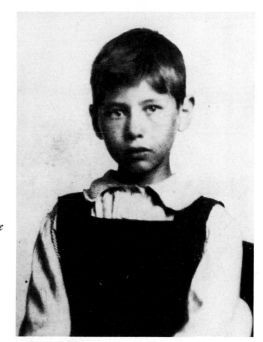

Lily Shiel, age nine, in the Norwood orphanage.

Lily at seventeen.

e.e. cummings' portrait of Freddie, painted in 1942.

On the facing page: My mother and her first husband, John Graham Gillam, dressed for presentation to King George V and Queen Mary at Buckingham Palace, 1931.

At left, my mother and F. Scott Fitzgerald on their visit to Tijuana, Mexico, early in 1940. The picture was taken by a sidewalk photographer. At right, Fitzgerald as he looked shortly before my mother met him in Hollywood in 1937.

On the facing page, TWO JEWISH FAMILIES: *Above, the Shiel family, c. 1917. Back row, left to right: Sally, Morris, Iris, and Lily. Front row: Meyer, my grandmother, Sally's son Len, Henry, and Iris's daughter Cecily. Below, four generations of the Citroen family in 1912: Freddie, his mother, his grandfather, and his great-grandmother.*

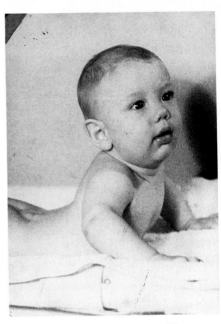

CONSTRUCTING THE WESTBROOK MYTH: *Above left, Wendy Frances West-brook, age six months, 1943. Right, Robert Trevor Westbrook, age six months, 1946.*

At Malibu, 1947.

MOTHER AND DAUGHTER: *Christmas 1942.*

1944

1947

SHEILAH GRAHAM, HOLLYWOOD COLUMNIST: *Left to right above, the late thirties and the early forties. Below, the early fifties and publicizing the carpet.*

presence four or five years later after my mother had remarried. "It's perverse," said my mother. "Why is he visiting now? He never comes otherwise." We agreed that she was right, but without any bitterness. I have no memories of missing my father or of thinking he should be part of our household. His role was to live in England and to visit occasionally, though years later, staying with him in England and browsing though his old photographs, I found a letter that my mother had sent him around the time of their divorce. Chiding him for his neglect of the children, she enclosed, for what it was worth to him, one of the notes that I, aged four, had dictated to my nurse. "Dear Daddy, When are you coming on the airplane to give Wendy a big kiss?" Such expectancy surprised and touched me. I couldn't remember ever worrying about his coming or not coming. Our household seemed complete without him.

Why should we need a father when we had a mother who could be mother and father in one? She, in turn, had her able female lieutenants, the housekeepers in the kitchen, the secretaries in the den, who joined in the campaign to sustain the household and ensure our happy childhood. As for the place of men in our life, we knew them as helpers: the television show writers, the masseur, the "leg men" who fed my mother items for the column, the Japanese gardener. Or they came to the house as family friends—and some of these I'm sure were lovers. But they were not integral to the house. The only male resident within its walls was Robbie, my little brother, bearing his heavy burden as sole defender and representative of his sex. Once as we sat listening to my mother talk with a friend about some other friend going through a difficult menopause, Robbie, mishearing, intervened, "There you go again—'Men of course!'"

And then my mother remarried.

It has always seemed to me a bitter joke that our dog Tony had a human name whereas our stepfather, whose real name was Stanley Wojtkiewicz and who called himself Wojciechowicz Stanislav Wojtkiewicz and pretended to be a famous All-American football player, was known to one and all by the nickname of a dog. My mother married "Bow Wow" on Valentine's Day 1953, when I was ten, and then "kicked him out," to use her language, three years later. I weathered this marriage as my stepfather's enemy, waiting for him to be gone. And at last he was, an acknowledged mistake and as such not, to my mother's thinking, to be dwelt on. As she wrote in *The Rest of the Story,* dispensing of this marriage as if it were the most fleeting of clouds to dim the California sunshine, "Except for one brief period the years at 607 North Maple Drive were very satisfactory." At most she would say that her third husband had been a Polish-American whose name was unpronounceable. I too did not like to utter his name, and was more intent probably even than my mother to stamp him out of our collective memory. There is no stepfather in my dreams about 607 North Maple Drive. And yet Bow Wow is very much a part of what happened there.

At the time that he met my mother, Stanley "Bow Wow" Wojtkiewicz was a football coach in a California prison. He was already friendly with a number of movie people, and someone—perhaps it was Glenn Ford—had given him an introduction to my mother, whose help he sought in raising money for a pet project. This was his plan to create a home for delinquent boys that would be called Bow Wow's Boys Town, and he brought with him a blueprint of this pipe dream—the words BOW WOW'S BOYS TOWN printed across the top—that I graphically remember.

Bow Wow was a large man in his mid-thirties. He had the build of an athlete whose muscles have turned a bit to fat but who still gives the impression of energetic athleticism. The tragedy of his life, my mother later insisted, was that his small hands and feet had prevented him from having the success as a football player that he had hungered for. Bow Wow did the next-best thing, which was to pretend that he was the famous

All-American Alex Wojciechowicz, whose name he blurred with his own. My mother called him a "pathological liar." If she ever paused to compare his lies with her own, I think she would have said that hers were more pragmatic and that she had never confused them with the truth. Bow Wow, a much less successful liar than my mother, seemed confounded in his own delusions. To the end of her life my mother talked about writing a short story based on Bow Wow to be titled "Athlete's Foot." It would end with the protagonist dying himself to save a drowning woman and thereby achieving the heroism that had eluded him in life.

On the day that Bow Wow first visited our house, Robbie and I met him before my mother came down from her room, and the next thing we knew we were playing catch with him in the living room, throwing the ball over sofas and chairs. I remember my exhilaration to be encouraged and protected by a grown-up in such a forbidden activity. My mother always told the story that her first thought as she came down the stairs was, "Oh my God, the furniture," and her second one, "What a wonderful father for the children." Six weeks later, they were married before a justice of the peace in Ventura County. Robbie and I were present at the ceremony, and we continued along on the few days of honeymoon at the Santa Barbara Biltmore.

It is painful to remember, given all that came afterwards, how pleased I was about my mother getting married. She consulted with us in her bedroom, first of all breaking the news, concealed from us for over five years, that she was already divorced from Trevor. As she explains in *The Rest of the Story*, "I had not told them of the divorce until I was able to say, 'And now I can give you an American father.' They were delighted and danced a little jig around my bedroom. Wendy was ten and a half. Rob was seven."

I remember dancing that little jig. The divorce from Trevor seemed insignificant, since his presence had been so insignificant. What "having a father" meant was vague to me; yet I liked the idea and was happy and excited to think of having one in-house. My mother presented marriage to Bow Wow as a family project, something we were doing all together. Later she would assert that she had married fifty percent because she was in love and fifty percent because she wanted to give us, particularly Robert, a father.

My enthusiasm to have a live-in father quickly cooled as the stranger intruded. Already I was ill at ease as Bow Wow and my mother were getting the license. My mother wrote down on the application that her age was thirty-six. Standing next to her and observing this, I pointed out her mistake. "That's not right," I said. "You're thirty-eight." Bow Wow then took me outside while the business was completed. In truth, my mother was a decade older than even I knew. Guardian and defender of what I thought were the facts, I was highly indignant when in 1956, at the time of her divorce, *Time* magazine pegged her at fifty-one. "How outrageous," I said. "How can they do this to you?" It was only years later that I realized *Time* had got it right. My mother once explained to our friend Larry Van Gelder that she had lied about her age because she hadn't wanted her children to have an "old" mother. I wonder if Bow Wow knew her real age, which made her thirteen rather than three years older than he was.

My actual detestation of Bow Wow began on the honeymoon in Santa Barbara. I must have been in a generally anxious state of mind, for I remember how often, walking either behind or ahead of the newlyweds, I kept stepping on my mother's heels and toes. It also bothered me to find myself with Robbie in the backseat of the car—my mother, my brother, and I had always sat all together in the front seat of our little Studebaker. But now we children were in the back, I directly behind Bow Wow, who was driving, listening to the two of them plan the gala wedding reception shortly to be held at our house. Addressing my mother, I asked if I could have a few of the invita-tions to show to my friends at school. Bow Wow intervened. "Why doesn't she ask me?" he said, turning his head towards my mother with never a glance at me. That was it, a small enough thing, but the moment at which I swore eternal enmity; and I more or less kept my vow.

The wedding reception at our house was so splendid that one Hollywood paper called my mother "Hostess of the Year." My mother wore a lovely pink sequined gown and a tiara crowning her head. Marilyn Monroe put in an appearance, hours late as usual, and had her picture taken kissing Robbie. She was also photographed with my mother, who holds her own very nicely in the inevitable comparison of the two blond beauties. I was there too, wearing a white dress and curtsying as I was introduced to guests—Darryl Zanuck and Robert Taylor, Greer Garson and John Wayne. I was not unhappy, though by then Bow Wow had moved into our house carrying innumerable shoes in cardboard boxes up our curving staircase and on to my mother's bedroom. I had sat on the stairs, my habitual outpost, and watched his intrusion. Later, I would perch at their top, waiting for the 7:00 A.M. time when I was now allowed to go into my mother's bedroom, or sit with Robbie, halfway down them to be safely out of sight, listening with horror and fascination to the quarrels that shortly ensued. Three weeks after she married Bow Wow, my mother already knew that she had made a terrible mistake.

It's hard to imagine how the woman who had spent three and a half years with F. Scott Fitzgerald and had had a child by Freddie Ayer could consider Bow Wow a suitable father for her children and mate for herself. The match was utterly incongruous—as one family friend recently put it, "It would be like saying that Cary Grant and Ma Kettle were an item." But then my mother was not at all snobbish about people. To understand better why she married Bow Wow, I think I would have to know what her hopes and disappointments had been before he came along. All that is apparent is that she succumbed to his whirlwind courtship, believed he would be a great help to her and her children, and surely knew that he could never displace her in our affections.

My policy towards Bow Wow was to have as little to do with him as possible. Our relationship was simple: we were enemies. Yet having an enemy involves awareness of his presence. Etched in memory is a vision of Bow Wow, clad in one of his football jerseys with their cut-off sleeves, seated at our kitchen table and, his mouth wide open, biting into a juicy red apple. My mother built him a dressing-room annex to her bedroom and also an office over the garage, where he would spend much of his time, but doing exactly what, no one quite knew. He gave up his job in the prison and became my mother's full-time helper in what were in fact her busiest years. In 1954, for example, in addition to her daily column, she had responsibility for a five-day-a-week radio show *and* a five-day-a-week television show, broadcast live from Hollywood Monday through Fridays at 7:30 A.M. and including filmed features on the stars. My mother describes her schedule of this time in *The Rest of the Story:*

After the morning show we had a meeting to discuss the next. Then I wrote my column. The afternoons were for filming. At 5:30 the radio show. After dinner with Wendy and Rob, I helped Rob with his homework, discussed the day's adventures and problems with my daughter, memorized the television show and tried to be asleep by 10:30.

There is no mention of Bow Wow in this description—he had been written out of the story—but he was indeed there, helping my mother to do all that she had taken on. He ran interference for her, though some of the fights I remember were expressions of her anger about phone calls he had made in her name. He told lies constantly, and she worried about his ability to injure her position in Hollywood. Nonetheless, he offered something. Warmth, I think it was, and even some protection. He gave her a birthday party, something no one in her life had ever done before (and no one would again until I gave her one at eighty). And then too, there was sex. My mother always said that she had been physically in love with Bow Wow. I used to wonder what this meant, though I don't think I really wanted to know too closely. Talking recently with Gerold Frank, a sprightly eighty-two, who had been my mother's collaborator on *Beloved Infidel,* I asked him what my mother had said to him about her third husband. He grinned and answered, "I guess it's all right to tell you this now. She said, 'I always went to sleep with a smile on my lips.' " Was this, I wondered, the embellishment of Gerold Frank, whom my mother had always accused of thinking in clichés? Or was it—I still shuddered slightly—really my mother's own thoughts and words?

For me at age ten, eleven, twelve, thirteen, Bow Wow's presence in my mother's bedroom was a cause of ill-understood but nonetheless powerful jealousy and rage. Once by mistake I walked in on him when he was naked—he was sitting on the bed with his back to me—and I remember the broad stretch of flesh from shoulders to bottom lacking any definition of a waist. He turned his head and told me sharply to leave. Basically I avoided him, trying to will him away, and while he remained, to pretend he didn't count. We did little together, and he liked me as little as I liked him. We attempted not to clash, though I am sure I was enragingly contemptuous. Once when he had hit the dog, I openly defied him, and my mother, watching the scene, feared that he would hit me. That time he didn't, though I have a memory that he did hit me once. My mother always insisted this couldn't have happened, since it would have been a violation of the unspoken rules that protected me from his interference. I, however, remember him bursting into my room where I was reading with a flashlight under the covers—it was after my fairly strictly enforced bedtime—and slapping me as I cowered there, indignant but defenseless in the face of his intrusion.

On the other hand, I have not forgotten that it was Bow

Wow who brought us our dog Tony as well as lots of other animals—ducks, pigeons, chickens (Bow Wow was a country boy)—that we kept in the backyard until my mother put her foot down and all except the dog disappeared. It was he who taught me to recite the presidents of the United States in order, something I can do to this day. And finally, I recall a single afternoon when we were friendly. The family was set to drive back from Malibu to Beverly Hills. But instead of the usual arrangement, Robbie going with Bow Wow in his car and me with my mother in hers, Bow Wow, who was angry that day with Robbie, his general favorite, invited me instead of my brother to go with him. I accepted; he was nice to me; and I melted instantly. The memory of this capitulation has often led me to wonder if the story could have been different. If Bow Wow had treated me with more indulgence, with more considered and consistent kindness, might we have been better friends?

I suspect not. My jealousy was strong—I think it would have been of any man who came between me and my mother— and Bow Wow was easy to despise for his lack of manners and education. Quite apart, though, from these easily labeled deficiencies, he was not a good man. He lied and he cheated. He was out to cheat my mother. Finding his diary, which—no respecter of privacy—she had come upon and read while he was on a trip out of town, my mother took us to stay with friends in Ojai, then went back to L.A. to meet Bow Wow at the airport and to "kick him out." I never saw the diary, but by her account it had terrible things to say about us all, including my mother. Also she learned that Bow Wow had been secretly making a few mortgage payments on 607 North Maple Drive, a ploy that enabled him to claim in the separation hearings that he had put all his savings into our house.

I was exultant when I heard that Bow Wow was gone. I had known that I would outlast him, and now I had. Occasionally in the terrible divorce proceedings that followed, my overwrought mother would say, "Oh, it's just too much for me. I think I'll take him back." This would strike terror in my heart, and I would insist, "You can't do that," wondering what power I had to prevent it.

Harassment ensued. Bow Wow sent the ASPCA to our house on a tip that a dog was being mistreated there. He wrote a letter to our school headmistress saying that Sheilah Graham was a Communist. My mother kept having to go to court and ended up paying him alimony during the separation. He also got to live in the beach house that my mother had built at Trancas Beach, just north of Malibu, with the profits from *The Sheilah Graham Show.* In the end she changed to a less scrupulous lawyer who put detectives on Bow Wow, and they nailed him on adultery, bursting in with a photographer and taking pictures. The divorce was settled out of court with Bow Wow buying the beach house from my mother but getting to live in it for a year before beginning his payments. He sold it right before the first payment was due.

I never saw Bow Wow again after he left 607 North Maple Drive. My mother, as I have said, simply cut him out of the story. She destroyed all photographs of him, mainly photographs from the wedding, even cutting some pictures in half to keep the half he wasn't in. We almost never mentioned his name or his nickname. If he came up at all, it was my mother's habit to refer to him as "the monster."

My hatred of Stanley "Bow Wow" Wojtkiewicz remained fierce. I had a fantasy shortly after he left that he appeared on our street and to protect myself and our house, I simply stabbed him to death, thrusting a knife into his slightly beefy stomach. In time I came to admit that there was a comic as well as tragic element to the drama, and I recognized its oedipal dimensions. Basically, however, it remained my position that I had hated my stepfather—and that he had been hateful.

"What would you do," asked my brother at the time of our mother's heart attack, "if you were to run into Bow Wow?"

"Oh, I don't know," I answered with a laugh, at least recognizing that what I was about to say was in obedience to an old reflex. "I guess I would kill him. What about you?"

"Oh, I don't know," said Robert. "I guess I would invite him out for a beer and ask him what he's been up to all these years."

My mother wrote Bow Wow out of the story, but, the custodian of her own legend, she was obsessed in the years right before her death with his theft of some of her Fitzgerald papers and also the filmed episodes from *The Sheilah Graham Show*. I found three notes in her safe deposit box, all addressed to her children and dated October 1984, October 1986, and September 15, 1987, her eighty-third birthday, that urged us to prevent Bow Wow's possible exploitation of these materials. The first note offers the fullest explanation:

For Wendy Fairey and Robert Westbrook, and other heirs to my estate.
In 1956 after I severed my relationship with Stanley Woitkiewich [sic], whom I had married on February 14, 1953, I took you both with me to Ojai for us all to get away from my house (at 607 North Maple Drive in Beverly Hills). This gave my then husband the opportunity to get into the house (he hired a locksmith and told him he had lost his keys), and during that time he took several things. His clothing, books of stamps, several important papers of mine including the lists Scott Fitzgerald had planned for what I called my "College of One," which was published in a book (I found the copies at Princeton). He also took the reels of film I had made for my daily television show for NBC in 1955. It is my belief that he still has all this material. If after my death he tries to use any of this you must take steps to stop him because he has no legal rights to any of it. It belongs to you. It was never given to him for his use. As you know he was a pathological liar which was one of the reasons I had to divorce him. When *Beloved Infidel* was published, he actually wrote to Princeton saying he had a trunkful of unpublished Scott Fitzgerald material. The head of the

Rare Books Library there came to Hollywood for this great "find" and of course it was a lie.

Signed
Sheilah Westbrook

I have thought a lot about the effects on our lives of my mother's unfortunate third marriage. Our little family survived Bow Wow. The house survived him. And yet, his coming and departing marked a change. Things were never quite the same after him, though surely if it hadn't been Bow Wow and the divorce, there would have been some other circumstance of our lives to serve as the needed explanation for a sense of loss that I suspect was inevitable. What I lost was my confidence in my mother's power to envelop and sustain us in a protected world of childhood. In my mind it was Bow Wow who was the destabilizing force. There were the pre–Bow Wow and post–Bow Wow years, and the literary character with whom I felt the closest identification was David Copperfield, whose early pre-oedipal paradise of a life with his pretty mother and their devoted servant Peggotty was brought to a cruel end by the intrusion of the wicked Mr. Murdstone.

Unlike David Copperfield, I had won. Bow Wow was gone. But still the damage seemed great. My mother lost some of her gaiety. She seemed to have lost her interest in men, though now I realize that she simply never sought to bring another man into our family triad. Bow Wow gone, Robert entered his difficult adolescence, and I continued essentially to do without an adolescence—not rebelling, continuing to excel at school and to pursue my newly formed determination to become an intellectual. No man stood between me and my mother, but, perversely, I found myself sometimes wishing for one—or rather wishing to have had one, a better stepfather who might, so my fantasy went, have rescued me from being so exclusively my mother's daughter.

Five

"BELOVED
INFIDEL"

Y MOTHER ONCE suggested to F. Scott Fitzgerald that they should have a child. As she remembered this moment, he was shocked. She thought he was going to faint, mostly, she conjectured, at the idea of further responsibilities. Given her own concern to observe proprieties—or at least to conceal improprieties—her wish to her was proof of the strength of her attachment. She wanted a child, Fitzgerald's child, and later regretted that there hadn't been one: "someone who might have looked like Scott." When she was pregnant with me, an acquaintance remarked to her, "Isn't it marvelous that you are pregnant with a child from Scott." The time frame, of course, made this impossible—Scott's death in December 1940 long preceded my September 1942 birth. "If I was," replied my mother, *"that* would be a real miracle." I think, though, that to her having the baby did seem a miracle with which Scott Fitzgerald was somehow hazily connected. She saw it as compensation for losing him, a consolation arranged through his intervention. "Obviously," she wrote in *The Rest of the Story,* "he had talked to the big shots in heaven and said, 'Give her a baby.' " Or as she put it in *The Real F. Scott Fitzgerald,* her last book about Fitzgerald, written thirty-five years after his death, "After I became pregnant, I fantasized that Scott had spoken to the powers that be and said, 'Don't let her love him [Trevor] but for God's sake give her a baby.' He knew how much I wanted a child."

Dying in my mother's living room twenty-one months before my birth, his death making way for my birth—for surely there would have been no Wendy Westbrook if he had lived— Scott Fitzgerald hovered over our lives as our own personal guardian angel and, strangely, as a ghostly progenitor. My mother strove in her stories about Fitzgerald not only to stress the depth and importance of their love but also to connect him with her children and with her own miraculous rebirth as a mother. Fitzgerald dead, she would not love "unreservedly" again, at least not love a man, but Fitzgerald would make up for having left her by blessing her in the project of bearing and raising children. Pregnant with me, she wanted a boy, and she wanted to name him Scott. When I turned out to be a girl, she gave me the middle name of Frances, since Scott had been Francis Scott Fitzgerald, and viewed me as a substitute for the love that she had lost—except that I, and then my brother, were "hers" in a way not even Fitzgerald had ever been.

It was one of those stories in which there are two priceless objects, things rich beyond compare, but you can't have them both. We came *after* F. Scott Fitzgerald, and it was as if our very presence depended on the tragedy of his absence. When Robert and I were small, my mother had a dream, she said, in which Satan or God or some unearthly spirit gave her a choice—she could have Scott Fitzgerald back in return for her children. "No, no," she shouted. Then waking in terror, she rushed from her room to see if we were still in our beds. She could imagine Scott smiling and reassuring her with the special nickname he had for her, "Sheilo, there is no contest."

So Scott remained in heaven, or wherever it was that he had access to the gods and could negotiate in my mother's interests, and we remained in our lives at 607 North Maple Drive, the recipients, as she put it, of all the love and devotion, all the anxiety, the anguish, the fear, the obsessive concern that had once been for Scott, who had taught her to love without reservation and then had left her. It was Scott Fitzgerald who had made her a loving person so that she could then love us. This was at the heart of her myth of herself, establishing her in a continuum of roles as lover, beloved, and mother, enhancing her credentials to serve as our only parent. If she could be both mother and father to us, dispensing so easily with any available father's assistance, in part this was because she had the guidance of the only father she really ever permitted us: our spiritual father, F. Scott Fitzgerald.

I have often been asked if I knew F. Scott Fitzgerald, and I have been asked if Fitzgerald was my father. I am always quick to correct the misperception of any overlap in time or biological connection. Yet how can I write the drama of my parentage and leave him out of the story? If my mother worked to link us with Fitzgerald, we children in turn believed in the link. It was a family myth, created by my mother, subscribed to by us children, that Fitzgerald could be claimed as our relation. As my mother recounts in the preface to *Beloved Infidel,* addressing Scott in the form of a letter:

Little by little I have told the truth about my background to my children. They have always known about you: they know you are something very precious in their mother's life. Only the other day Wendy, coming upon your name, asked, "Would he have liked me, Mother?" I tried to explain to her why we were never married. I said, "I could not marry him because his wife was very ill in a sanitarium and there was a daughter he loved very much, and he could not abandon them." I told her of your relation to Francis Scott Key and once when she sang "The Star-Spangled Banner," she turned to me and said, quite proudly, "I'm kind of related to F. Scott Fitzgerald, aren't I?" And then Robbie asked, "I'm related to him too, aren't I, Mom?" "Yes, you are, both of you—in a kind of a way." I told them that you would have liked them. Very much.

Thus the ghost of F. Scott Fitzgerald joined our family. Phantom lover. Phantom would-be husband. Phantom father. In answer to my question whether Scott Fitzgerald would have liked me, my mother explained to me why they couldn't marry. In other words, he liked *her* so much that, circumstances being otherwise, he would have been her husband and my father. "Scott's second wife," Edmund Wilson had called her, in acknowledgment of her important and sustaining role in Fitzgerald's life. Well, if she was Scott's wife, we by extension were his children. And as I might then have vied for the love of a living father, I cultivated my own relation with him and entered into covert rivalry with my mother, if not to possess him at least to make room for me in the equation. My means of being close to him began with listening to my mother's story but quickly progressed to some skepticism about her version and the sense that somehow I knew better what had happened and who Fitzgerald really was.

Hearing my mother talk about her love for Scott Fitzgerald, I believed it had been real and deep. What I wondered about, though, was the transfiguration of whatever had gone on between these two people into the legends of *Beloved Infidel* and the various Fitzgerald sequels. The experience had turned into a mythic story that exhibited all my mother's instincts for flattening out the twists and turns, the doubts and reservations of life into the broad lines of self-affirmation.

The story featured my mother as vulnerable, self-sacrificing, and heroic. She had broken her engagement with the Marquess of Donegall in order to take up with the quiet pale man whom she first espied behind the veil of his blue cigarette smoke, sitting aloof from a party in Robert Benchley's bungalow at that fabled Hollywood halfway house of actors and writers, the Garden of Allah. She learned he was the writer Scott Fitzgerald, down a bit on his luck, poor in money and health, his books out of print, but, as she presented him to us and to the readers of her autobiographies, the most charming man in the world, a man who gave you his complete attention and could make you feel through the intensity of his interest that *you* were important and as marvelous as he. And so for three and a half years she gave him her love and her loyalty, writing her column but otherwise curtailing her social life, deflecting the advances of Gary Cooper (though not without a twinge of regret), avoiding old friends and lovers to humor Scott's jealousy, "negating herself," as Fitzgerald's psychiatrist noted in a letter to Gerold Frank, "to help this man with whom she had obviously fallen deeply in love." The psychiatrist had "never seen a more devoted, dedicated person." My mother quoted his letter in *The Rest of the Story,* as if to persuade the reader—and herself— that she really had been this paragon of selflessness.

What she also said she gave, and gained, was the trust and benefit of candor. She told Scott the truth about herself—not just about the poverty and the orphanage but also the Jewishness. And what a relief this was, she stressed, after all the lies that she had told. But it's as much a part of the myth that Fitzgerald abused her trust as that he won it. It was in the great drinking binge of 1939 that he screamed, as she put it in *College of One,* "all the secrets of my humble beginnings" to the nurse taking care of him, then, ashamed of what he had done, kicked the nurse in the shinbone. This was also the day that my mother and Fitzgerald grappled over his gun and my mother made the pronouncement of which I think she was rather proud: "Take it and shoot yourself, you son of a bitch. I didn't pull myself out of the gutter to waste my life on a drunk like you." What Fitzgerald had screamed to the nurse, my mother eventually told me, though she never brought herself to write it in any of her books, was that she was a Jew.

After that binge, Fitzgerald was contrite, and the story ended with the stability of the final year. He wasn't drinking. He and my mother lived on adjacent streets in North Hollywood. They dined together nightly, quiet and contentedly domestic, on the meal prepared by their shared housekeeper. They were immersed in the College of One education that had begun in mid-1938 when Fitzgerald found my mother trying to read the first volume of Proust. He had taken her in hand and drawn up the two-year plan of study. Now my mother spent hours each day reading books and discussing them with her teacher. The curriculum had history in it—the aim was to work up to reading Spengler—and art and music, but above all it was the study and appreciation of literature. Fitzgerald and my mother recited the poems together—Keats, Swinburne, T. S. Eliot—and pretended to be famous characters from the novels: Grushenka and Alyosha from *The Brothers Karamazov,* shortened to "Grue" and "Yosh"; Natasha and Pierre from *War and Peace* (my mother had rebelled against being cast as the worldly, jaded Helene); Swann and Odette from Proust; Esther Summerson and Mr. Jarndyce or the Smallweeds slumped in their chairs from *Bleak House;* Becky Sharp and Rawdon Crawley from *Vanity Fair,* or for a change of pace Scott would become fat Joseph Sedley. I loved the account of the education. It conveyed such a vivid sense of intimacy.

In the last year of his life Fitzgerald was also working on his novel *The Last Tycoon.* He had hopes that the book would be the best he had ever written, and my mother was very proud of the ways that she was part of this project. Remarks that she made got included in the text: "the stars are like ping-pong balls"; "I have nice teeth for an English girl." Also the heroine, Kathleen, was based on my mother—a woman "dower[ed] with a little misfortune," "the only woman whose life did not depend on him [the hero, Monroe Stahr] or hope to depend." Fitzgerald offered to bequeath her the manuscript of *The Last*

Tycoon, but she refused to accept this, saying Zelda and Scottie needed the money more; she could take care of herself.

And then Fitzgerald died, and she did indeed take care of herself—and of others. She bought Scottie Fitzgerald her wedding dress, even though it had been eighteen-year-old Scottie who had pained her in the aftermath of the death by pronouncing what she herself knew already: "You know, Sheilah, you can't come to the funeral." She advised Edmund Wilson in his editing for publication of the manuscript of *The Last Tycoon.* She went back to England as a war correspondent. The Marquess of Donegall still wanted to marry her, but she couldn't bring herself to do this; it was too soon, she said, after Scott's death. And then she met Trevor Westbrook, and what she imagined as Fitzgerald's wish for her came true. At the point that so much seemed lost came the miracle of having children, a compensation for her suffering, a reward for her courage.

It was not until 1951, ten years after Fitzgerald's death, that my mother first ventured to talk to anyone about him. She was lunching at Romanoff's with a friend from New York, the theatrical producer Jean Dalrymple. Jean asked about Scott, and thinking that she would be able to talk calmly, my mother launched into the story. When it came, however, to speaking about his death, she burst into tears. It was part of the Fitzgerald saga as we knew it that what had happened had affected my mother so profoundly that she did not talk about Fitzgerald, she really could not talk about him, for all this length of time. She had corresponded with Arthur Mizener to answer questions for his Fitzgerald biography, *The Far Side of Paradise.* But as she explained in *The Rest of the Story,* "Very few people knew of my association with Scott. I only discussed him when I was asked direct questions." Just as she considered herself an outsider to Hollywood, my mother always thought of herself, liked to think of herself, as a very private person. She was keen to stress to the world the strength and depth of the reticence it was necessary to overcome in order to share with the world this important chronicle.

But shared it was. It all started—the telling and selling of her great romance and her life—in the autumn of 1955 when Woody Wirsig, an editor from *Woman's Home Companion,* approached my mother with an expression of interest in her story, both the Fitzgerald part and also her experience as an English girl who had come to America and made good. This was, after all, at the height of my mother's own fame and power as a columnist, so the story had the double interest of the stature of her lover and her own celebrity. About the same time, Jerry Wald, a film producer at Twentieth Century–Fox, got the idea to make a movie about Scott Fitzgerald, and learning with surprise of my mother's history with Fitzgerald, he wanted to buy the saga of her romance to be made into an original screenplay. And finally, just to add to the stir and frenzy, an editor from Simon & Schuster was interested in the project as a book.

Never one to miss an opportunity, my mother set to work, first writing a one-hundred-page account of her life, from the orphange through Fitzgerald, then when both *Woman's Home Companion* and Simon & Schuster said this material wasn't good—she had been too hard on herself—taking one more try on her own in a deal with *Woman's Home Companion* and pouring 100,000 words in seven days onto a dozen reels of tape.

It was in the context of all this activity, which to me often seemed like commotion, that I heard more at times than I cared to know about Scott Fitzgerald and my mother's early life. Perhaps it is true, as my mother stated in the preface of *Beloved Infidel,* that we children had always known about some sort of connection with Fitzgerald—my brother recollects our mother taking him into our den when he was very young in order to look up Fitzgerald's name in the *Columbia Encyclopedia.* Suddenly, though, there loomed a momentous story with all its claims to romantic legend. I don't recall if it was imparted to us in a dramatic hour of disclosure or simply absorbed by us, piecemeal, nonchalantly, from its pervasive presence in our household. When I went to visit our old housekeeper, Anna Bayer, she told me how my mother had taken *her* aside and said,

"Anna, I want to tell you what I am going to write in my book about F. Scott Fitzgerald and about my life." Anna was pleased to be considered worthy of being told all this directly, but in fact she knew the story already. She had heard my mother discussing it with her secretary, or explaining it to us children, answering the questions that I, in particular, was eager to ask her about her life.

"Was I so eager?" I asked. "I don't remember."

"Oh yes," Anna said. "You were very eager. Robbie went by, and he heard and he didn't hear. But you asked many times about everything."

My own memory is not of learning about my mother's life but of simply at a certain point, like Anna Bayer, having possession of this knowledge in a household that was now beset by the *Beloved Infidel* project. In terms of our family chronology, *Beloved Infidel* came right after Bow Wow, and I think that its concentration on her tie with Fitzgerald served to bolster my mother's confidence, which had been shaken by the marriage and divorce. The idea of the project arose before Bow Wow left, but it was when he was gone that my mother set to work in earnest. She had never before looked back, and I doubt that she knew she was launching what would become the obsession of the rest of her life: the chronicling of her own history, the writing and rewriting of autobiography, the validating of her past and self.

It was both her past and a commodity called *Beloved Infidel,* the title borrowed from the poem Fitzgerald had written in homage to her charms. It used to bother me that my mother spoke about "the girl"—herself—and "Fitzgerald" as if they were characters in a novel or items in her column. "But didn't this happen to you?" I would insist. The more pressing question of the moment was what would happen to the story. Would my mother sell it to Fox? Would it first be a magazine piece? Would it first be a book? Should she have a collaborator? Woody Wirsig lost his job at *Woman's Home Companion,* but he owned the tapes, which my mother now had to buy back from him. Henry Holt & Co. supplied the cash, because this was the publisher that in the end bought the book. Fox bought the movie, and on the basis of there being a movie deal, my mother secured Gerold Frank as her collaborator. His credentials were that he had been coauthor with Lillian Roth of *I'll Cry Tomorrow,* the story of her struggle against alcoholism, and with Diana Barrymore of *Too Much Too Soon.* Both had been best-sellers, and *I'll Cry Tomorrow* had been made into a successful film.

When people subsequently asked my mother why she had felt in need of a collaborator, she always answered that it was because she wasn't sure she could do Fitzgerald justice on her own and she wanted an expert to help her put the book together. Her stated mission in writing the book, the almost sacred duty that caused her to overcome reticence and scruples, was to correct the impression created by Budd Schulberg's *The Disenchanted,* and even by the Mizener biography, that Fitzgerald had died a drunk and a failure. My mother knew he had not. Fitzgerald was not "the poor son-of-a-bitch"—Dorothy Parker's quotation at the time of his death of the line from *The Great Gatsby*—but a hopeful, dignified man, not drinking, working on what he believed would be his best book, enjoying the stability and warmth of his intimacy with my mother. Never one, however, to hide behind overly pure motives, my mother also acknowledged that her desire to set the record straight about Fitzgerald, to show he had died dignified and productive, had not been the only thing on her mind. "I wonder," she mused in *The Rest of the Story,* looking back to the stir of writing of the earlier volume, "at what moment the money becomes interesting and you want to make a profit on what began as a noble idea." What she failed to wonder about was that the "noble idea" of redeeming Fitzgerald also involved the issue of her own redemption. No mere Hollywood columnist, she now asserted herself as the woman who had loved and rescued the great American novelist, and whose love for her in turn confirmed and underscored her worth.

I did not like the *Beloved Infidel* project. It entered our lives at a point when I was already angry with my mother. Anna Bayer may remember me as asking eager questions, as always having a smile on my face and being my mother's great friend. What I remember is the intensity of my guilty, muffled rage that my mother had made such a mess of things and now seemed to be falling apart. The strain on her nerves in getting rid of Bow Wow was great. She talked compulsively about the divorce and kept announcing in a very dramatic way that she was about to have a nervous breakdown. This frightened me, and I held tenaciously to my belief that she was really as tough as they came. Then it simply seemed cruel of her to scare us with her hysteria.

As *Beloved Infidel* took shape, it replaced the divorce as my mother's obsessive focus. The actual writing of the book took place in 1957 and 1958 when I was not much at home, this being my first year at boarding school back East. Still, from my holidays and summer vacation in California, I remember the book as taking over 607 North Maple Drive. Gerold Frank— "the ghost," we called him, though really he was the collaborator—moved in for weeks at a time, playing chess with Robbie when he wasn't closeted with my mother, eliciting into his tape recorder all the details of her sad childhood, adventurous young womanhood, and great romance. As in the past, we could always interrupt her with our concerns, and she would patiently give us her attention. But in my eyes she had changed. She had wanted us to believe in her as a mother who could anticipate and meet our every need, who lived to make us happy and had the power to do so. Now I saw an anxious, erratic person who seemed surprisingly centered on herself. I was resentful and angry, and then guilty about feeling as I did.

It occurs to me now, though it didn't consciously at the

time, that *Beloved Infidel* must have confronted me in ways that were disquieting with my mother's sexual past. Here we had just evicted Bow Wow, I at fourteen and fifteen was dealing with my own timid and confused first romantic attachments, and suddenly my mother was inviting the world to see her as Scott Fitzgerald's "Beloved Infidel." Scott wrote the poem after asking my mother to number her past liaisons. "Eight," she said, picking, as she described it, an "approximate" figure. Fitzgerald was shocked, and the Beloved Infidel figure of his poem is not just the poet's lover but a woman with a history of lovers:

> That sudden smile across a room
>> Was certainly not learned from me,
> That first faint quiver of a bloom
>> The eyes initial ecstasy,
> Whoever taught you how to page
>> Your loves so sweetly—now as then
> I thank him for my heritage,
>> The eyes made bright by other men.

So goes the first stanza, with subsequent stanzas ending "A heart made warm by other men," "On lips made soft by other men," "The tale you told to other men," and so on.

My mother loved the poem. "It was a poem for me and about me," she wrote in *Beloved Infidel*. "I had never read anything so beautiful. I read it again and again, now to myself, now aloud, lingering on the words." She loved the title, which confirmed that she was Scott's beloved. Also to be an infidel fitted nicely with her sense of herself as an unbeliever, an outsider. That the poem is obsessed with her sexual experience and allure was something she never remarked on. Perhaps she liked that too. She certainly liked seeing herself as a woman whom men found irresistible, at the same time conveying *her* ability to resist *them* and her pride that, sought after as she was, she had never compromised her independence.

What Fitzgerald thought is difficult to decipher. Once in a drunken rage he had scrawled the word "paramour" across the back of my mother's picture—a strangely old-fashioned word to describe a lover or mistress, and his use of it points for me to the mixture of feelings he seems to have had—fascination, boastful pride, jealousy, and shame—at being linked with a woman of experience and with his own role as her adulterous lover. He was puritanical, my mother always said, or at least had a puritanical side.

I am tempted to say that I was puritanical too, though I don't think this quite accurately describes me. It wasn't a matter of a general outlook or philosophy. I simply did not want to think about my mother's eyes or heart or lips made bright or warm or soft by any men, and I did my best to wipe out from my life every aspect of her story that disturbed me. My method was simple. I did not read my mother's book. I did not go to see the movie. Why should I read the book since I knew the story already and did not need to reexperience it through the medium of Gerold Frank's prose? As for the movie, my mother said it was rotten—"I had but one life to give my producer and Jerry Wald ruined it," she quipped. She thought the casting was all wrong—Gregory Peck too wooden to be a good Fitzgerald and Deborah Kerr too ladylike for "the girl." Better choices, she insisted, would have been Richard Basehart and Marilyn Monroe—she thought that she and Marilyn had the same quality of vulnerability. Why, I said, should I go to see a bad movie? And so I stayed away.

I did not need to read my mother's book or to see the movie to know about F. Scott Fitzgerald. I absorbed him from my mother's stories and then reshaped him as an intimate of my own. I took the things my mother presented—little things, by and large: Fitzgerald looking at her "with such love" with his head cocked to one side, the two of them lying at opposite ends of a sofa with their shoes and socks off and massaging one another's toes, the two of them at Malibu Beach scooping into buckets the tiny fish called grunion that come onto the beach at night to spawn (Robbie and I had been allowed to stay up once for a grunion run). And from these and other images, I built my own picture of the man my mother had made such a presence in our household. I knew what Fitzgerald had been like. I almost felt I *became* him and could share his vision. We both knew what it felt like to love my mother, to be enchanted by her warmth and beauty, to seek in her the radiant center of the world.

And so, imagining him loving her—the alternative would have been to imagine him loving me—I drew close to him, and he became for me an ideal, a model, an alter ego. Not that I wasn't aware of his faults; I am sure they even attracted me: the drinking, the jealousy, the immaturities. But I understood the quality of his charm—that wonderful sensibility, the capacity to give another person his undivided attention—and I wanted to possess such charm even more than I wanted someone to lavish it on me. I understood his values: his love of language, his love of the books that had shaped his own imagination and intellect and now had such an important role in shaping mine. I had no time to read *Beloved Infidel* because I was too busy reading the volumes of Dickens and Thackeray and Tolstoy and so many other marvelous books in the College of One library. And then I started reading Fitzgerald's own books, and his letters, and I listened to his voice. He was a dreamer; he believed in the glory of illusions. Yet he was also a realist, never forgetting, as he put it, the value of "making an effort," never losing sight of what in a letter to his daughter he had called "the wise and tragic sense of life," by which, as he explained to Scottie,

I mean the thing that lies behind all great careers, from Shakespeare's to Abraham Lincoln's, and as far back as there are books to read—the sense that life is essentially a cheat and its conditions are those of defeat, and that the redeeming things are not "happiness and pleasure," but the deeper satisfactions that come out of struggle.

Scott Fitzgerald helped to define for me an alternative to Hollywood. From my earliest reading—*Black Beauty* and *Little Lord Fauntleroy* onward—I had imagined myself in a world that was different from my own. It existed, I believed, back East and in England, a world of green landscapes and century-old houses, of greater rootedness and civility. It was a world where people had family histories and saw life more philosophically than seemed to be the case in Beverly Hills—perhaps where they had "a wise and tragic sense of life." Learning about Fitzgerald, who had both loved my mother and known what books to give her so that she could pass them on to me, I felt I had gained a personal guide for my own cultural and intellectual odyssey away from Hollywood, away even from my mother.

My mother once said that she felt like the madam who had educated her daughter to be a lady only to have the girl turn in contempt on the profession that had paid for her gentility. It was part of our family myth that my mother slaved away in Hollywood so that we, her children, could do something better. If you ignore the issue of comfort and money, you could substitute "sweatshop" for "Hollywood" and believe that we were not so different, really, from the immigrant Jewish families on New York's Lower East Side or in London's East End. By dint of my mother's labor and at the price of distancing us from her, we were to have an education, a passport to our cultural transfiguration.

To say, though, that Scott Fitzgerald was my guide in my escaping Hollywood and my mother is, of course, to ignore my mother's role in shaping my aspirations. It was my living mother, not the dead Fitzgerald, who helped me to choose which book to read next, who handed me *Tom Jones* when I had finished *Bleak House* or who thought it might be time for me to read *Zuleika Dobson* or *War and Peace.* It was my mother whom I knew and admired as a political liberal—Scott had had her read Morton's *People's History of England,* which she said had changed her from a conservative to a liberal in a week—and who taught me to abhor Joseph McCarthy and to idolize Franklin Delano Roosevelt and Adlai Stevenson. Not that there weren't other Democrats in Hollywood. But the majority of other people's parents were Republicans, and our status as Democrats was one more thing that seemed to set us apart from Hollywood's opulence and assumptions. My mother was not a crusader. She had been frightened when, after she allowed her name to appear on a list of prestigious supporters of the First Amendment—Archibald MacLeish and Gene Kelly among them—a series of anonymous letters appeared in the *Citizen News,* the very Hollywood paper that then carried her column, denouncing her as a Communist. Subsequently, she refused to put even an Adlai Stevenson sticker on our car for fear that this would draw unwanted attention when she drove the car to the studios. Still, it was my mother, not Fitzgerald, whom I knew in our household as the voice of political liberalism; it was my mother who I knew hate inequality, loved literature, and above all, respected education. It was only, so it seemed, that her pursuit of high ideals got muted by the daily exigencies of writing the column and holding her own in Hollywood.

Fitzgerald had educated my mother, but not to the point that she had any real confidence in herself as an educated person. Though she was always a reader of books, she did not continue with any systematic pursuit of knowledge. And somehow her sense of having missed out on an education was always stronger than the sense of having been able to catch up on one, perhaps because education brings conviction of belonging as well as of knowing, and my mother never felt she belonged anywhere. What Scott Fitzgerald's gift of education to my mother therefore seemed to amount to was that she could educate, really properly educate, me and my brother. Like Fitzgerald's daughter, Scottie, I would go to boarding school in Connecticut and to an Eastern college. I would be part of a world of culture and intellect where I could feel I belonged. I would have the skill to talk about literature and ideas, to analyze the novels of Scott Fitzgerald and other authors, to study math and science and languages and philosophy as well as litera- ture and history. I would have all the knowledge, the confi- dence, and the privilege that my mother imagined education to confer. I tacitly agreed that this should be my destiny, and accepted that my mother should make it possible through her own self-sacrifice—her lucrative but ignoble profession as a Hollywood gossip columnist.

The process of my leaving Hollywood, of us all leaving and moving from 607 North Maple Drive, began even before Scott Fitzgerald became such an integral part of our lives. I think the first step was the trip my mother and I, then age eleven, took to Europe in the summer of 1954. My mother had not been back to Europe since her time there with Trevor during the war. Our expedition inaugurated a tradition of family travel abroad, other trips following in 1956, 1959, and 1960. On this initial trip, it was just my mother and me. Bow Wow, still living with us, stayed behind in California. Eight-year-old Robbie, thought too young to appreciate Europe, would spend the six weeks we were gone at summer camp in Arizona.

An increasing number of Hollywood films at this time were being made abroad on location, and the idea of our trip was that my mother would visit the locations and interview the stars while I would have the chance to see some of Europe. Aside from a few weeks spent at the same camp Robbie was now attending in Arizona, I had never traveled outside of Califor- nia. Going to Europe seemed momentous, a rite of passage. I had just finished sixth grade and was eager for something seri- ous and important, what it exactly might be I wasn't sure. We set out on a TWA propeller plane, sharing a berth for the over- night flight to New York. I have a picture of us standing to- gether by the door to the plane, both fresh from the hair- dresser, smiling and waving goodbye to California.

For all the anticipation of new horizons, there was a way in which our trip to Europe was simply an extension of Hollywood, with me tagging along while my mother did her work. Granted the setting was different. I was astonished first in New York, and then again in London, Paris, and Rome, the cities we visited, at how dirty the buildings were. Europe surprised and stirred me with its dirt and crumbling edifices, with the sight of horse-drawn milk wagons in London and donkeys in the roads outside of Rome, with its monuments and its languages. Still, much of our activity was the familiar and embarrassing round of going with my mother to studios and restaurants while she interviewed the stars. We went to see a drunken Errol Flynn in his dressing room at Shepperton Studios. He angered me by speaking insultingly to my mother. But when I stood in front of her chair and glowered at him, he threw back his head and roared with laughter at "the cub defending its dam." Another day we lunched at Les Ambassadeurs with Zsa Zsa Gabor and her current flame, Porfirio Rubirosa. Rubirosa kissed my hand and kept exclaiming, *"Ah, qu'elle est belle; ah, qu'elle est mignonne."* I wiped off the kiss and ate my sole amandine. It was more fun in Paris when we went to watch him play polo in the Bois de Boulogne. Zsa Zsa said that she exercised his horses.

Perhaps it's more accurate to say that here again was Hollywood but interwoven with the sights and culture of Europe. I kept a diary and took great pride in my powers of observation as I recorded what I had done and seen. In Paris, for example, I noted my impressions of the Bois de Boulogne, the Eiffel Tower, tea at the Ritz, and going with my mother to see Ingrid Bergman in a French translation of Shaw's *Saint Joan* and then to interview her in the bar at the elegant old Hotel Raphael while her three children by Rossellini played on the floor of the large, dark, oak-paneled room. I knew about the Ingrid Bergman scandal—her running off, the illegitimate baby, her daughter Pia Lindstrom left behind. And now here was the woman who had stirred all that trouble, her hair cropped short for the part of Saint Joan, asking me questions about my

school, which Pia had also attended. I found her attractive and
was pleased that she seemed to like me.

In Rome I was impressed by poverty, the Catacombs, the
beauty of Linda Christian (just separated from Tyrone Power),
and the wooden horse on the set of *Helen of Troy,* before which
we were photographed. The photo documentation of the trip
is extensive. Aside from the publicity pictures—of my mother
and me boarding the plane, posing with the Trojan horse, walking together into the dining room of the *Queen Elizabeth* on
our voyage home—we have our own snapshots, which my
mother took of me in front of just about every major monu-
ment of London, Paris, and Rome. Looking at these pictures, I
see a sober, self-possessed young person, not happy, not unhappy—the same person whom a few years later a boarding
school housemother would sum up as "neat, quiet, studious,
and reliable."

I must have been pleased to be off on my own with my
mother—without Bow Wow and without even Robbie. One
picture of us standing together on a bridge that crosses the
Seine shows me nestled against her mink stole, and I can remember how comforting that felt. What I remember just as
vividly, however, is the discomfort of being too closely cooped
up with her. I did not like sharing a berth on the airplanes. My
mother tossed and kicked, and I couldn't sleep. Also, my insistence that I could fall asleep only in total darkness made sharing
a room difficult for us both. To accommodate me, she would
normally go into the bathroom to read until I was asleep. One
night, though, at the Georges V in Paris, after she had logged a
long stretch sitting on the toilet seat with her book, I made the
mistake of greeting her in my most wide-awake manner as she
crept back into the bedroom. It surprised me when she said I
would just have to put up with the light.

I also remember in Paris a taste of what seemed like daring
independence. One evening we attended the paratrooper show
of the Grande Armée—the French Foreign Legion. At inter-

mission, when my mother wanted to leave and I didn't, she arranged for the young French woman who was our public-relations contact to bring me back to the hotel. I remember staying on with the Frenchwoman and her friends to the end of the show, then sitting in the backseat of their car listening to them converse in French as we drove through the lamp-lit streets of Paris—across the Seine, around the Place de la Concorde, up the Champs-Elysées. Back at the Georges V, my mother was waiting up for me, distraught, she said, that she had left me with virtual strangers in a strange city. Her anxiety startled me, for I had been so free of anxiety—happy to feel I could enter and navigate another culture, at ease with life's expanding scope.

Perhaps no city that we visited confirmed in me such feelings more than London, where we began and ended the trip. London was special in that we were connected with it through family history. Trevor lived here; my mother had grown up here—that much I knew—and being in London gave me a sense of almost belonging somewhere other than Hollywood. We stayed at the International Sportsman's Club on Upper Grosvenor Street, which my mother had joined as a founding member in the 1920s during what later she dubbed her "society period." She had known all the young bloods of her day (she liked to tell me how handsome Randolph Churchill and Tom Mitford had been) and had captained the club's women's squash team. The same porters from the twenties were still opening the front door, hailing taxis, and carrying suitcases up the tiny bird-cage elevator to the rooms that were available for out-of-town members. They greeted my mother with deferential recognition and told her who was still alive and who was dead. We had tea in the lounge with Jack Mitford—uncle of Jessica, Unity, Nancy, and Tom—with whom my mother had gone skiing in St. Moritz in 1929. Another old friend, sporting top hat and tails, took us to a cricket match at Lord's. And I remember a drink with Lord Beaverbrook, an old admirer of my mother as well as Trevor's boss during the war, a compelling gnomelike little man who asked me how I had liked Rome. My mother tried to intervene and answer for me, but he silenced her with a peremptory "Let her speak for herself." I answered, "Rome is ruins," and both of them found this amusing.

It's odd that I don't remember seeing Trevor on this trip. Perhaps I saw him and have forgotten; perhaps he was away somewhere and not available. On every other visit I made to London—and I must have been back there at least fifteen times before his 1978 death—I always did something with him; at the very least we had lunch or dinner together or I went with him for the day to his country house in Sussex. Looking back to this trip, however, I can't even remember expecting to see him or being disappointed not to.

My lapse of memory about Trevor seems all the more telling in light of the men I do remember seeing and doing things with apart from my mother. John Graham Gillam, my mother's first husband, introduced to me as "Uncle Johnny," took me on a daylong excursion to view the changing of the guard at Buckingham Palace and visit the Crown Jewels in the Tower of London, to which we traveled by tube. Johnny was courtly and full of interesting information about the queen and her style of life. I don't think I knew at this point that he had been my mother's husband, the man who had taught her table manners and sent her to train for the theater at the Royal Academy of Dramatic Art, but whose failure in business and in bed—a month after their marriage he was both bankrupt and impotent—had been the spur to her realization that she had better get on with taking care of herself. I am sure I learned all this only at the time of the *Beloved Infidel* project two years later. My mother did tell me that Johnny was poor, and therefore she liked to invite him to tea in the Sportsman's Club lounge, where, without loss of dignity, he could eat his fill of the little sandwiches and cakes.

I liked Johnny, a gentle whimsical fellow, but he never became my particular friend, perhaps because he was so declaredly and wholeheartedly attached to my mother. Someone I liked better—best of anyone I met on the trip and best perhaps of any grown-up I knew as a child—was introduced to me as family friend, professor of logic, and the man who, as fate and history would have it, had taken my mother to the hospital the night that I was born. This, of course, was Freddie Ayer.

I never thought about it at the time, but I realize that Freddie was not particularly interested in my mother, nor she in him, and I readily appropriated him as *my* special friend and admirer. My mother took me to his little flat above a tailor's shop on Whitehorse Street in Shepherd's Market. Then either all three of us, or just he and I, went to lunch at one of those out-of-the-way little restaurants in Soho and Mayfair that Freddie always knew about. The menu was always in French, and Freddie, who boasted of being bilingual, would show off by ordering in that language with the same incredible rapidity that he spoke English. I am sure that it was just Freddie and I who went off after lunch to the bookstore. I remember him standing with his hands thrust into the trouser pockets of his habitual three-piece suit, questioning me in his rapid and animated manner about what I had and hadn't read, then taking down the Hardy from a shelf. When I got back to California, I lay on my bed immersed in the sad tale of seduction and its consequences: the tragically timed encounters, concealments, and revelations that ensnare poor Tess and Angel and Alec. Freddie then wrote me letters in his tiny, almost indecipherable script, and it seemed perfectly natural to me that we should be friends. After all, wasn't I an intellectual too? Thus ours was the affinity of like-minded people.

By the time of our return to California, I had acquired an English accent, which I maintained for several months until my mother gently but firmly urged me to "drop it." My accent was symptomatic of a new restlessness with my old identity and horizons. The trip to Europe had stirred in me the desire to have a wider, more noble existence. Unable to move to London or New England, where I imagined such lives could be led, I did what I could. I asked my mother if I could go to private school rather than continuing at my old school, Hawthorne Elementary, for the final seventh and eighth grades. The idea came to me as I was in my room, just a week or so back from Europe, rereading *Little Women*. In a distinct and crystalline moment of resolution, I felt the need for change and new opportunity, and I realized that I wanted to go to private school. At Hawthorne, fine Beverly Hills public school that it was, the boys were beginning during recess to roughhouse with the girls, to run after them and grab at their clothes while the girls giggled and made a loud flirtatious show of wanting to escape. Cliques abounded, and although I belonged to one, its gossip and titillations—expelling someone from our circle or going into the playground bathroom to look at Cynthia Niven's size 34B bra—now seemed constricting and mundane. A private school, I thought, would be different—more rarefied and intellectual, more commensurate with my sense of life's possibilities.

The Bel Air Town and Country School, a semicircle of low white wooden buildings perched atop a bluff in Bel Air, was run by Mr. and Mrs. John Dye, a rabidly Republican couple whose only son had been killed in World War II and who had founded the school in his memory. A full-length portrait of the son in his Air Force uniform hung in the school's main hall and inspired student respect for the loss the Dyes had suffered and the seriousness of their mission as educators.

Known to the student body as Auntie Catherine and Uncle John, the Dyes ran the school, which went from first through ninth grades, as a kind of extended family, which I now joined. We sang school songs to them:

> Oh Uncle John, we sing-a-ling-a-ling
> With all out hearts to you . . .

And:

> Hail to Auntie Catherine,
> Hail-a Hail-a Hail-a,
> There's nothing that she cannot dooooo . . .

Also every morning, assembled around the central green in front of the buildings, clad in our blue-and-white-checked uniforms designed by Lanz, we would face eastward, stretch out our arms, and intone a Hindu salutation to the dawn. This was the special Bel Air prelude and embellishment to the ensuing Pledge of Allegiance. All American schoolchildren recited the Pledge of Allegiance, but we at Bel Air, perched on our California hillside, joined rituals of East and West in lofty ecumenicism.

I remember the ways that Bel Air was silly and pretentious, and no less than Hawthorne, a school for movie people's children. Our morning ride on the school bus was rather like a tour of movie-star homes, as we stopped to pick up the three noisy sons of Gregory Peck; Larraine Day's Michele and Christopher, who vaunted their double distinction of being adopted and belonging to the Mormon Church; Paul Henreid's pretty blond Monica; Dean Martin's pert brunette Claudia and Gail; and at the Lana Turner–Lex Barker home his Lynne and Stevie and her daughter, Cheryl Crane, who was expelled at age twelve for telling lies and who was later indicted for stabbing Johnny Stompanato.

Still, Bel Air did not altogether disappoint me in my quest for transfiguration. The school communicated that students were special—perhaps private schools always try to do this—not because we were the sons and daughters of well-known and successful people, but quite aside from this, almost despite it. We had a sense of being noticed and recognized for individual merit. Mr. and Mrs. Dye as well as our teachers seemed intimately to know us. If we excelled, we were honored, our names called out before the school as we came forward to sign special books that would preserve the record of our good citizenship or academic achievement.

It was in seventh grade at the Bel Air Town and Country School that I entered the stretch of years, lasting through high school, of being always the best student in my class. At Hawthorne I had been a good student, but there was the occasional B on my report card, and there were other good students as well. Bel Air was smaller; I felt galvanized by exciting teachers; and suddenly I found myself both deeply engaged in my schoolwork and rather strikingly, self-consciously, an academic star. I gave an oral book report on a Dorothy Parker short story and was amazed at my ability to control the presentation and elicit laughter from the class. We read *Julius Caesar;* I loved the language and felt exhilarated to sense my mind engaged with it. I started French and Latin and found them easy. In Social Studies we had to do reports on Egypt, Greece, and Rome. I rode my bike to the Beverly Hills library, researched the topics exhaustively, and felt boundless energy and commitment as I wrote up my findings and drew carefully detailed freehand maps to accompany what I wrote. My grade on each assignment was A+.

My success bolstered ego and confidence. It also made me anxious since it seemed to me most unlikely that I could really be so smart. Bel Air was small, I told myself. The teachers favored me. The other students weren't that bright. Thus I vacillated between arrogance and insecurity, and it's no wonder that as successful as I was academically, I was not particularly well liked by my classmates. Compounding my difficulties, the school decided my second year there to put a small number of the good eighth-grade students in the same classes with the ninth-graders. Since I was the only girl moved up like this, the arrangement effectively separated me from the eighth-grade girls I had left behind, yet kept me at a distance from the ninth-graders, whom I held in too great awe to make into friends. At home this was the era of getting rid of Bow Wow and the divorce. So all in all, it was a lonely, unsettled time.

The idea took shape that I should go to boarding school.

My mother worried about my social backwardness, perhaps more than I did, and thought that going away would give me a chance to have a fresh start, unhampered by my current reputation. Going to boarding school was also presented as a privilege that I had earned by my achievement.

It was the night before my scheduled departure to begin ninth grade at the Bishop School in nearby La Jolla. My trunk was just about packed, and Wendy Westbrook labels had been sewn on every last sock and washcloth. My mother, brother, and I were together in my room when suddenly my brother burst into tears. "She's going away," he said. "And then she'll go on to college. And then she'll get married. And I'll never be with her again." His outburst was surprising, and it moved us all. None of us, probably not Robbie himself, knew that he cared so much about me.

The next morning it occurred to me to ask my mother if I really had to go away. I didn't think she'd back down; I wasn't even sure what I wanted. Yet it seemed worth a try. "No," she said. "You don't have to go. Unpack at once."

And so I spent another year at Bel Air, back with the previous year's eighth-graders. That was the year I lost the school election to be May Queen (there were only four ninth-grade girls, and it came down to between me and Judy Rackin). Pepa Ferrer, the previous year's May Queen and my idol, came back to the ceremony of dances on the green and gave me a little gift with a card: "To the girl who should have been May Queen." My mother, stung by my defeat, bought me a beautiful yellow dress at Bonwit Teller for my role as ninth-grade attendant to the May Queen and to the end of her life told the story of how Deborah Kerr, another school parent, thought I had been the May Queen because she had been so entranced by my dazzling smile.

Plans were now forming in earnest for me to go to boarding school. It was out of the question that I would go to Beverly Hills High, or even to one of the private day schools that most all my classmates were headed for. I was different from other girls—special, more difficult, more talented. Our choice now was between the Katherine Branson School in San Francisco and a school in Connecticut called Rosemary Hall, both of which had admitted me. Katherine Branson was closer to home, but Rosemary Hall had the allure of the East. Unable to decide between them, I spent a stretch of mornings getting into bed with my mother to discuss with her the pros and cons of each. If my mother began to favor one school, I would immediately stress the advantages of the other. One morning I went into her room to continue the vacillation, and she startled me with the announcement that I was going to Rosemary Hall. So that was that.

The only member of my Bel Air class to go to boarding school, the only one to leave California, I prepared for my departure. We bought the Rosemary Hall uniforms—the wool skirts and blue blazers, the tams and the sports tunics. We bought "free dress" clothes—wool skirts, sweaters, and coats to keep me warm in the Eastern weather. We bought a complete set of Eastern riding clothes, including the boots and a hard hat, since I had chosen horseback riding as my fall sport.

When my mother was initially negotiating the movie sale of *Beloved Infidel,* she came up with the whimsical idea that her price was a cottage in Connecticut. Connecticut to my mother, no less than to me, represented an enviable and idealized world of old, unostentatious houses and families within these houses secure in all the ways she wasn't. Now I would become part of this world, the first member of my family to leave California and the vanguard of our general exodus. In 1959, right before my last year at Rosemary Hall, my mother, having just remodeled 607 North Maple Drive, suddenly put the house on the market. Robbie was set to follow me east to boarding school, and my mother decided it was time for us to move as a family. She had second thoughts, but not before the house was sold. The buyers were the Hollywood agent Warren Cowan and his bride-to-be, the actress Barbara Rush. They would be married in the house; it would be Barbara Rush, not I, who came down the curving staircase as a bride.

My mother bought a house in Westport, Connecticut, and rented a small apartment in New York. Her notion was to continue writing her Hollywood column but from a base in the East. As it turned out, this arrangement proved impractical. After a couple of years, my mother decided it was impossible to write a Hollywood column from Westport, Connecticut, sold the house there, and bought another house back in California.

In the ensuing thirty years my mother bought, sold, and rented over two dozen houses and apartments in New York, Connecticut, California, London, and Palm Beach. She was always looking for the best place to live, and always restlessly moving on. I, meanwhile, the product of my education and aspirations, became an Easterner, adopting and adapting to the settings I had so clearly wanted to be part of. As for my past life growing up in Beverly Hills among the film people, this became the life that I had left behind me, as emphatically, though often it also seemed as incompletely, as my mother once left behind the East End of London.

Six

TREEING
THE CUB

HE FIRST TIME I beat my mother at tennis, she threw down her racket, called me a bitch, and stomped off the court. Perhaps I had swaggered in victory, and this provoked her. I was twenty-two and she was sixty. Later she turned the memory of her tantrum into one of those stories she used to tell against herself with such amiable zest. "I misbehaved terribly, just terribly, the first time Wendy beat me at tennis." I don't think she had any idea how large to me loomed her inability to be happy that I had won. "Your day will come," she had insisted when she used to sit with me at bedtime in my room at 607 North Maple Drive, soothing, consoling, and rallying me in the face of my social miseries. Well, I thought, hadn't it? Couldn't she accept that it had?

Among our family myths, the stories my mother and I shaped about ourselves to help us deal with one another and the world, are the myths of my passage to adulthood. My mother's version of this process, as I piece it together from the things she wrote and said, is a variation on the Walt Disney bear story, the mother bear treeing the cub. My mother had hovered over our childhoods, never, as she put it, allowing us to make mistakes. She liked to recount how I was asked to write an essay at school entitled "My Greatest Mistake" and how she and I spent hours trying and failing to find one. I don't remember this, but perhaps it happened. She also liked to stress the dependence that *she* had then helped me to break, to tell how I sang a solo, "Shenandoah," in a program put on for the Bel Air Town and Country School parents, then looked questioningly towards her, asking for approval with my eyes—she nodded and the other parents smiled—or how my first term at Rosemary Hall I telephoned home to California to ask if I had time to wash my hair before dinner.

"I sent Wendy to boarding school," said my mother, "to make her independent."

I believe that she considered her strategy successful, but it always irritated me to hear her take such credit for the process. Hadn't I, guided perhaps by my father's genes no less than by my mother's exhortations (not to mention the encouragement of the ghost of F. Scott Fitzgerald), had an idea of a different kind of life for myself and set out to realize that life? This was *my* version of the story, a kind of *Bildungsroman,* a tale of development: my coming into my own through the force of internal growth and vision, *desiring* my independence, claiming my own scope.

As *I* present the story, I did indeed telephone home from boarding school to ask about washing my hair or about selecting what dress to wear when we had the freedom of not wearing our uniforms. And I wrote my mother constant letters—particularly the first year—describing every move I made and sore throat I had and grade I got on tests. But I also made a few good friends, grew attached to teachers who encouraged me, and did well academically in a way that reflected not only my grubbing for grades but a genuine intellectual fervor that made me happy to live within my own mind and self.

It was also, ironically, at my Connecticut boarding school that I first learned how my link with Hollywood could serve to enhance me in other people's estimation. If, despite my being shy and rather mousy, I quickly gained a certain odd cachet, it was not only because of my standing as the girl with the highest marks in the school but also because of my ability to obtain autographed photographs of their movie idols for my starstruck classmates. I conveyed the "orders" in my letters home to my mother. *"Margy* would like Marlon Brando, *Ann* would like Jeff Chandler, and *Valerie* would like Deborah Kerr." Or again, "I know you already got one 'Audrey Hepburn' but the girl who requested this is a good friend of mine. Her name is Joan." One friend, Candy Schrafft, home with me over a vacation, actually lunched with Rock Hudson at his studio. We have a photograph of the occasion: a resigned Rock Hudson seated between the two girls, my friend looking joyous with excitement, me looking blank. Indifference was my personal necessity.

I let people know I was from Hollywood, but also that it was a place I had no use for. I suppose this was a way of enjoying the status of the connection and at the same time asserting the superiority that I imagined my outlook conferred on me. To have a connection that so awed other people and to take it so in stride—this seemed the beginning of a certain style of my own. I was a self-proclaimed intellectual and also a terrible snob. When my mother, again over one of my vacations, invited me to come along and meet Elvis Presley, I declined and stayed home to listen to my recording of *Madame Butterfly*. And so I entrenched myself in my chosen path, excited by Jane Austen and Racine and Shakespeare and algebraic equations and the direct and indirect causes of World War I. The reward was my own kind of stardom. At the June 1960 Rosemary Hall graduation my mother sat in the audience and watched as I was called repeatedly to the platform to receive the English Prize, the French Prize, the History Prize, the Math Prize, the Highest Average Award, and a special cup for love of learning. My classmates were all in tears at the thought of leaving Rosemary Hall, but I felt triumphant. It only occurred to me years later to wonder how my mother felt. Was she proud? Did she think, "Poor Wendy, all she has is her grades"? Did she think about herself and about what she might have done if she had had the same advantages?

My mother had toured with me the preceding fall to look at colleges. There was no question but that I would stay in the East (by then, in any case, we were all living in Connecticut), and we had visited Wellesley, Radcliffe, Swarthmore, and Bryn Mawr. Vassar, where Scottie Fitzgerald had gone, was no longer considered an absolutely top school and I applied to it only as my fallback. I ended up not applying to Radcliffe, and Swarthmore turned me down, so my essential choice lay between Wellesley and Bryn Mawr. Wellesley in my mind had a strike against it because the person conducting my interview had invited my mother to join our conversation. Also I had a fuzzily defined impression that Bryn Mawr was more my kind of place. The students whom I encountered walking across the campus seemed friendly but also pleasantly eccentric. Not all wore plaid skirts and McMullen blouses. I sensed tolerance and liberality.

And so in the fall of 1960 I entered Bryn Mawr College. A tea was held for the new students at the home of President Katharine McBride, an imposing woman rumored to have a wooden leg, who informed us that we were the *"crème de la crème"* and exhorted us to great achievement. I was thrilled but anxious. In awe of Bryn Mawr's history and standards, I was sure I would now be found out for the mediocre intellect I suspected I really was despite all my straight A's and prizes. When, however, this didn't happen, I felt I could relax a bit. I made friends, dated boys—boarding school, despite the occasional dances with counterpart boys schools, had been very cloistered—and joined the college theater. What I loved about Bryn Mawr was that it brought together people who seemed to share both talents and problems—we had all been at the top of our high school classes and many of us had also suffered, as I had, as social misfits. Coming together at Bryn Mawr, we were transfigured into something positive and powerful. For the first time in my life, I felt a part of a community that I respected and in which I could freely express myself—in my work, in the plays I acted in, with my friends. To be sure, there were times of upset and depression—I was certainly not serene—but I did not feel out of place.

Also I was growing apart from my mother. Fifty-six years old the September I entered college, she too was adjusting to change, though less positive change, it often seemed, than mine. If I think of my mother's life in terms of broad epochs, I would divide it into her childhood, her heyday lasting through my childhood, and the last third of her life, the years after leaving Hollywood. She herself guides me in this division with a fragment she wrote titled "ON THE SUBJECT OF LOVE." "I'm an expert," she declares. "As a child I longed for it; as an adult I was drenched in it; and now that men's eyes pass me by, I observe it." It was this last stage, my mother's postsexual years (or so I believe them to have been), that coincided with my becoming and existing as an adult, and much of what oppressed me—what I both resisted and accommodated—was her abiding need, though she was no longer an object of men's desire, to feel powerful, central, and unrivaled. She turned, as she acknowledged, to food and buying houses as substitutes for sex. So these were the years of great weight fluctuations and the frenetic buying and selling of homes. She was restless and never really at peace with herself. Still, she had her old exuberance. Also, there was work—her column, the books and articles, the appearances on television. As long as she could work, my mother could almost regain the feelings that had stirred and soothed her when she was younger.

What she couldn't bear very easily was watching me exist apart from her, particularly in the arenas that most emphatically had been hers. She came to see me in a play at Bryn Mawr—*Venus Observed*, by Christopher Fry—and sent my boyfriend backstage at intermission to tell me to speak more softly—it seemed that I was louder than the other players. She came again when I played Ophelia in *Hamlet*, this time found me very good, and then decided on her own to write to Richard Burton's press agent—Burton at the time was casting his Broadway production of *Hamlet*—to say, without revealing my connection as her daughter, that she had seen a marvelous Ophelia in a college production at Bryn Mawr. I was flattered by her enthusiasm, but also deflated. Why wasn't it enough for her that I was good at Bryn Mawr? We never heard back from Richard Burton.

It grew increasingly clear to me that I would be infinitely better off if I could limit my mother's influence in what I considered "my own life." When I was twenty, I lost my virginity in a short-lived and uncertain affair with a Hungarian refugee who was a student at nearby Haverford College. Rather quickly I pulled out of this and then made the mistake in a phone conversation with my mother of telling her about the experience. The next thing I knew, my Hungarian friend was calling in great consternation to ask what I could have said to my mother. She had phoned him after speaking with me, threatened him with deportation, and said outrageous things, most memorably, "Why don't you stick to your Hungarian whores and leave my daughter alone? What did you come over here to do? Rape all our virgins?"

Chagrined, humiliated, furious, I tried to call her back, but she was out. By the time I got hold of her a few hours later, I had regained sufficient calm to realize that simply by virtue of confiding in her, I had played a role in what had happened. "Did you expect me to do nothing?" she asked me. I had, but that, I realized, was unrealistic. She didn't know proper limits. Subsequently, I did my best to confide in her much less.

My mother came to my 1964 Bryn Mawr graduation, bringing Trevor with her. He said little but seemed impressed with the college and the ceremony. I overheard her telling him that while my name was on the program as graduating *magna cum laude*, I probably could have graduated *summa* if I hadn't acted in all those plays. "How can you know that?" I retorted, but she held to her conviction. I had written my senior English honors paper on F. Scott Fitzgerald, a choice that I worried ran counter to my desire to forge an independent destiny. I had started with "The Lost Generation" but somehow was drawn back to Fitzgerald. Writing on Fitzgerald, I explained to myself, was a coming to terms with my spiritual father; I knew too that it was more than that: a complicated negotiation to be loyal to my mother and simultaneously compete with her. She, I think, knew little of my motives and was flattered by the academic prestige that my project seemed to her to confer on both Fitzgerald and herself.

After Bryn Mawr (to sketch the rest of the story), I worked for a year as an editorial assistant in the textbook department of a New York publishing house—the kind of boring, low-level job available to graduates of elite women's colleges—and then returned to school to get a Ph.D. in English literature. Columbia University offered me a three-year scholarship covering tuition and a modest living stipend, and on the strength of this degree of financial autonomy, I rented my own little apartment on the Upper West Side and felt happily independent. I had intense friendships with women, all of whom in some way reminded me of my mother, and a few love affairs with men who reminded me of her much less.

In 1969, at age twenty-six, I married Donald Fairey. He was not exactly the man that my mother, author of among her other books, *How to Marry Super Rich* (published in England as *Love Stories*), would have chosen for me. The previous year she had bought me a mink coat to outfit me for "catching" a good husband, and I felt she must have been disappointed with the return on her investment. Donald was not a lawyer or a doctor and would never make much money. Nonetheless, he was amusing and kind—to her as well as to me—and that counted for a lot. An Englishman who had grown up on a farm in Essex, put himself as an adult through college, and ended up in jobs—first as foreign student adviser at Columbia and later as a trade-union organizer—that involved helping other people, he seemed calm, unspoiled, not interested in being a star. A year after the wedding I was a mother. Donald proved a marvelous father to small children, we both loved having a family, and we forestalled and muted our difficulties by making the family rather than the couple the unit that counted.

Also I grew adept at navigating the world. I got good jobs, and we lived in far-flung places. First there was Hawaii, where I was hired to teach at the university and where we moved with one-year-old Emily. There Sean was born, and sitting at my typewriter on our screened porch, gazing out at a backyard of plumeria blossoms and banana trees, I wrote my dissertation on George Eliot. I traced a recurrent story that Eliot keeps telling: of the need her heroines feel for some meaning to life beyond the egotistical self. They search, though not always success-fully, for a focus or activity—helping others, involvement with community—that will give them what Eliot keeps calling a "larger" existence. My topic seemed to me covert autobiogra-phy. I too was seeking a larger existence, as afraid as George Eliot of unrestrained hungers—for love and attention, acclaim and preeminence. At the back of my mind was a generalized specter of Hollywood vulgarity and self-absorption, at times taking tangible form in the person of Zsa Zsa Gabor as I re-membered her in our Maple Drive living room, talking about her lovers and her jewels. I felt an urgent need to turn my own egotism to more civilized and intelligent account, yet remain-ing always a bit afraid of what I might want, what I might be, if I ever relaxed my diligence and discipline. At the back of my mind was also the specter of my mother, whose energy, cour-

age, and capacity I admired, yet whose untrammeled individu-
alism had caused me so much anxiety and confusion. In so
many ways I wanted to be like her, but I also quite desperately
needed to be different. Now a teacher, scholar, wife, and
mother, I could feel myself a success but not a rank egotist. As
my mother had done, I was constructing a self, but it was a self
with a different relation to society.

After a few years, we moved to Maine. Donald got a job
unionizing hospital workers; I became an assistant professor of
English at Bowdoin College. We bought an old farmhouse,
rambling and decrepit, where we grew vegetables and raised
chickens and turkeys. Friends visiting from New York were
amused at my new incarnation. But I was very happy. After my
first year on the Bowdoin faculty, I was recruited, starting in
the fall of 1977, to be the dean of students. And so began the
twelve years in college administration of the person my mother
liked to boast about to her friends as "my daughter, the dean."

"The most interesting question about your book," said a
friend who is also a writer, "is who you are going to be in it. We
know who your mother is. But what about you? I mean, are
you going to present yourself as Goody Two-shoes Dean
Wendy Fairey?"

I didn't know what to answer her. At issue in part was my
right to keep my own secrets even as I was exposing those of my
mother. But the figure of Dean Wendy Fairey was not a phony.
In an odd way (notwithstanding my mother's enthusiasm for
the title and cachet) she represented my expression of rebellion.
Would anyone ever have ever dreamed of calling Sheilah Graham a Goody Two-shoes? Certainly not.

I had struggled hard to construct a self who could be dif-
ferentiated from the famous Hollywood columnist, the Most
Beautiful Chorus Girl of 1927, the lover of F. Scott Fitzgerald's
last years. It had seemed important to cultivate balance, self-
containment, and continuities, to have one rather than multiple husbands, to make sure my children had a father. And I had

done all this. I really had. At a certain point, my project seemed successful (much more so than it does now). I wish I could say I then felt more at peace with my mother, but that didn't really happen. I was, however, at least able to look back to Hollywood, the place I had needed to get away from, and to see it with less contempt and hostility.

It was when I was visiting my mother in Palm Beach over the 1979 Christmas holidays that I had a shift in thought about Hollywood, specifically about the women of Hollywood, that was almost a moment of epiphany. Palm Beach resembles Beverly Hills in the sparkling stillness of its pastel-colored mansions enclosed by their well-tended lawns and high walls and hedges. But since we never owned one of those mansions and since it annoyed my mother to be poor by Palm Beach standards, she used to retaliate with the pronouncement that it was an indignity to be, as she put it, a second-class citizen in a place where the first-class people are so third-rate. Palm Beach, she liked to point out, is not a place where people work or necessarily owe their wealth to any personal talent or exertion. The women organize charity balls and dress for parties.

The contrast, of course, is that Beverly Hills was an industry town. Its residents, including women like my mother, were successful professional people. And if sex was often a blatant issue in their lives, gender at least was not a prohibition. The names of the female stars who had crossed my path in childhood—Anne Baxter, Dorothy Lamour, Marilyn Monroe, Ingrid Bergman, Maureen O'Hara, even Zsa Zsa Gabor—were, I realized, the names of working women, successful working women. They may have been helped or hindered by husbands or lovers or studio moguls; they may have appeared on the screen as every man's desire and right. But these nevertheless were women who made their own money and as often as not bought their own mansions. Perhaps a third of the houses on our block were owned by women—not just the stars but women writers, costume designers, agents, and others.

My understanding of all this crystallized in a peculiar image. My mother invariably had out on the coffee table in her Palm Beach living room a few of the Hollywood biographies and autobiographies that publishers kept sending her. On the occasion in question, one of these was *Mommie Dearest,* Christina Crawford's best-selling memoir of her relationship with her mother. I picked it up and read it through, though uneasy at the encroachment into my vacation of such a vituperative tale. A mother's monstrosity was not for me a comfortable subject, and I was happy as I read to contrast Joan Crawford with my own mother, who, simply to launch the list of differences, never drank. But there was one image in the book that touched a familiar chord of memory. Christina Crawford describes the care she and her brother took when they played outside in their backyard in the mornings not to make noise that might disturb their mother sleeping in her bedroom upstairs. Although my mother always woke up early, the part of the description that was utterly familiar to me was the mother in her bedroom as focal point, her presence radiating from that center and asserting its force over the rest of the household.

And thinking about women's lives, I realized that growing up in Hollywood had given me a valuable perspective on women—on who they were and what they could do. It never occurred to me from my experience as a child to think of women as at a disadvantage or as tactically located outside the center of power or of interest. Hollywood showed me women as effective agents in shaping their own lives. I knew the dominance of my mother, who for so long sustained our household, ably seconded by those subsidiary figures of female authority, the cooks and the secretaries. I felt the presence of the women stars, living up and down the streets of Beverly Hills in their mansions. I noted other women too, less famous ones but merged for me in a general impression of female effectiveness: the clever woman who produced my mother's radio show; the woman screenwriter, a family friend, with a house and tennis court at Malibu and a charming unemployed husband; yet another friend who owned a lingerie shop in Beverly Hills that specialized in silk and satin nightgowns for the stars and whose retired husband, nicknamed Pops, took long naps after lunch. I did not want a Hollywood life. I had different ambitions, different values. Nonetheless, the achieving female self loomed from my childhood as a bold conception. And since I did indeed want to work and to do well, and, all in all, to lead a life in which my own efficacy mattered, this conception, the residual imprint of Hollywood, with its mansions and its palm trees long behind me, was proving, I realized, a legacy of substance.

Thus ends one version—I have called it the *Bildungsroman* version—of my passage to adulthood and maturity. In all that I have said I have tried to be truthful; yet my effort makes clear to me how difficult this is. The story that I have told conceals another story, another self, perhaps another myth of the self. *"Je suis mon ancêtre,"* my mother had said of herself, and she reinforced the plausibility of this declaration by suppressing even her parents' names. I, on the other hand, was Sheilah Graham's daughter. Her name, her identity, drew me in, an undertow, a whirlpool, dangerous and often oppressive, dangerous because so enticing. Much of my life had been a struggle to climb onto my own little mound of individuality and proclaim my territory: the fragile island of the self. But all my straight-A report cards, all my good jobs, all my pleasure with my own family and friends, never really gave me the sure sense that I had managed this. Sometimes I wondered if I even wanted to. I seemed a person who remained—worse still, had even chosen to remain—captive and unrealized.

It is not easy to be the child of a celebrity. Unlike money or property or social standing, celebrity such as my mother had, that is, celebrity based on her individual luck and determination and achievement, cannot be bequeathed to children. The example, as I have suggested, can inspire, but the legend overwhelms.

True, my mother was never a major figure and, as much as for her own life and accomplishments, was known for the circles in which she moved. In a sense, hers was a reflected glory, glory by association. But if this is so, she nonetheless had her part in the pageant and earned the luster of her connections.

I did not. Yet the luster rubs off on me, still glowing at third remove. On learning who my mother was, a woman I met recently, granted a rather silly woman though utterly sincere, went on and on until overwhelmed by emotion. "I can't believe it," she marveled. "Your mother was Sheilah Graham! My God! You're a living link. I am in the presence of a living link. A link to the Golden Age of Hollywood. To Scott Fitzgerald and all that era." She put her hand over her eyes to stem the tears. I, meanwhile, fighting hard not to be terse or rude, reproached myself inwardly for once again having let the cat out of the bag, once again having invited such embarrassment.

There is a game—the revelation of my mother's name—that I have played ever since I went east to boarding school. Most commonly, it begins with my response to the question of where I come from. I know that if I say "Los Angeles," I can keep my secret, for to be from Los Angeles rarely leads to follow-up questions. If I say "Southern California," the generality of the answer may lead the questioner to ask, "Where in Southern California?"—at which point I still have the option to say "Los Angeles," but it is likely that I will now confess to Beverly Hills—the game's decisive move. Ordinary people aren't thought to live in Beverly Hills, so the mere fact of it being my hometown suggests some interesting connection with fame and glamour. The ensuing chain of questions and answers goes something like this:

"Ah, Beverly Hills! Was your family connected with the film world?" or "Oh, really? Beverly Hills! Did you know any movie stars?"

"Well, yes. My mother wrote a column. A Hollywood gossip column."

"How interesting. What was her name? Would she be any-one I might have heard of?"

"Perhaps. Her name is Sheilah Graham."

"Why, of course! Your mother is Sheilah Graham? *The* Sheilah Graham?"

Assent given by a nod or carefully unexpressive "Yes." If I like my interlocutor, I may also smile wryly and give a little shrug.

Occasionally people haven't heard of my mother, but this is rare; sometimes, too, they are not particularly impressed, but my own offhandedness protects me from the embarrassment of seeming to have wanted to impress them. There are also alternative routes to the revelation. The lead-in topic may be working mothers—if I say it was my mother who supported us, I am likely to be asked what she did—or even the life or works of Scott Fitzgerald. Here I have to be a bit more forthcoming, but still it feels like an act of concealment not to explain that my mother knew him and that as a matter of fact . . .

In recent years I have worked to be less coy and to tell about my mother more directly. I think the double motive behind my coyness has been to make my ultimate revelation through its buildup as dramatic as possible and at the same time to reduce the inherently dramatic to the ordinary. Pretending innocence of the interest of the name, I focus on a mother, just your typical mother, though there are these few tidbits of her life that might be worth mentioning. . . . Perhaps too, I have wished to forestall what always feels like a moment of renewed bondage. Once I am known as Sheilah Graham's daughter, the game is over and I have abdicated the control, lost the option that playing it gives me to suppress my mother or reveal her. There she is again, irrefutable, and I, redefined as her daughter, am enhanced by the connection but also somehow skewed, distorted, thrown off center. A friend of mine who also has a famous mother—she is the daughter of the South African liberal MP Helen Suzman—told me a story that for her encapsulated our shared predicament. She went to a party where, introduced by her married name, Francie Jowell, she met new people who shook her hand and said how pleased they were to meet her. Then someone interjected, "Francie is the daughter of Helen Suzman." Again the people shook her hand; again they said how pleased they were to meet her, as if, said Francie, they were meeting an entirely different person.

It has interested me to observe that my children also play the game of naming my mother, but buffered by the generational remove. At the time that my mother was planning her hip-replacement operation (this became the time she bolted from the hospital), Sean, then fifteen, wrote her a letter:

Dear Granny,

I hope you are recovering quickly from your surgery (I think this will get to you after the surgery). If you haven't had it yet, don't worry, you'll be fine.

Today in school I was speaking to the teacher and the topic of grandparents came up, so I said that my grandmother's name was Sheilah Graham. The teacher didn't believe that "the great Sheilah Graham" was my grandmother (I quote). She thought that you were dead. I told her that you were alive and kicking. I also told her that you were still globe trotting.

She said that her favorite book was *Beloved Infidel* and that she was in awe of having the grandson of a celebrity.

So keep a stiff upper lip about all this unpleasant business. You'll be fine as I said.

Your loving grandson,
Sean

My mother, of course, loved this letter. Reaffirming her dual status as luminary and granny, it granted her both preeminence *and* connectedness with others—and neither at the other's expense. I admired and rather envied Sean's breezy ability to flatter and also his unclouded pleasure in the teacher's response.

For me, to figure more interesting as Sheilah Graham's daughter inevitably made me feel less interesting as Wendy Westbrook or Fairey—my mother had inculcated by her example such respect for absolute individuality. And yet didn't she write me into her story, just as I accorded her a place in mine, not just as any old daughter but as an impressive personage, a relation well worth owning? There I am in her narrative, from the child who asks questions about Scott Fitzgerald in the preface to *Beloved Infidel* to "my daughter, Wendy W. Fairey, Ph.D., who helped me so much in the organization of this book" *(The Real F. Scott Fitzgerald)* to the person quoted in the opening sentence of "One Damn Thing After Another": "My daughter, who is the Dean of a College in New York, said to me recently . . ." I always suspected that these references were a way of pulling me into the construction of the celebrated self that was so centrally her activity, and thus I felt more used than flattered. But surely, if it comes to talk of using, I used her too.

At the time of my mother's first hip replacement back in 1981, I had a strange and vivid dream about her. The dream occurred the night before the surgery, and on waking, I recorded its details:

I dreamed that I was in the operating room during the performance of the operation. At first I was at the foot of the operating table, which was cranked up with my mother on it. She moaned with this movement, and I had the sense of registering her movement and her pain with the most profound empathy. She seemed very large, hovering above me on the cranked-up bed, taking up all the space but in a suffusing rather than a suffocating way. She was like a cloud that settles over one. And then I was no longer at the foot of the bed but rather at the head, cradling her head in my arms and against my chest while the surgeon cut into her. She moaned a lot and again, in a fluid and connected fashion, I was moving with her moves and with her pain. I kept thinking that perhaps I ought to leave because visitors/observers are not permitted in the operating room during surgery. But it was not my inclination to leave. I wanted to stay where I was with her head in my arms. When I woke up and thought about this dream, it struck me that it was the first time in a long time in which I have been at peace with her, strangely at peace, and able to express my affection.

Blurring the lines between us as well as nearly killing my mother off, drawing me back, but endowed with compassionate maturity, to an imagined primal scene, my dream brought a release of peaceful feeling that was rare in waking life. I understand why I couldn't, but it still makes me sad that I did not, in fact, do more to reach out to my mother as she aged. She accepted help from people, but always in the interest of reaffirming herself as the center of attention, and I resisted being helpful on these terms. I think too that she had a great deal of difficulty with the notion of her own mortality. She had almost believed she was immortal, or so she avowed only half in jest, until in her mid-sixties a detached retina put her for a month in the hospital, her eyes bandaged and sandbags immobilizing her head. Even then, she dictated her column from her hospital bed and did not falter. But she said the experience taught her respect for her body's frailty. She was not afraid of dying, but what she had glimpsed—and hated—was the prospect of enfeeblement. Her sense of herself depended not on physical beauty—in contrast to many beautiful women, I don't think she worried about the physical effects of aging—but on her stock of energy, the fuel of her resourcefulness.

As for me, I stayed close to my mother, but often it seemed at great cost. I had a tendency, in the interest of not losing her, to pretend to be smaller and more helpless than I was. Thus, if I could not do much to take care of her, she at least could retain the role of helping me—and then we got on very well. My other tendency was sullen opposition—turning myself to stone in the face of her demands. And so we moved on, at times great friends but with many treacherous undercurrents, through the last decades of her life.

What I hoped for from my mother, and, not surprisingly,

never got, was her enthusiasm and respect for my independent life. I didn't need her to protect and rescue me. I didn't want to be sent up a tree and have her walk away. I wanted to be a grown-up daughter who had a mother. It was my mother's fear that if I didn't need her, I would abandon her, and as a measure of self-protection she made plans to abandon me first. Ritualistically, then, would follow the sudden outbursts and even dramatic gestures of flight. Most memorably, she ran away to England right after I got married. The wedding took place in a house she had rented for the off-season, October to May, in Westport, Connecticut. When everyone was gone—the bridal couple off on their honeymoon, the guests having waved goodbye from their cars—she had sat under a tree and looked at the debris on the lawn, the abandoned half-drunk glasses of champagne, the bits of sandwiches and wedding cakes, the crumpled paper napkins. As she later told the story, she experienced a sudden surge of loneliness.

"This won't do," she said aloud to herself. "Go to London, see some plays, stay at a hotel, see some friends." She was packed and off to the airport before she could change her mind.

I remember my return to New York from my five-day honeymoon at a country inn on the Delaware River. Eager to see my mother and be together with her as her married daughter, to have her accept me in my new life and new status, I found that she had run away, gone for the summer. I was stunned and hurt. She had left me a letter, which explained her actions:

Dear Wendy,

It was too quiet in the country after all the excitement, so I came in [to New York] this afternoon and decided I will not go back. . . . I feel kind of lost and want to go where it's cool, so I am leaving Tuesday for London where I hope to relax a bit before my book comes out. . . .

The letter continued with instructions for me to send my mother her telephone book, which she had forgotten to take with her, and also to bring in linens from the country, since the lease was up on the rented house. Finally, it ended with some thoughts printed around the edge of the page when the rest of the space was full: "I BROUGHT IN ALL OTHER SHEETS. YOU HAVE THE FURNITURE. IT WAS A LOVELY WEDDING. LOVE TO YOU AND DON, MOM."

My marriage, perhaps to her surprise, turned out for my mother rather well. It offered her gratifying new roles—mother-in-law to Donald and Granny Sheilah to Emily and Sean—that she played with all her gusto and charm. Also she liked the idea of me being settled. I had the sense that I was where she felt she could find me, not elusively on the loose and free in ways that she had always claimed for herself. All her life, as she put it, she had decided "what I would do, how I would live, where I would go, who I would like, who I would love, who I would hate." I always felt that she feared my having the same options.

But I could not stay married just to please my mother. Shortly before her heart attack, after a stretch of great difficulty, Donald and I separated. I did not regret the nineteen years spent in the marriage, though I know I had held on to it less for reasons of abiding love than as a way of seeming, and feeling, substantial. Finally, I had the courage to leave it. My sense was of both liberation and loss.

Nor am I still Dean Wendy Fairey. Two months after my mother died, I was asked to resign as dean of Brooklyn College. I had a moment of tearfulness as I drove home that day. I'm glad, I thought ruefully, that my mother is not alive to see this. But my basic feeling was of relief. I had believed in the value of the work but never thoroughly enjoyed it; it had always felt like something I ought to like more than I did, and I welcomed the return to full-time teaching. "Anyway," said Sean, doing his best to cheer me up, "who came first, the teacher or the bureaucrat?"

So there I was, not a wife, not a dean. Such labels had never in any case proved too effective in persuading me of my separate life. I never sorted out if what I was doing was to please my mother or to get away from her, and in a way it didn't matter. Either motivation confirmed the same entanglement. The irony too is that much as my mother enjoyed having a daughter who was a dean, I know that she would have adjusted to the new circumstances and found a way to boast about me still. I can imagine her talking with her friends. "Wendy could have been a college president, but she preferred to be a professor. . . ."

I know the question I ask implicitly with everything I remember and write is whether my mother loved me. The answer, I think, is yes, but it is not a simple answer. My mother, creator of herself and of her destiny, made up Sheilah Graham, mythic individualist, and to this creation, as Fitzgerald says of the Great Gatsby, was "faithful to the end." She also created Sheilah Westbrook, mother of Wendy and Robert, grandmother of Emily and Sean and Robert's son, Gabriel, and it was the essence of Sheilah Westbrook that she loved her children and grandchildren with all the heart and feeling and vision she could muster. The love was real and it went far. Only there was another part of her, another self—to give her a name we can call her Lily Shiel—who was incapable of loving other people. Cast into an orphanage at six, fatherless and effectively motherless, Lily needed all her love for herself because she knew that other people couldn't be counted on.

Perhaps the more interesting question to ask about my mother is not whether she loved me but whether she knew that I loved her. And here I think the answer is no.

Her short story "One of the Family," published in 1981 in *Harpers & Queen,* presents the history of "a widow with grown-up children" who finds herself a bit lonely. She goes back to her old job as a journalist and is then "too busy to miss her children." Also she can count on friends who welcome her into their homes for Sunday lunch or who take her out with them to dinner, and always she is reassured that she is "one of the family."

As the protagonist and her circle of friends grow older, she senses that her visits have become an intrusion. Her friends are settled in their own lives, and she is aware of the greater effort "for them to entertain her and for her to be amusing and to give all the latest gossip about people they were no longer interested in." Gradually the visits stop.

Stricken with arthritis, she retires to a nursing home in Brighton. At first the friends come to visit, but quickly the visits fall off. Nor are her children around. Her daughter, the story explains, "was now living with her family in Scotland; her son had emigrated to America."

Scotland seemed to me an odd choice for the daughter's remove, though perhaps my mother was thinking of my years in Maine, another distant northern location. Brighton had more direct associations—it was where my mother had worked at fifteen as a skivvy, where both her sisters had lived in old age, and where she herself had even talked of buying a nice flat and "retiring." In "One of the Family," however, it is not a comforting place for the heroine to find herself. The final paragraph, terse and desolate, presents a painful vision of abandonment:

The nurse who looked after her wants tried to be sympathetic. When other people's visitors were milling around, she would look in and straighten the bed covers and pat her arm and say, "What, no visitors today? Ah well, never mind. Perhaps tomorrow."

The story as it appeared in *Harpers & Queen* was accompanied by a glamorous photograph of my mother decked out in her Howard Hughes brooch and George Delacorte watch and wearing her best wig, "as befits," commented my mother, "this upmarket magazine." She had attached a note to her copy of the story: "I just hope I don't end up in the same way as my heroine." But the very act of writing the story and posing for the picture were ways of forestalling such an outcome. Not a person to sit back and wait for the worst, my mother countered her fears of loneliness and abandonment with her abiding, irrepressible optimism that something good might turn up tomorrow, with her energy for any new project that did turn up, and with her pleasure in herself, which never waned.

I have a favorite story about my mother in old age. We were lunching together at the Russian Tea Room, our ages respectively seventy-eight and forty. We sat at my mother's special table, the booth nearest to the restaurant entrance, and we had ordered our usual fare of borscht and pirogi. My mother sat opposite me and was chatting away in her habitual fashion when suddenly she paused and seemed to be peering either at me or at something behind me. "You know," then came the explanation, "I am looking at myself in the mirror behind you, and I *must* say, I am *so* pretty."

Her face was mottled and she looked her age, but she *was* so pretty; there was no doubt about it. In part it was a question of her features—the nose, the eyes, the mouth, the cheekbones. And of that marvelous skin, which despite wizening and markings of age was still lovely. But this doesn't really suffice to explain her allure. Marlene Dietrich at eighty refused to appear in Maximilian Schell's film about her and teasingly allowed only the recording of her voice. I think that if someone had asked to do a film about my mother, she would have donned her wig, sat with pleasure before the camera, and believed that she looked great. It occurred to me that at a certain point narcissism becomes a successful mechanism for survival, a love of oneself that is sustaining in the face of pain, disease, diminution. My mother seemed triumphant in her pleasure in herself. It made her beautiful, and I admired her.

I am not sure if our joustings and negotiations as mother and daughter came to any climax or resolution, but for me we reached a kind of milestone on the occasion of my mother's eightieth birthday. No one other than Bow Wow had ever given my mother a birthday party when I decided that I would like to organize one in celebration of her turning eighty. Though I was living at the time in Virginia, I wanted the party to be in New York, and when a friend offered the use of her East Side townhouse, I knew I had what would be an acceptable setting and I proposed the idea to my mother. At first it pleased her, and we enthusiastically began to make plans. As the party, however, grew nearer, she grew afraid of it. She feared it would embarrass her; she feared I could not be counted on to do it right; and at a certain point the only way I knew it was still going forward was that my mother had taken it upon herself to invite most of the guests. Also my mother suspected my motives. "You're just giving this party so that you can have a trip to New York," she said. Then Robert, invited to come from California, couldn't make it, and my mother's gloom deepened. "Why don't you just be done with it," she said, "and bring in the coffin with the cake?"

On the day of the party, September 15, 1984, as I stood in the midst of the party preparations, waiting nervously for my mother and the invited guests to arrive, I wondered how I had got myself into such a miserable situation. The party seemed unlikely to be nice for anyone, particularly me or my mother. Hers was the first ring at the door. I noted in greeting her that she seemed in fine spirits, and I realized that in the crunch she could be counted on—star of *The Sheilah Graham Show,* she had always been a pro. Taking a seat on the living-room sofa, which she made into her birthday throne, she welcomed the guests—her friends and mine, people ranging from their eighties to their forties—who had come to honor her. "I'm eighty," she announced to one and all. "I used to lie about my age, but now I'm proud of it. I think it's an accomplishment." I had a sense, as I did later at my mother's memorial service, not only of our connection, mother and daughter, with one another but of the durability of our connections with other people. There was my mother's close friend Jean Dalrymple, whom I had known since I was sixteen and who had been and still was my mother's equal in toughness and beauty; there were a few of my mother's old boyfriends, now cautious and slow in their movements but more elaborate than ever in their compliments to women. The younger crowd, those under sixty-five, included Dee Wells, now living in New York after the dissolution of her marriage to Freddie Ayer; Professor John Kuehl, a Fitzgerald scholar midway in age between me and my mother and a great friend to both of us; and then the people who were my friends but had become friends of my mother as well: the owners of the townhouse, Marcia and David Welles; my Bryn Maw roommate Helen Dimos; my old boyfriend Larry Van Gelder.

I phoned my mother from the airport as I was flying home. "It was a wonderful party," she said. "I didn't think I would like it, but I enjoyed every minute." We gossiped about the guests, she thanked me for the trouble I had gone to, and I felt very happy that my effort to do something nice for her had succeeded. I remember thinking too: This probably won't last, but we have had this moment.

I like to believe that my mother felt the same way. Among the papers I found after her death, there was a little scrap of paper headed "Wendy—My 80th Birthday Party." It lists the names of the two dozen people who had attended. And at the end of the list is a brief acknowledgment:

"A very good party."

Seven

EXIT
TREVOR

THE FIRST OF MY PARENTS to die was Trevor West-brook, the man I no longer know how to name. I've taken to calling him Trevor, though that's not who he was to me during the thirty-six years that we were alive together as father and daughter. He was "my father" or, if more of an explanation seemed in order, "my father who lives in England." The letters I wrote him began "Dear Daddy," and his to me were signed "Love, Daddy" or "Your loving father." Now he is Trevor, a better choice, I think, than "my old father," "my former father," or "my putative father," though perhaps this last has the virtue of greatest precision. My impulse is still to say "my father." That's who I thought he was, how I experienced him when he attended my Bryn Mawr graduation or came to my wedding or when I spent time with him in England. I didn't experience him as a putative father. But as soon as I slip and say "my father," the very words remind me that this is what he is not.

I have stressed as a part of my story how unimportant Trevor was in our lives. This assertion is true; yet at the same time it is an inadequate representation of the truth and even a distortion. To call Trevor unimportant is inexact because it fails to suggest the importance of his unimportance. His absence, what at times seemed his defection, was not an offhand matter, though I tried on the whole to make out that it was. There he was, my father, someone I could conceivably know and love. And I did not know him; I did not love him; and he did not know and love me.

A good illustration of our failure is the rather absurd business of the handkerchiefs. At Christmas and on our birthdays, Trevor dependably sent a small gift. In particularly flush years this might be a traveler's check, but mostly it was handkerchiefs—year after year of monogrammed handkerchiefs, first for me and my brother and then, when I married, for Donald and the children as well. And throughout all those decades of handkerchiefs, Trevor never thought to ask whether I liked or used them, and I never ventured to express anything other than my grateful pleasure for his "lovely and useful" present. The handkerchiefs were a joke among the recipients. "Have you received your handkerchiefs yet?" we would ask one another. And somehow they always got lost before the next batch arrived.

At Christmas we also received his card with its formal greeting: "Best Wishes for a Happy Holiday Season from T.C.L. Westbrook," except the one year that he felt too up against it and Christmas cards became a dispensable extravagance. But even that year I think we got the handkerchiefs.

A better word for Trevor than "unimportant" would be "auxiliary." We were our mother's children, and then there was our father. We could talk about him, make fun of him—the man whose zeal in fixing little things led us to call him "Clever

Trevor"—and he slipped in and out of our lives. He came to visit for Christmas when I was two—that was our first meeting—and then came back the couple of times I've mentioned to our house on North Maple Drive. "I never knew much of either of you when you were young," he admitted in a letter written at the time of my pregnancy with Sean. When we started going to Europe, I saw more of him. I stayed with him in London and at his country house in Sussex; I met his mother before she died; I reencountered his sister, my aunt, and her three daughters, my first cousins, who had spent those five wartime months with my mother and me in California. But neither Trevor nor these relations nor any of Trevor's friends— what few friends he had—became people we felt akin to or on whom we in any way depended.

In terms of child support, Trevor had agreed to provide £600 a year per child until we were each sixteen. He lapsed from contributing even this, and my mother would occasionally focus on getting him to pay up. Once when she succeeded, we went on a wonderful buying spree at Harrods. Trevor had given her the money in pounds; it couldn't be taken out of the country; we resolved to blow it then and there. In a way it was play money—we didn't really need it. I realize that much more valuable to my mother than receiving Trevor's financial or emotional contribution was what his failure to give this permitted her: the full psychological reappropriation of her children. If memory serves me correctly, the time he gave her the money was also the time he welcomed us—me, my mother, and my brother—to his house in Eaton Mews South for what was supposed to be a three-week stay, giving up his bedroom to my mother and providing her with blue satin sheets. These were a failure since she found them cloying and heavy. He removed them obligingly if uncomprehendingly. But somehow we found it impossible to settle in. Less than a full week into our visit, we devised a change of plans and departed, guilty and relieved, for Paris.

The one essential that Trevor offered us—the contribution that we children took for granted and I am sure my mother did not—was his name. It was the name my mother used when she wanted to be someone other than Sheilah Graham. On her tax returns, on her bank accounts, to her housekeepers, to her children's friends, she was Sheilah G. Westbrook, the name she resumed after her brief interlude as Sheilah Wojkiewicz and kept to the end of her life. It was also the solid, Gentile, Anglo-Saxon name that launched me and my brother in the world. We were Wendy Frances Westbrook and Robert Trevor West-brook, our father a substantial Englishman, a collateral de-scendant of Harriet Westbrook, the poet Percy Bysshe Shelley's first wife. Sometimes we played a game with our mother of imagining what our lives might have been if she had married the Marquess of Donegall. I then would have been Lady Wendy Chichester and Robert the Earl of Belfast. But with this different father, how could we have been our same selves? No, we were Westbrooks. "Westy Windbrook," I was sometimes taunted in grade school. I used to think about my name and wonder if I really liked it. It wasn't inherently embarrassing, but it seemed a bit prosaic, connoting such specificity of place, a brook in the West. It was adequate, I decided, but not a wonderful name, and when by marrying I had the chance to move on from it, I did so without regret or nostalgia. My new name, Wendy Fairey, always made people smile, but I remained determinedly undaunted. Later, with more feminist awareness, I would explain that if I had to have a man's name, I was a lot fonder of my husband than my father. My history and continu-ity as a Westbrook seemed adequately denoted by a middle initial.

It was my wedding that offered the name Westbrook its most impressive and persuasive validation. The engraved invita-tions went out:

> *Mrs. Sheilah Westbrook*
> *Mr. Trevor Westbrook*
> *request the pleasure of your company*
> *at the wedding reception of their daughter*
> *Wendy Frances*
> *and*
> *Donald Macrae Fairey*
> *Saturday, the third of May*
> *at half after three o'clock*
> *361 Greens Farms Road*
> *Westport, Connecticut*

And everyone who wrote back in a formal manner was either accepting with pleasure or expressing regret at being unable to accept Mrs. Sheilah Westbrook and Mr. Trevor Westbrook's kind invitation.

It meant something to me that Trevor came to the wedding, and I think it did for him as well. Eager not to make too much of this—or too little—I have looked over the letters that he wrote to me in anticipation of this event. Congratulations on my engagement are accompanied by an initial evasiveness about his participation. "Of course I will try to come over but things are a little more difficult as I have lost ⅖ of my income and this year passing I had to draw on my capital." Trevor was a constant complainer about money losses, but since he always seemed just as well off, we tended not to pay these much heed. Then at a certain point he says he is coming for sure, worries what clothes he will need—should he bring a white dinner jacket?—and tells me he is on to a money-making scheme in Monte Carlo. He is pleased that Donald is an Englishman and wants to know more about him. He hazards that Donald "is obviously good in bed, otherwise I don't think you'd be fond of him," an observation that I remember startled and discomfited me. Finally, in a letter that sets forth his travel plans and totes up the cost of the trip (by combining it with a business detour to Cleveland, he hopes to get half his fare paid), he makes a

typical Trevor kind of joke, penuriously, misogynistically cheerful: "You can tell your husband to be that you are expensive,
but you are I hope worth it."

And then there he was at the wedding, bustling to get people drinks and having a good time. He behaved much better
than my mother, who was nervous and imperious and not at all
at her best. I remember my appreciation of his undemanding-
ness. He did not need to be the center of attention and seemed
happy as the father of the bride.

The wedding was probably our nicest encounter. Trevor's
enjoyment of it pleased me, and I glimpsed what it must be like
to have more than one parent to turn to. Attending his daughter's wedding, Trevor was not a shadow or a fifth wheel but a
legitimate participant in the occasion. And somehow we could
express the affection that ran like an underground spring—or
perhaps only a trickle—in both of us, struggling, though not
always successfully, to surface through the firmly packed
ground of our alienation.

At least I can say that he was always pleased to see me. I like
to think so, and there are supporting images—flashes of contact usually at airports or in doorways, greetings and partings—
that sum up our bond at its most promising. He was an expect-
ant man despite the remarkable stiffness in his every word and
gesture, the result of some extraordinarily successful stifling of
self that made it hard to be other than stiff oneself in his presence. He comes to mind careful, compact, his rebelliously wavy
gray hair mustered into place, standing at the slightly forward-
leaning angle that suggested both eagerness and restraint. He
often would meet my plane when I arrived in England, and I
could sense a pressure of feeling as he carried my suitcase to the
Bentley, and then in later years when he was economizing to
the Jaguar, or "Jew's Bentley," as he once referred to it, giving
vent to the anti-Semitism that was one of his few articulated
opinions.

Also I remember the narrowness. When Robert's son, Gabriel, was born, he wrote to me, "So glad Robert's child has at last come off, but why call him Gabriel I don't know. It just makes one feel one has a Jew as a near relation." His niece's husband, a Jew, had once "diddled" him of £20,000, which he never abandoned the expectation of recovering. I think that almost every letter he ever wrote to me once I was grown up and could appreciate such matters rambled on about H——, "a real so-and-so," and the lost money. Trevor's world was full of people like H——. They fooled you and then cheated you; they led you into sudden loss. He seemed to relish his disappointments. They confirmed that others were not to be trusted. I wonder what he would have said had anyone ever told him about my mother being Jewish. I don't believe he ever found out.

Trevor was proud of my getting a Ph.D. and equally proud of my possessing good teeth. It's hard to know what having children meant to him. It often struck me that he lacked the instinct for fatherhood. Children did not seem an answer to his concern with his own loneliness, and anyway we were clearly our mother's responsibility. Nor did he seem to get much pleasure from his grandchildren. "I must say I am not very fond of being a grandfather," he wrote to me at the time of Emily's birth, though he did ask me to send him a picture of the baby before slipping back into his more habitual grumbling: "Well there is really no news here except that the stock exchange has gone to Hell."

I like to explain—it somehow makes him more coherent for me—that Trevor Creswell Lawrence Westbrook, the person I knew as my father, was a study of the self-made man. Born at the turn of the century, the youngest son of a widowed mother whose circumstances were constrained and genteel, he had left school at sixteen, gone to work as an apprentice in the aircraft section of Vickers-Armstrong, and by the age of twenty-eight risen to be company manager of aircraft production. Later he came to the attention of Lord Beaverbrook, minister of air, who put him in charge of aircraft production for the war effort. Supposedly Beaverbrook had once said to him, "This war will be won by three Brooks—Tobruk [the North Africa campaign], Westbrook, and Beaverbrook." Whatever contempt my mother expressed for Trevor as a man, a husband, and a father, she respected his professional achievement, and wishing to give him his due, used to tell us, his American children, of England's debt to him. "Trevor Westbrook produced the plane that saved the nation in the Battle of Britain." It was one of those stories that foster abiding awe for our parents' capabilities. The designers had brought in the plans for the famous Spitfire. Other engineers had pronounced it an impossible project. But Trevor Westbrook, to whom "It can't be done" was like "a red rag to a bull," had pursed his mouth in determination, muttered, "We'll see," and set about proving them wrong. He felt, at least according to my mother, that he ought to have been knighted after the war. But he had been so untactful to some of his colleagues, those he considered incompetent, that he was eased out of British aviation, acknowledged with the lesser honor of Commander of the British Empire, and otherwise overlooked by his country.

Photographs of the Spitfire, the Wellington, and Trevor's other planes hung on the walls of his austere little room—the smallest bedroom at Little Brockhurst. He had created Little Brockhurst at Lurgurshall near Petworth, from two adjacent laborers' cottages, which he had knocked together into one three-story, six-bedroom, four-bathroom, ivy-covered mansion. The house embodied the conflict in his nature between social aspiration and resolute penuriousness. Little Brockhurst had all the trappings of grand country living—flower beds, swimming pool, tennis court, a picture window and patio overlooking the Sussex Downs. But Trevor refused to heat the swimming pool, no matter how cool the English summers. The tennis court was of the type that required a top covering of pebbles to ensure a smooth surface, and once the initial load of green pebbles wore thin, they were never replaced. As for the flower beds, they were Trevor's special province since one of his few pleasures in life was "to work" on tangible projects with intense, taciturn absorption. The gardens were lovely. I remember looking out through the picture window at a panoply of roses, violets, irises, gladioli, against the lawn, the sky, the downs. But then Trevor got too old to cope with them by himself, and since he refused to hire any help, they too, along with the frigid swimming pool, the unplayable tennis court, the decrepit old armchairs in the living room, and the kitchen linoleum, which was dotted with bits of green adhesive tape to cover the cracks, became a sign of his miserliness and of Little Brockhurst's decay.

Trevor lent himself to caricature, and it was a family pastime of my mother, brother and me—the family that defined itself by excluding him—to collect anecdotes about his penny-pinching, his glumness, and his zeal for self-denial, which meant that luxury was for others and as for himself, well, it sufficed to sit alone in his inelegant kitchen with a tin of Dinty Moore Beef Stew, eating from the tin with a plastic spoon. I had also seen him rescue a hunk of indisputably stale bread from the rubbish bin where I had tossed it and moisten it under a tap. "That's good bread," he had grumbled. "For the birds?" I had asked. "No," he had said. "For me." He was capable of quite reckless extravagance when in pursuit of a business deal or a woman. But I think he was happiest when he felt "hard up" and called upon to make his little economies.

So this was the peculiar father whom we believed our mother had given us because she couldn't face the anniversary of F. Scott Fitzgerald's death. It had always seemed to me, even before I knew about Freddie, that the affair begun during that 1941 English summer, when she was a war correspondent and he at the zenith of his career in aviation, should, in keeping with her life's normal logic, have been a passing thing. True, she went back to America with his ring on her finger, but she never suggested that this was serious. After her death, I learned by reading *A State of Heat,* the autobiographical novel that the *Times* obituary had referred to as "steamy" and that my mother always said she was sorry to have written, that the "engagement" to Trevor was but a part of her effort that year—the year after Fitzgerald's death—to see how many men she could get to ask to marry her. If the book is to be believed, Trevor's proposal was one of six in a twelve-month period, and it restores some of my faith in her judgment to think she never would have given him a second thought but for his opportune reappearance at the time she needed a father for her baby. Poor Trevor, who was always being conned, fell an easy and willing victim to my mother. I am sure that she considered him duly recompensed. After all, didn't she give him two lovely children? Trevor was over forty, this was his first marriage, and we were the only children who ever bore his name.

What I have come to realize about Trevor is the depth of his isolation. He had been bullied as a little boy at school. An older brother (father of my cousin Ann, who lived in New York) had drowned at sea. He had been very attached to his mother, the constrained, genteel widow, who had ruined him, said my mother, by encouraging him to think he was always right. She did seem an inhibiting sort of woman, though I say this having encountered her only once, shortly before her death, when I paid a visit to her Eastbourne nursing home on my first trip to England at age eleven. I have said that I don't remember Trevor from that trip, but it must have been he who took me to Eastbourne, and I remember clearly the meeting with his mother. Scraggly and austere, she gave me a strand of tiny pearls, a family heirloom, which I was instructed to hand on to my own daughter and which, sadly, I lost years before I had the chance to do so.

A framed photo of his mother sat on the dresser in Trevor's bedroom. He also had photographs of his two ex-wives, my mother and the subsequent one, and one of me. But depending

on how he felt about us at the time, a given photograph would
be either facing the room or stuffed into the back of a frame.
He had only two frames, so it was impossible to have everyone
face forward at the same time.

My own mother's picture had its moments of being in
favor, not, I suspect, because he really liked her but because she
was glamorous. He never said anything against her, but I'm
sure he considered her a "rum customer." Subsequent women
in his life struck me as all rather dreary. There was one nice one,
but she, he said, just wasn't "quite quite." As for the others,
they were cold and flashy, all carefully blond and ingratiating.
But invariably these involvements would end in some betrayal
or disappointment, and Trevor would be back again on his
own, eating out of tins, wearing the old tweed jackets he was
proud to have preserved for thirty years, and puttering about
Little Brockhurst.

It was in his periods of "disappointment in love" that he
showed the most interest in his children. He never, however,
gave up on connecting with a woman, and in the end, in a
strange parallel to Freddie, he got back together with his former second wife. Twenty-five years after running off with another man to Australia, thereby enshrining herself as one of
Trevor's prime betrayers, the second wife, Carmel, came back
to take care of him in return for the inheritance of the estate. It
was for both of them a prudently calculated arrangement. He at
seventy-five needed someone to look after him; she, twenty
years younger, must have reasoned that he wasn't such a bad
old fellow and, anyway, he couldn't last that long—though
once confined at Little Brockhurst (he at this point had given
up the London address as too expensive), she clearly disliked it
and him. She complained to me that his chewing, that meticulous, relentless chewing of his food, simply drove her to distrac-
tion. So Carmel spent much of her time up in her room on the
third floor, drinking gin and typing long letters to her relations
in Australia, whom, in my more suspicious moments, I imag-

ined as accomplices in an elaborate conspiracy to gull my poor
old father. Trevor lasted three years, though in the final
months, I gather, he was very senile. "He spends all his time
just sitting in front of the fireplace or the television," explained
my cousin Ann's son, who had gone to Little Brockhurst to
check things out. Somehow it made sense to me that in old age
Trevor should atrophy. The stiffness that was so inculcated in
his character had simply taken over until he ended up a fixture
in one of his old armchairs, not even looking out the picture
window.

Eight years earlier—about a year after my wedding—when
Trevor was still spry and the flower beds at Little Brockhurst
were all in trim order, he had communicated to me that unless
he remarried, I was to be his principal heir. My photo was face
forward in the second of the bedroom frames, and I, in turn,
tried my hardest to make sense of a father's significance. I used
to ask myself as a test of feeling whether I would miss Trevor
when he died. I didn't know the answer, and it was less perplex-
ing to think about the inheritance, for which I was sure I would
feel very grateful. My brother was in the will for only a few
thousand pounds, a distinction that embarrassed me, and I
determined to split whatever I got between the two of us—
there would certainly be enough to provide comfortably for us
both. For five years I enjoyed my fancies as the prospective heir
of Little Brockhurst, the Jaguar, and other untold assets of the
T.C.L. Westbrook estate. Then the second wife resurfaced,
and that was that—I like Robert would be remembered with a
few thousand pounds. I wasn't surprised. Nor did I really feel
cheated. I had only been heir *faute de mieux,* aware even in the
midst of my expectancies that the connection with Trevor was
fragile. Our efforts to strengthen it had never been more than
halfhearted, though certainly we both had tried.

Mine had begun at sixteen when I had made it my project to
get to know Trevor and like him better. It had struck me rather
forcibly that no one is by nature a caricature, that we had acted

towards Trevor in ways that were both unfair and unkind, and that it was not too late to try to deepen the relation of father and eldest child.

That was 1958. For the twenty years from then till Trevor's death, I tried to keep an open mind about him and never expressly pronounced my project a failure. But we were always so awkward together that it was all too easy to slip back into disaffection, and I cannot, in fact, remember a truly comfortable moment spent in his company. I am convinced we both hoped for something from the other, so that I, for one, would be heartened by any flicker of a bond—the expectancy in his greeting, his gaiety at the wedding, even a grunt of pleasure on his part that my school grades or my teeth were looking good. But there were too many small fiascos and disappointments. He took me for dinner at the Royal Thames Yacht Club, treating me to grouse, which he considered a delicacy. I nearly gagged on each raw and gamy bite; nor did I feel free to confess I didn't like my meal. I introduced him to a boyfriend of mine who was Italian, but afterwards wished I hadn't when he made disparaging xenophobic remarks and bluntly told me he thought I could do better.

Another memory is the evening of dining and dancing at the Savoy. I was twenty at the time and passing through London—though not staying with Trevor—on my way back to college. We had a nice outing as I listened to the elliptical narrative of his business deals and losses and at the same time could look about me at a group of English debutantes and their escorts in the ballroom. But then, on the way out to the car, Trevor disconcerted me. In response to my thanks for the evening, he rested his hand very suggestively on my bottom. Then two days later in the mail I received a disquieting plea. He had always been so lonely, he said. He had such hopes we could be closer. I could mean so much to him.

The letter frightened me. I did not want the responsibility of this lonely man's emotions, and it angered me that he did not know how to be fatherly, that his overture was so fraught with sexual stirrings. My reply was evasive, and our relationship slipped back to its habitual constraints.

Neither of us ever totally gave up on the other. We corresponded, we saw each other every year or so, and occasionally he helped me out with a little money—though always with clearly expressed reluctance. Then about three years before his death, when Carmel was already entrenched at Little Brockhurst but off for a while with friends on the Isle of Wight, I asked for £1,000 of which I stood particularly in need, and he gave it very willingly and graciously. The idea of his helping me like this was so gratifying and surprising that I went around for days exclaiming to myself, "My father has given me £1,000."

I visited him at Little Brockhurst to thank him for the gift, and we sat together in the living room drinking afternoon tea. Carmel had left him in charge of her dog, a noisy little terrier named Tina, which yapped at our feet and for which he had developed an obvious affection. He told me a story about a dog he had had as a young man when he lived in a lodging house in Bournemouth and was just getting his start in aviation. It was clear that the dog had been his great friend, and I felt in listening to him that this was perhaps the most personal revelation he had ever made to me. He was also very grateful for some jars of peanut butter and jam that I had brought him. As I went down the red macadam driveway, which years earlier he had built single-handedly, I could see him on his way out to the overgrown garden, the little dog scurrying at his feet. His loneliness was palpable, but there seemed nothing I could do about it. About six months later, when I was settled back home in the States, I received the first of several inquiries: when would I repay the £1,000?

Carmel's presence a Little Brockhurst made it harder than ever for me to feel at ease there, though I did manage to visit twice in what turned out to be Trevor's last eighteen months.

On the first of these occasions, I dined with him and Carmel at the local pub, our party also including a cashiered stockbroker and his wife. I sat beside Trevor, who concentrated on each mouthful of his dinner with that slow, meticulous intensity that Carmel found so bothersome. Having cleaned his plate, he dozed intermittently while the others chattered, mostly ignoring him, though every now and again Carmel would turn his way to urge, "Come along, Trevor. Wakey, wakey." I could see that her life at Little Brockhurst was an incarceration from which she sought whatever relief possible elsewhere. I could also observe Trevor's decline. He wrote out a check for our dinner as deliberately as he had eaten. A palsy was beginning to affect his hands and legs.

It was dreadful to see "my father" at the mercy of this woman who treated him with visible impatience; yet this was the situation he had chosen. It seemed best to distance myself from it, and I accepted that I would probably never see Trevor Westbrook again, particularly when he failed to send his usual greeting at Christmas. Nonetheless, that next June, when again I found myself in London, something nagged at me to go to Little Brockhurst—a sense of duty or the old habit of touching base or perhaps my realization that this truly might be the final chance to spend time with him. I did not want to be alone with him and Carmel, so my mother, also in London, agreed to accompany me on a Sunday expedition. We would go down by train and take a cab to Little Brockhurst from the station. A colleague of mine from Bowdoin was in town, and we cajoled him to come along on what we assured him would be a bizarre excursion.

It was drizzling lightly when our cab deposited us on Little Brockhurst's red macadam driveway. The grass was uncut, and the flower beds were a tangle of weeds. No one answered our ring at the large oak main door, but finding it unlocked, we made our way to the living-room armchairs to wait for someone to appear. Initially, when Carmel had taken up residence at the house, she had made improvements: rooms were painted, the kitchen linoleum was replaced, fresh flowers brightened up the living room. Now everything was shabbier and in greater disarray than ever. I wandered into the kitchen, where a chair was propped against the broken-latched refrigerator door. A terrible stench permeated the room, which I traced to nine bottles of sour milk—the refrigerator's only contents.

After about twenty minutes, we heard a loud roar in the driveway. Carmel's car, one further emblem of decay, was missing its muffler. It was a shabby little Simca, the Jaguar having met its end when Trevor, confusing the gears, had spurted forward in the garage instead of reversing. Carmel had just left him at the pub, where he was holding the table for lunch. But first, fetching down the gin from the third floor and turning up a bit of sherry from the kitchen, she insisted that we have a drink at the house.

Carmel wanted us to know the details of Trevor's senility: his incontinence, his addled memory, his sporadic lapses of consciousness. Once, most dramatically, he had wandered into a field, collapsed, and lain there undiscovered for twenty-four hours. Still, the man refused to keep a nurse. And what, asked Carmel, could one do with him?

"Hmmm," said our friend Bill. "It sounds like my grandfather, and he lasted until ninety-four."

"Well," said my mother, "if Trevor is in such a bad way, perhaps we shouldn't leave him alone at the pub."

Our shared anxiety was not to be resisted, and off in the mufflerless Simca we went to join him.

Huddled in his old overcoat at the head of a long, empty table, Trevor acknowledged our arrival with an eerie smile and a futile attempt to rise. The deterioration in his appearance since that other pub dinner the previous year was striking. His hands were more gnarled, his voice huskier, and it was now a task for him to form his words. But the horror did not really lie in these particulars of physical decrepitude. What made me start involuntarily to cry in the midst of my effort at sociable chatter was the shock, not of his paralysis, but of his pathetic and stubborn aliveness. I could feel the pressure of an inner intensity that survived within the painfully arrested body and that asserted some claim on those around him. It was the same pressure of feeling to which I had always been sensitive, still insistent though more frustrating and unanswerable than ever. For what response, sitting next to this wreck of a man with his occasional inquiring smile, could I now make to him? He asked after Donald, whose name, I noted with a sense of triumph, he had not forgotten. I responded with news of my husband and children, though clearly to talk and even to listen exhausted him. He ate with more doggedness than ever, mustering his resources of energy and attentiveness to cut, raise to his mouth, and chew each bite of food. I made sure that he got the salt and the bread and a second glass of cider, and when it came time for him to make out a check, I reminded him where the sums should be written. Carmel was gesturing from the other end of the table that I should fill out the check and just have him sign it. But it seemed more loyal to bear with his slowness.

My mother and Bill were also very kind to him, attending to his wants and helping him to shuffle back to the Simca. He had trouble lifting his legs, and Bill eased them through the car door. We had been joined for lunch by two blowsy ladies, evidently pub friends of Carmel. They seemed good-hearted, and their presence helped to mask the sadness of the occasion. One was to take us to the station, but first the whole party stopped at Little Brockhurst, where Trevor with our help struggled out of his car to his feet, and there on the red macadam driveway we said goodbye to him.

It was Bill's comforting comment on the train ride back to London that my father had "good color" and that strangely winsome smile that made his plight seem less intolerable. Carmel, we all concurred, had a drinker's unhealthy bloatedness. Perhaps Trevor would outlast her. Or if not, and his death seemed suspicious, we should be sure to insist on an inquest.

Trevor Westbrook died in September 1978, a few months after our visit. I learned of his death quite by chance about a month after it occurred. Someone who had read the obituary in the *Times* told my mother, and she, of course, called me at once. He had died in the nursing home to which he had been confined since August. His solicitor, whom I then contacted, apologized that he had not known where to reach me or my brother.

It was from the solicitor that I learned the provisions of the will. Little Brockhurst went outright to Carmel, who had already put the property on the market. There were a few cash bequests, the largest being £2,000 for me and £1,000 for Robert. The remainder of the estate would go to Carmel, but Trevor's affairs were in disarray and the extent of assets beyond Little Brockhurst was unclear. The estate would be in probate for six months to a year, and it was not certain that there would be enough, once all debts were paid, to cover even the cash bequests.

I had never imagined that Trevor's death could stir in me such bitterness. Robert, whom I phoned with the news, was more dispassionate. "What a sad life," he said. For me there was a more acute, personal disappointment. My ignorance of Trevor's move to the nursing home, the delay in my hearing of his death, the loss of Little Brockhurst and Trevor's effective disinheritance of his children, all pointed to our definitive failure as father and daughter. I had never been of help to him, nor he to me. Now he was dead and nothing more could happen between us.

There was a single clause in Trevor's will that attested to fatherly sentiment. I was to have first choice of a memento from among Trevor's furnishings and personal effects, by which, he had specified, I might cherish his memory. The gesture bemused me. To be provided so scrupulously with a memento but otherwise remembered with so little care some-

how called to mind the years and years of handkerchiefs that I
had never had any use for. When I received the Little Brockhurst inventory, I decided to choose an item I then might sell.
This would call us quits with no lingering pretense of connection. On the list and valued at £200 was the canteen of Trevor's
silver, each piece engraved with the mail-boot Westbrook crest,
that Robert and I as children had dubbed "the order of the
boot" and always found so pompous and funny. I would send
for the silver and sell it. Despite the boots and the three pieces
missing from the sixty-six-piece set, it would probably fetch a
good price.

And then one night, as I lay in bed wondering if my canteen
was by now on some transatlantic freighter, my thoughts
turned to Little Brockhurst, and as one does sometimes before
sleep, I started to play a game of remembering, trying to picture
the rooms in Trevor's house. Beginning with all the musty
rooms downstairs—living room, kitchen, dining room, hall
toilet—I moved on then to the second floor, to Trevor's little
bedroom at the head of the stairs, which I could see as it used to
be, tidy and austere. I recalled the narrow bed, the dresser with
its competing photographs of mother, wives, and daughter,
and the photographs on the walls of the airplanes. There were
other photos, too, taken mostly on airfields and featuring Trevor at high moments of his career. Several commemorated an
encounter with King George VI, in each of which Trevor could
be picked out, dark-haired and neat, one of a group of men
escorting the king on an inspection of a wartime airfield. Another that I remembered showed Trevor in his early thirties.
He strides along a runway, young, vigorous, slightly wind-
blown, carrying a duffel bag for the man a few paces behind
him. That man is Charles Lindbergh, whom Trevor hid out
from the press in the aftermath of the Lindbergh baby kidnap-
ping case. It was a picture I had always liked because it captures
Trevor in a burst of such purposeful motion. He moves free of
all the tentativeness and constraint that I could detect in his

posture as he waits on King George. And lying in my own dark bedroom, remembering this photo of two attractive young men, both aviators and one of them "my father," I felt a terrible sadness that I had missed the chance to claim it as my memento.

Afterwards I learned that Trevor's sister, Adrienne, had requested some of his photographs. It occurred to me to write to her to ask if she had taken the one of him and Lindbergh, but somehow this seemed difficult—I had not seen or talked to her for so many years. In any case, the canteen arrived, and I decided to keep it. The wooden case was very handsome, and I noted its brass-plate inscription that identified the case and its contents as a gift to T.C.L. Westbrook from the directors of the Heston Aircraft Company on the occasion of his marriage to my mother. We used the silver when guests came to dinner, and their inquiries about the unusual mail-boot engraving would lead me to talk a bit about Trevor Westbrook and his bequest to me of a relic from Little Brockhurst. I always did my best to maintain a wry perspective, but in truth I found an odd and heartfelt comfort in the possession of my memento. Then in January 1989, ten years and a few months after Trevor's death and forty-seven years after the marriage that the canteen commemorates, it was the canteen of silver, with its "evidence" of the wedding date, that helped me to know that Trevor Creswell Lawrence Westbrook was not my father.

And so I lost a parent, a connection, a point of reference. But what did it mean that Trevor Westbrook, the father I had enjoyed so little, was now officially relieved of the role he had hardly played? I did not miss Trevor after his death. Relieved of the duty of writing him letters or visiting him at Little Brockhurst, I more or less, if truth be told, forgot him; he faded from my thoughts. Trevor dead and my mother, as Sean had said to his English teacher, still "alive and kicking" and making her claims felt at every turn, it became all the easier to persuade myself that I had never really had but one parent. To learn then after her death that he wasn't my father seemed only a final act of divestment.

Yet changing fathers also stirred the memory of Trevor, and it was a memory that now caused me pain. Had Trevor and I been close, I think that losing him as my biological father might, oddly, have seemed less bleak. That's what he had been—not a close father, not a loving father, not an understanding father, just a biological father. But this status imposed responsibilities that we both had made an effort to fulfill. I remembered the years of trying to forge a bond with dour, anti-Semitic Trevor, trying so hard to like him, wishing he were different but accepting that this was my father. And he, poor man, saddled with me as I was with him, thinking I was his daughter, disappointed, I surmised, that I had given him so little, yet sending his handkerchiefs and writing his letters to "My dear Wendy" from "Your loving father." We did these things because we were biological father and daughter. And in the end we were not even that. We had made do with one another because of our blood relation. And it didn't even exist. Our effort lost its meaning. This was a loss I felt very keenly.

And how can my mother, knowing the truth, have watched us and not at some point intervened? Perhaps not while Trevor was alive. I can understand the many reasons why at least for his lifetime our sticking with the father we had started with would have seemed to her best for all concerned. Yet the lie lived on for a whole decade after Trevor's death. I wonder if my mother was ever tempted to undo it. I wonder what she felt when she read my story "Nothing Can Come of Nothing," which set forth so clearly what a sad time I had as Trevor's daughter. She criticized the story's point of view as being too exclusively that of a disappointed child. Then when "Nothing Can Come of Nothing" got published, she took pride in it being well written—my mother respected success—and from that time on encouraged me as a writer. For both of us, Trevor had faded to a fiction, a set of paragraphs.

Probably I give my mother credit for too much subtlety in my thinking that she understood my hopes and burdens. She had recruited Trevor as a nominal father for her children, and *she* didn't need much else. How could she, fatherless herself, have imagined the needs stirred in us by a living but disappointing father? Or if she had any glimmer of these, perhaps she felt that she could assuage them.

I think too that I underestimate the importance to her of having secured our legitimacy. Trevor believed I was his child, and while he suspected Robert wasn't—my guess is that this was a factor in his wanting a divorce—he had given Robert his name and acknowledged him as his son. My mother once mentioned to me Trevor's doubts about Robert, but only to dismiss their credibility. By her account the marriage had ended when she refused to have the second baby in England and when Trevor had met and wanted to marry Carmel. Perhaps it was part of the bargain they struck, not necessarily even discussed, that we would both be Trevor Westbrook's children.

This, then, was how we grew up. I knew I was Trevor's favorite—he never much liked my brother, whose gentle and imaginative nature so differed from his own, but then it didn't seem to me he really liked me either. That Robert might have another father seemed to me not out of the question. My mother, however, was persuasive in her denials, and I gave the matter little further thought. Then the year before Trevor's death, on my next-to-last visit to Little Brockhurst, an incident occurred to bring the issue into sharper focus. I was sitting in the kitchen with Carmel, Trevor not present, when suddenly the conversation turned to Trevor's new will. I would now get £1,000, Carmel informed me, and Robert nothing. "Why Robert nothing?" I asked. Carmel then told me, though Trevor never had, that my father believed Robert was not his son. I asked if Trevor suspected who Robert's father might be, and she answered with some assurance, "Robert Taylor." This seemed to be based on the common first name—I explained that my brother had been named for Robert Benchley—and on the fact that both Robert Taylor and Robert Westbrook had a widow's peak.

I communicated the substance of this conversation to my mother, who responded with considerable alarm. It was bad enough for Trevor to cut Robert off without a penny, but more worrisome still was that the will might contain a clause to justify the disinheritance. Defending her cubs and her honor, she went into action. She was in London and I back in Maine when I received from her the following long letter:

Dear Wendy,   June 30, 1977
    I took the bull by the horns and phoned Little Brockhurst. After a long ring your father answered and I decided to talk to him rather than Carmel. I asked if he had put "anything derogatory about Rob in his will." He said "absolutely not." So then, just in case, I mentioned the affectionate letters and cables he had sent Rob over the years. I read the ending of one of them to him. Actually I have 4 letters which I have clipped with 2 cables and the signed photograph he gave Robert "YOUR LOVING DADDY" and put them in the top drawer of my filing cabinet should the need ever arise to use them. When he said, "Absolutely not," I said, "That's good, because if you had, I would reluctantly have to take some action." That's when I mentioned the letters and cables. Rob probably has a lot of them. I have these because when I moved and you and Rob were away, I automatically brought them with me. . . . Oh yes, when I said that I was naturally upset that Carmel had told you of the £1,000 and nothing for Rob and that a previous will had left you £5,000 and Rob £2,000, he said, "Ah, that was when I had £7,000." "Are you really broke," I asked him. "Yes," he replied. "How are you managing?" I asked him—almost on the point of offering him some money—I restrained myself—"Only just," he replied. . . . I've been hearing stories like this ever since I met him so who knows. I told him to call me when he comes to London. He sounded so husky on the phone, like I do now [my mother had a cold], but I hope eventually to sound like my clear well-modulated voice. My love to you and Donald and the children.

                    Mom

I am sure one reason my mother never told me about Freddie is that then she would have had to come clean about Robert. Who knows what that story is? Perhaps for all our sakes it was better not to tell it. My mother made a point of being evenhanded, and she would not have wanted to give me a new father without giving Robert the same. Robert and I have talked about who his father might be, and he declares that he has little interest in pursuing the investigation. Initially, his response startled me, but on reflection I understand it better. Why should he unsettle himself for such an uncertain outcome? "I prefer," he said, "to think that my father is Trevor Westbrook."

Eight

"I AM YOUR
FATHER"

*I*N MID-FEBRUARY 1989, I received a letter from
Freddie Ayer. Written on a blue aerogramme and
mailed from the South of France, it was the letter
in which he told me who he was.

Dear Wendy,

Your asking me to write to you is presumably the outcome of the
conversation that you had with Dee after your mother's funeral. You
were then feeling your way towards the truth. I am your father. Your
mother and I became lovers in New York during the winter of 1941–
42. When she found that she was pregnant, she disappeared for a few
weeks without saying anything to me. When she returned to New
York, she told me that she had married Trevor Westbrook in order to
legitimate her child. I was still in the process of divorcing my first wife
and anyway, as Sheilah knew, was not prepared to marry again so
soon. We remained on very good terms until Dee wrote a hostile
review of her book about Scott Fitzgerald for the Sunday Express. It
is odd that they should have become such good friends in later years. I

very much regretted the break because it put an end to Sheilah's bringing you to visit me in London but there was nothing I could do about it.

It was an accident that I took your mother to the hospital for your birth. You arrived a few days earlier than you were expected and I just happened to be dining with her that evening. I understood her wanting to suppress it [Freddie being my father] back at that time but don't know why she kept it a secret from you for so long. Perhaps she thought that you would be shocked. From the way you talked to Dee and to me on the telephone, I infer that you are not. For my part, I am happy and proud to own you as a daughter. I regret only that I have seen so little of my grandchildren.

Much love,
Freddie.

I am hard put to express the effect on me of Freddie's letter. I already knew he was my father (by the time the letter reached me, its content presented me with few surprises), but hearing it from him directly moved me deeply. I felt rescued from my old life and self, from the pain of association with Trevor and Bow Wow and even my mother, transfigured by Freddie's acknowledgment into someone new and better—or perhaps someone who had been there all along but unperceived and unappreciated—a person who deserved this father. A very sore spot in me felt touched and soothed; a mantle of lead seemed lifted from my shoulders.

I also felt startled and numbed by the confirmation of so much subterfuge in which Freddie as well as my mother had taken part. I saw that he presented himself as a helpless, even somewhat detached bystander and as a father who had felt no responsibility for his child. The letter was thrilling and powerful, yet it also revealed Freddie as disappointing.

Not wanting to dwell on this, I countered his evasiveness with my own. It may seem odd, but what I responded to most directly, what I found myself noting and then thinking about afterwards, was Freddie's use of language. I had always admired him as a writer, and the letter became my text to study the precision in his choice of words, the graceful economy of his sentences. I remembered his reputation for lucidity and conciseness. "I am your father." What an extraordinary statement to be making to another person. Yet I am sure that Freddie had simply sat down with his sheet of aerogramme paper, collected his thoughts, and begun to write his admirably to-the-point sentences. I knew this was the way every morning he worked on his books. He didn't make drafts. He didn't revise. He knew what he wanted to say and simply proceeded to say it. If some of Freddie's statements seemed spare, this was the virtue, I persuaded myself, of a precise and uninflated style, a candid and rational intelligence.

Freddie's letter also needs to be put in the context of the ongoing drama of my paternity. Much had happened since that moment on the 23rd of December when Dee Wells had posed her question to me about Freddie in my car. She had joined him as planned in the South of France, got herself and her cat settled in, and then, true to her promise, proceeded to raise with him the issue of his daughter. Still wishing to conceal her own initiative, she had concocted a story that it was I at my mother's memorial who had brought Freddie up. I had asked about dates, said Dee, and discussed how curious it was that Freddie had taken my mother to the hospital the night of the birth and then shown such interest in me when I was young. The irony, of course, is that these things had never seemed curious to me at all; they had seemed perfectly natural. But Freddie found the account of my suspicions plausible, and Dee now suggested to him that it might be time to make a declaration. After all, I was not exactly a baby, and as Dee said she had put it, I had a lot of equilibrium. To all this Freddie, whom Dee reported as being less ill than she had feared, had readily assented and then asked her for my address. Dee wrote first, her letter a precursor of Freddie's. "And think of the genes," it ended. "F's brains plus Sheilah's sweet nature and ability to survive in no matter how shark-filled an ocean."

I cried with relief when I received Dee's letter. It arrived a few days after I had seen the photographs in Volume 2 of Freddie's autobiography. Thus, I knew he was my father, but did not know what he was prepared to do about it. Perhaps he was too ill, and to write to me now would seem too taxing and involving. Or illness aside, it could be he preferred things as they were or would think it an embarrassment to come forward so belatedly as my father. For forty-six years he had made do with our current situation. What desire would he have to change it? I worried too about Dee. Perhaps she would regret her disclosure and choose not to follow through. I had never been sure she really liked me. She had a blunt, aggressive manner that often made me uneasy, and I certainly didn't count her among my warmest friends. I knew she was a staunch champion of good causes, tough and fair-minded in her support of the deserving and oppressed. But could I be considered a good cause? Why would she want to do me this good turn? How did it serve her interests? In short, I was full of fears and doubts, beset by fantasies of my own impotence and unimportance.

And then Dee had written, and suddenly I was the princess in a fairy tale—and she my rescuer and fairy godmother. Still anxious, however, about what would happen next, I decided to telephone her in France in order to thank her for her letter and establish direct contact with Freddie. Dee's confidence in my equilibrium notwithstanding, I felt at this point in great turmoil. Still grieving the recent loss of my mother, exhilarated and unsettled by the prospect of my new father, I clung to a modicum of calm by asking what difference it all made anyway. Half my life had been lived without Freddie as my father. Whoever I was, I would continue to be. Somehow, though, having this father seemed to make all the difference in the world.

Donald and I had once visited Dee and Freddie at their house in the little hillside village of La Migoua. It was a hard place to get to, making our way as we did by car from Italy, winding along the Grande Corniche, then continuing inland on narrow, unilluminated country roads. When we finally arrived in the middle of a very dark night, we had felt ourselves quite at the end of the earth. Now, pushing a few buttons on a telephone, I was in contact with Dee as if she were still in New York. We exchanged a few conspiratorial words, and then she passed me to "my father."

"How are you, Freddie?" I asked him.

"Not bad," he said cheerfully, "but I don't breathe right"—this was announced almost with pride. "Dee has a woman coming to teach me how to breathe. It seems that I breathe all wrong—through my mouth when I should be breathing through my nose."

How amazingly ordinary this conversation seemed. Here I was—in touch with my long-lost father. I knew who he was and he knew that I knew—and on we went chatting, warmly but casually, about the yoga lady coming to teach him to breathe. I ended by encouraging Freddie to write me a letter. "I will," he said. "And so nice to hear your voice." Not a word was spoken about his being my father.

I tried to keep in mind—both at this moment and later when I saw him—that what was new to me wasn't new to Freddie. Whatever pleasure "owning me," as he put it, gave him, he had always known who I was; he had, as Dee said, been "fond and proud of me"; and he had accommodated himself with little further ado to the essential separateness of our lives. When later I asked him if he had minded having a daughter he couldn't be more in touch with, his reply to me was "Not really," though he said he had been sorry not to be able to acknowledge me. Such matter-of-factness hurt my feelings, but I didn't show it. Eager to please and be pleased, I respectfully noted Freddie's candor and then prudently took care, at least in our direct contact, not to make too much of the change that my knowledge and his acknowledgment created. Perhaps this was the kind of equilibrium that Dee knew I could be counted on to display in just this sort of tricky situation. She knew, as she put it, that I would not "go all hysterical." In all our dealings with each other, Freddie and I were friendly, casual, and essentially reserved. I felt the strain of this, but I am not sure what realistically would have been preferable.

In any case, the reserve was not all Freddie's. It was mine as well. On an unexamined level I was deeply angry with Freddie, and the reserve was a safeguard against both feeling the anger and expressing it. Asked by people if I was angry with him, I invariably answered, "Not really," and felt I was being sincere. To bog in resentment seemed pointless. A better expression of hope in the future was to do what I could to claim my father now that I had found him.

One way for a person like me was to read the two volumes of Freddie's autobiography. First there was *Part of My Life,* the account of family background, education, first marriage, and early career. It brought Freddie to 1946, the year that, aged thirty-six, he gave up his lectureship at Oxford to become Grote Professor of the Philosophy of Mind and Logic at University College, London. *More of My Life* took up where the first volume ended, continuing the saga of work and career, amours and friendships, up to 1963, the year of the birth of Nicholas, now oddly my half brother, when Freddie was fifty-two and I—not a figure in either volume—was twenty.

I suppose that I was looking not only to understand the life that had occurred so largely apart from me but also for hints of my existence. There were none to be found, though their absence gave a peculiar resonance to the moments in Freddie's life when, had he chosen to include me, I would most likely have been mentioned. I read of thirty-one-year-old Freddie's arrival in New York in November 1941, two weeks before Pearl Harbor. He was on assignment with the Special Operations Executive of British intelligence, training to be a spy in South America. He never got there, remaining instead for a sociable year and few months in New York before returning to England. I figure that I was conceived less than a month after his arrival, so clearly he can't have wasted much time before taking up with my mother.

Later he told me how they had met the previous summer in England and been attracted to each other though without beginning an affair. When he arrived in New York, aware she was there but not having her address, he happened to be talking to two men about not knowing any girls in New York except one—Sheilah Graham—and found that one of the men had traveled with my mother on the boat returning to America and could tell him where she was staying. Freddie then, as he put it, "rang her up" and got right to the point. "We've got some unfinished business," he announced to her. Telling me this story forty-seven years later over lunch in a London restaurant, my father beamed with pleasure at the memory of his tactics and success. He paused a moment for effect. "And then we finished it!" he said.

"Did you know about F. Scott Fitzgerald?" I asked him.

"Oh yes," he replied. "And I was the first to console her."

This is not a story that appears in Freddie's autobiography, though he writes with both frankness and zest of a number of other liaisons. It seemed to me he might at least have mentioned my mother as someone he encountered that year in New York. He was so very sociable, and he cites so many of his acquaintances and friends. Her name, however, is not included among these. Nor, of course, if there any mention of my September 1942 birth.

Turning to the time that Freddie and I first met in London, I read of his life in the mid-1950s. He was pleased with the move to University College, London, in sympathy as an atheist with the school's staunchly secular tradition—it had been founded in 1826 to accommodate students denied admission to Oxford and Cambridge because they did not belong to the Church of England—and gratified by the success of his efforts to build up from virtually nothing a first-rate department of philosophy. All in all, this seems for Freddie to have been a happy period. He writes of the revisions in his philosophical thinking; his belief that *The Problem of Knowledge* (1956) was a better book than *Language, Truth, and Logic;* his participation in prestigious international conferences; his travels to Russia and China as a member of a 1954 British cultural delegation; and, beginning in 1956, his appearances on the BBC television show *The Brains Trust* (a panel of intellectuals whetted their wits on questions ranging from "What are the possibilities of civil defense?" to "Do you believe in the devil?"), which made him, as Freddie put it, "something of a public figure." The autobiography also describes his ever-active social life: the evenings of witty banter with friends, the affairs with attractive women. Philip Toynbee once said of Freddie that there were two different persons. There was A. J. Ayer and there was Freddie Ayer; they were quite different and never quite got together. I'm not sure that I agree with this characterization. The person I encountered in 1954 when my mother took me to his Whitehorse Street flat (Freddie writes about the flat but not our visit) seemed an intellectual who could laugh at ordinary things and did not look down on other people.

I realized the extent of my parents' discretion: neither is so much as mentioned in the other's volumes of autobiography. One way, of course, to see this is as a reflection of how little they meant to each other, how supremely casual was their affair. My guess, though, is that each might have liked naming the other as a sexual conquest and that they refrained from doing so principally because of me. It was Freddie's later boast to have had affairs with 150 women. A far cry from Don Juan's *mille e tre,* this was nonetheless a record he took pride in, and surely it would have pleased him to acknowledge my mother among the women who had succumbed to his charm. As for her, the concern with respectability necessitated a general policy of more assiduous concealment. Still, she was proud of her appeal to intelligent, cultivated men, and I think it showed some restraint on her part not to include Freddie among such admirers. She does allow herself one oblique reference to him in *College of One*. Discussing the benefits of her F. Scott Fitzgerald education, she tells how she once won a bet from a professor of logic at Oxford University because she knew the author of *Les Liaisons Dangereuses* was Laclos and he did not. Later I asked Freddie about this incident, and I was interested to see he hadn't forgotten it either. Perhaps for both of them winning or losing such a wager was as memorable as sexual conquest. Still, it was only my mother who found a way to write about it.

More than an opportunity for inserting myself and my mother back into Freddie's life story, what reading his books offered me was the chance to establish an intimacy that circumstances had otherwise denied me. I had never heard Freddie tell his favorite stories about himself; I had not absorbed from him his family history or his sense of how he functioned in the world. The autobiographies offered me a means to do this, and I read eager for details of Freddie's history. I wanted to know what he had felt and thought and read, what he had done, whom he had known, what he had said to people, all of which information Freddie was now providing with his characteristic precision and lucidity.

Here finally I could trace my ancestors, precisely named and dated. The Ayers were French Swiss. My great-grandfather, Nicholas Louis Cyprien Ayer, had been born in the canton of Fribourg in 1825; my grandfather, Jules Louis Cyprien Ayer, born in 1867 in Neuchatel, had come as a young man to England, where he later became private secretary to Alfred Rothschild. His son, born in London on October 29, 1910, was baptized into the Church of England and christened Alfred Jules, Jules after his father and Alfred after Alfred Rothschild, who consented to be his godfather. This, notes Freddie, was not a fortunate choice, since Rothschild soon dismissed his

Above, my fifth birthday party. I am in front of Bozo the Clown, left of Claire Trevor's Charlie. My mother is at top holding Robbie. Below, my seventh birthday party. At the Disney Studio, back row, left to right, Joe Pasternak's son Mike, myself, my mother, Robbie, and Stella.

Six guns at the draw. Robbie, Hoppie, and me in front of the Christmas tree at 607 North Maple Drive.

Robbie and I at RKO-Pathé with Tarzan (Gordon Scott), Cheetah, and the trainer.

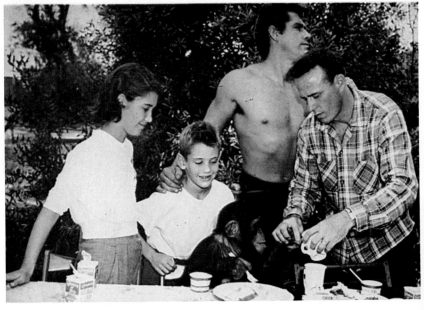

On a weekend at Palm Springs, 1951.

SUMMER 1954: *Above, on the set of Helen of Troy in Rome. Below left, on a bridge crossing the Seine in Paris. Below right, home in the backyard with our dog, Tony.*

On horseback at Sun Valley, Idaho, summer 1958.

OUR FATHER TREVOR WESTBROOK: *Above left, on his first visit to see me, 1944. Above right, at Warwick Castle, 1959. Below, with me in Biarritz, 1971.*

My mother with Marilyn Monroe. The picture was taken at the 1952 wedding reception for my mother and Bow Wow.

My mother lunching with Deborah Kerr to discuss the movie version of Beloved Infidel, *1959.*

Lunch with Rock Hudson at Universal, 1958. A treat for my Rosemary Hall classmate Candy Schrafft.

My junior year at Bryn Mawr, 1963.

THREE GENERATIONS:
*Mother, Emily, and myself,
1970.*

THE FAIREY FAMILY IN
HAWAII, 1973: *myself, Emily,
Donald, and Sean.*

FATHER AND DAUGHTER: *Freddie with Raymond Carr and Hugh Trevor-Roper, 1962. Below, on Fire Island, 1982.*

Age forty-six, in Prospect Park, Brooklyn, 1989.

Freddie, age forty-six, with Elizabeth von Hofmannstal at Zell am See, 1957, the photograph that convinced me Freddie was my father.

Dean Wendy Fairey, with Governor Mario Cuomo, Police Commissioner Benjamin Ward, and Robert L. Hess, President of Brooklyn College, at the 1986 Brooklyn College commencement. PHOTO BY GEORGE BING

Robert Westbrook at the time of the publication of his first detective novel, The Left-Handed Policeman, *1984.* PHOTO BY H. WAYNE STIERLI

On the steps of the Marylebone Registry Office, on the occasion of Freddie and Dee's remarriage, April 1989. Left to right: myself, John Bayley, Iris Murdoch, and Freddie.

Freddie, Dee, and Gully at their London home, early 1960s.

Freddie and Dee on the day of their remarriage.

607 NORTH MAPLE DRIVE: *In 1947 when we had just moved in: Robbie and me in front of the house. Below, in 1990 on my visit back to Southern California.*

Granny Sheilah with Emily and Sean at Disney World, 1981.

Sean at eighteen.

Emily at eighteen.

SHEILAH AND FREDDIE IN OLD AGE: *Sheilah at the Ritz Hotel, London, 1987.*
Below, Freddie in the South of France, 1988.

father, and my father was stuck with a name that, he asserts, "I do not like and have never been called by until I became Sir Alfred. To my family and friends I have always been known as Freddie."

It was on his mother's side that Freddie's background was Jewish. He traces his mother's family back to Jacob Moses, an itinerant fruit merchant who was born in Amsterdam in 1740 and died in 1814. Towards the end of his life Moses adopted the surname Limoenman, which his son then changed to Citroen, the Dutch word for lemon. This, Freddie explains, was at the request of his wife's socially superior parents—"they being wholesale jewelers and he only a goldsmith"—who thought the name of Citroen more genteel. Freddie's grandfather, Dorus, later David, Citroen was born in Amsterdam in 1860 and made a modest fortune as one of the earliest manufacturers of motor cars. He ran the English branch of the Minerva motor company (it was a French cousin who founded the firm of Citroën) and set up as a family patriarch who exercised a considerable influence on the life of his grandson.

I reveled in such specificities of name and place and social differentiation. How different from my fuzzy grasp of my mother's background and also of Trevor's. The documentation, however, of name changes on the "Citroen" side of the family led me back to thoughts about my mother. I had tended to view her renaming of herself as an individualistic act of defiance; yet how habitual name changes had been as a strategy of assimilation and survival for European Jews. I also decided that Freddie and my mother had salient points in common in their attitude towards being Jewish. The first paragraph of *Part of My Life* seemed an aggressive, though indirect, repudiation of the claims of this background. "My Jewish grandfather," Freddie begins his book,

had no liking for Judaism or indeed for any form of religion. He also believed that the Jews, throughout their history, had brought many of their troubles on themselves by their clannishness and their religious obduracy. He himself had married a Jewess, but he wished that his children, all three of whom were daughters, should marry gentiles. As usually happened in the family, his wishes prevailed. My mother was the eldest daughter, and I was her only child.

I could hear the echo of my mother. "Why should I identify myself with being Jewish? I don't believe in any religion, and I don't want to be stuck in a ghetto." Freddie, unlike my mother, did not seem ashamed of being Jewish, but he did not seem proud of it either. I have often wondered how much his militant atheism—not to impugn its philosophical foundation (the atheism was consistent with Freddie's belief that propositions are meaningless unless they can be verified)—was a convenient way out of the cultural dilemma of having to identify with one group or the other. Freddie had become an atheist at Eton, where he used to irritate his schoolfellows during chapel by muttering a running commentary on the fallacies he detected in the sermons. Reading this reminded me of my own phase as an atheist at Rosemary Hall, where from my very visible pew as a member of the choir (since we too were required to attend chapel, it seemed better to sing than just to sit), I used to refuse to bow my head when we were called upon to pray and to peer with conspicuous detachment at my praying classmates. This was around the time I learned my mother was Jewish, though I don't remember connecting my atheism with her background. I soon lost interest in religious issues, unlike Freddie, who maintained his to the end of his life.

I compared myself with Freddie, but in many ways—by virtue of time and place, gender and genius—he seemed at an idealized distance from me, the brilliant father who had led a charmed and privileged life beyond the reach of my own. I admired not just him but his world—that Oxbridge-educated, rarefied world of the British intellectual and cultural elite. Freddie was not born into this world. His background was solidly middle-class, more bourgeois than elitist or intellectual. But from a secure and comfortable family base (his father was something of a failure, but his Jewish grandfather assured the family's stability), his was then a career open to talent. He was intellectually precocious, did well at his preparatory school, and won a scholarship to Eton, one of only ten offered to new students that year. Freddie might have gone free to Eton, but his grandfather insisted on paying the full fees, worried that being on scholarship would put Freddie at a social disadvantage. Eton was followed by Oxford, appointment at age twenty-one to a lectureship at Christ Church, early marriage to the beautiful, strong-minded Renée Lees, six months in Vienna of combined honeymoon and study with the Vienna Circle of logical positivists, and publication at age twenty-five of *Language, Truth, and Logic*. Thus Freddie early took his place in that inner circle of the English intellectual elite who assume that the world will find them as accomplished, witty, and rightly privileged as they do themselves. The assumptions and self-assurance of this milieu seemed to me to shine through every sentence that he wrote, and I, for one, found its aura immensely attractive.

How different, of course, all this made Freddie from my mother. The two of them began to loom for me as almost perfectly counterpointed figures: the Eton King's College Scholar and the cockney girl in the orphanage; the Oxford philosopher and the Hollywood columnist; the self-confident intellectual and the woman who always considered herself a fraud. Yet there was another side to Freddie's story, apparent from his autobiographical writing and known to me from remarks Dee and my mother had made as well, that shifted this perspective. Freddie too had suffered as a child and felt at a disadvantage. He had attended England's finest schools, but at these schools he had been bullied and socially ostracized. Ironically, my mother in her orphanage became just the kind of leader, captain of teams, idol of younger children, that Freddie yearned but never managed to be. Physically small and socially immature, he did not fit in well either at the boarding school to which he was sent at age seven or later at Eton. Though he tries in writing about his experience of these years not to dwell unduly on his misery, he nonetheless keeps giving it away. A classmate he still knows from his prep school "has a more vivid memory than I have of my being tormented and expresses remorse for his part in it." Eton evokes the comment:

In spite of its rough justice, there was much to enjoy. . . . If I was in the main not happy there . . . it was because I got on badly with the other boys. . . . This was very largely my own fault. I was too pleased with my own cleverness and I had a sarcastic tongue. As a result, I made enemies without knowing it. I do not think that anti-Semitism had anything to do with it, though one heard reports of it existing in some . . . houses.

Freddie had very few friends at Eton, though he is at pains to describe those he had and to explain that he was "not . . . altogether an Ishmael." How emotionally grueling Eton must have been for him emerges more frankly when he contrasts it with his happier time at Oxford. "Finding more people who were willing to be friends with me, I became much more of a social figure."

I am sure that I made more than he would have liked me to of Freddie's woes at school. They reminded me of my own, and I was pleased to seize on the ways that Freddie and I resembled each other, even if the resemblance lay in having the same problems. I also was struck by the parallel of my mother going to the orphanage at six and Freddie to the harsh atmosphere of boarding school at seven. Clearly his childhood did not rival hers in hardship. Yet Freddie too had felt forlorn and unattractive and excluded. And wasn't his later history, as was my mother's, a way of overcoming this? Why does a man boast of having 150 lovers? Why does he persist in always ranking himself in relation to other people? Using the categories, for example, of Scottish football, Freddie put Russell and Wittgenstein in the Premier Division of twentieth-century philosophers and himself, Ryle, Quine, etc. in the First Division. He never got on the college eleven cricket team at Eton, but he had made the team of twentieth-century philosophers and was pleased to define his achievement. Freddie once said that he was "vain but not conceited." A vain man, he explained, "is one who's proud to display his medals"; a conceited man is "one who thinks he deserves more medals than he's got."

Immersed in Freddie's account of himself, learning so many facts about his life and trying to fathom the feelings that went with them, I felt that I was getting to know him much better, and I had an ever stronger sense that I was indeed his daughter. He would say something about himself—for example, about doing things as a child with his mother, playing ping-pong and tennis with her and going to the theater, or about "having an unusually strong capacity to live intensely in the moment," or being obsessively punctual so that he always arrived early at airports. And I would think, "Yes, I understand that." It was my experience or character trait too, or simply something I understood, with almost conspiratorial intensity. At one point Freddie notes as part of the account of his first meeting with e.e. cummings: "I had been playing tennis in the Parks and I called . . . immediately afterwards, hot and tousled and still carrying my racket." This may be a small moment, but I knew exactly how Freddie felt when he entered the room with his racket. I knew his feeling of energy, the awareness he had of his body, the pleasure he took in feeling and looking the athlete as he came among the more sedentary people. It was his pleasure in this moment that must have caused him to remember it and to include the detail in his book. And it was I, Freddie's daughter, who had figured all this out.

Yet Freddie also perplexed and in many ways continued to elude me. I understood his charm and his cleverness and even his vanity. What I did not understand was his aloofness, the strain of dispassionate detachment that seemed to set him at an emotional distance both from other people and from himself. I felt it particularly in his comments on the death of family and friends. His father's death, for example, when Freddie was eighteen, is recounted in a short matter-of-fact paragraph; then the narrative moves on to that year's summer holidays. His mother's death in 1940 prompts the summary, "Throughout her troubles and illness, she had retained a youthful zest for life, and it was sad that, having found happiness in her second marriage, she was given so few years to enjoy it." That being said, we are back to the topic that the notation of the death interrupted, Freddie's training in the Welsh Guards. More dispassionate still is the description of an old girlfriend's suicide:

. . . she was subject to fits of despair and in one of them she killed herself. . . . She rang me on the night of her death, without giving me any hint of her intention, which may not yet have been formed. I do not think that I could have done anything to save her.

The man who could write this may have had a wise philosophical detachment, but he also seemed in some strange way untouched by life. It was e.e. cummings who had once referred to Freddie as "that stainless-steel mind." I believe that Freddie was not unfeeling, but I saw that he could insulate himself from almost all emotional discomfort, particularly the discomfort of any grief or regret. Not included in the autobiographies is a story Gully told me of an evening spent with Freddie in London in the summer of 1981. They went to a party, where Freddie seemed a bit subdued but still good company. Gully was surprised that Freddie had wanted to go to the party. His eldest child, Valerie, had died that day. Born in 1936, six years my elder, she lived at the time of her death in Providence, Rhode Island, with her second husband, a clinical psychologist. The cause of her death was a rare kind of lymph cancer. Though I never had the chance to meet her, I sometimes now find myself thinking about her and wishing that she were still alive. But what were Freddie's feelings for his daughter? The story Gully told was chilling.

I paid particular attention to anything in the autobiographies that touched on Freddie's children, Valerie and Julian from his first marriage and Nicholas from his second. Not a lot is said about them, but it did seem clear that Freddie cared for them, and I envied them their experience of him as a father. I think it was less painful for me to believe I had missed out on a wonderful father than that this father might not perhaps have been wonderful after all. "Valerie," Freddie writes in *More of My Life*, "remembers my reading the novels of Jane Austen to her, sitting under the large copper beech in [Wadham] College garden." This was when Valerie was at boarding school at Oxford and Freddie came to take her out for weekends. I could think of nothing that might have given me greater pleasure than to have my father read aloud to me the novels of Jane Austen in the garden of an Oxford college. There are fewer such stories about Julian, and Nicholas is mentioned only once, though very significantly, on the last page of the second volume. "My love for this child," Freddie concludes his book, "has been a dominating factor in the remainder of my life." This sentence made me very sad. It was not that Freddie hadn't loved me like this, though indeed he hadn't, but that I could imagine how I might have stirred his love—if only I had known him as my father.

My history as Freddie's daughter is the story of what didn't happen, the relationship I didn't have. Yet looked at slightly differently, it's striking what I did have, even without suspecting who he was. Perhaps this is not so striking, given that everyone except me knew who was who and worked to sustain the connection. Thus my mother, I have learned, sent Freddie pictures of me when I was little. "Doesn't she look like her father?" she wrote on the back of one. Then my mother took me to meet Freddie. And Freddie wrote me letters. And I wrote back and always wanted to see him when I went to London, unwittingly—or was it intuitively?—doing my part as well. There may have been a hiatus in contact after Freddie and Dee were married. But it did not last long, and then Dee too worked to stay in touch, one of our family friends, from a certain point more zealous than Freddie in keeping up the connection.

It is wrong then to say I had nothing. Freddie may have read Jane Austen to Valerie, but he bought me *Tess of the D'Urbervilles* and introduced me to the Tate Gallery, where we wended our way among the Turners and I was so happy to be with him as he paused before one painting or another to make a quick observation or ask me my opinion. We had our particular moments. They were not numerous but they were special, and my friendship with Freddie had always seemed to me important. It influenced me out of all proportion to the time I spent with him; it helped me to define who I was and wanted to be.

The odd and also sad thing is, however, that it was mainly a friendship of my childhood. The last time I can remember being with Freddie in a way that seemed to reinforce our particular bond was when he came to lecture at Bryn Mawr during my junior year there. He must have told his official hosts about knowing me, for it became my privilege to give him a tour of the campus and then to take him into the faculty lounge, where students were not normally allowed. I remember how proud I felt to be seen with him by my professors and to have them understand that I was his friend. After his lecture we took the train together to New York and had a drink in the city before going our separate ways. Somewhere, I remember, we passed a television set tuned to a football game, and Freddie made fun of the players' pink pants. I remember thinking how easy he was to be with and what fun he could create out of silly little things. My brother, Robert, who also knew Freddie, once described him as "unsnobbish and joyful," and that seems to me an excellent description. Robert remembers how Freddie invited him to lunch at a club in Pall Mall when Robert was eighteen and in

an informative, totally uncondescending way told him all about
the English school system. Freddie could talk to young people,
and listen to them too. He treated you as an equal; he made
you feel that you had something to contribute; he made everything fun. This was the Freddie Ayer who meant so much to me
in my childhood.

My relationship with Freddie then subtly changed. I can't
remember how it got arranged, but the year that Donald and I
married and then spent the summer in Europe, we stayed with
Freddie and Dee at their London house in Regent's Park Terrace and visited them as well in the South of France. The ironies
of this holiday now seem to me quite overwhelming. In a car
lent to us by Trevor, we drove from England to Venice in order
to join my mother, then to France to see Freddie and Dee,
finishing up back in England with a few final days at Little
Brockhurst. I think it was on this visit that Freddie observed to
me that Trevor really didn't seem a bad fellow. Boring, yes. But
wasn't he fundamentally decent?

My memories of Freddie, however, begin to be less distinct
around this period. In London Donald and I were included in a
dinner party at which Dee served a wonderful trout with the
word FISH formed with bay leaves along its length. The guest of
honor was Noel Annan, who held forth from his seat at the
head of the table about who in the Bloomsbury group had
buggered whom at Cambridge. I sat next to Freddie, but I
don't remember what we said to one another. What I do remember is my rather sharp anxiety that perhaps I was insuffi-
ciently witty and interesting to hold my own in such company
and, in particular, to be of abiding interest to Freddie. Grown
up, I feared I disappointed him, though why I came to think
this I'm not sure. Freddie remained perfectly cordial, though
with so many other people around, I had less direct contact
with him than in the past. Furthermore, although he loved
conversation and could be very outgoing in the company of a
group of people, he tended in the context of his household to

withdraw into his newspapers and books and the football games he loved to watch on television. I in turn, already more self-conscious about our friendship, felt diffident about intruding upon him and kept my distance too.

Thus Freddie became someone I knew at more of a distance. In the South of France I can picture him seated each morning at the outdoor table placed in the shade of a lime tree where he did his daily quota of writing. In the afternoons, with either Dee or Donald driving—Freddie had never learned how to drive—we all went to the beach at Bandol. But I have more vivid memories of eighteen-year-old Gully and six-year-old Nicholas than I do of Freddie on these excursions.

Still, the connection persisted. I have a letter that my mother wrote to me in 1970 at the time of Freddie's knighthood. There was a lot of joking among Freddie's friends about his accepting this honor, since it seemed so very inconsistent with his left-wing politics. Freddie said that he accepted for the good of philosophy, but clearly he enjoyed both the recognition and the title. My mother wrote to say that she had "just called Sir Alfred" and she wanted to send me the Ayers' address in Cambridge, Massachusetts, where Freddie had been invited to spend a year at Harvard. I did not visit Freddie and Dee in Cambridge, but when Freddie came down to New York to give the Dewey Lectures at Columbia, Donald and I went to hear him. Pacing up and down, hands shifting in and out of his pockets, Freddie delivered his talk so rapidly (it was pitched, moreover, to a sophisticated philosophical audience) that we hardly understood a word he said. The only point that was clear to us was an example involving black swans. This was the one time that I saw Freddie in action as a philosopher. He seemed a bit more businesslike than usual but basically the Freddie I knew. "Bring pencils next time," he told the audience. "We're going to do sums." After the lecture he warmly thanked Donald and me for coming, and we gave him a lift to a party in our car.

Our next few encounters brought Freddie together with his grandchildren. We traveled with one-year-old Emily to England, and took the baby one evening to Regent's Park Terrace. Donald remembers Freddie coming into the room where Donald was changing Emily's diaper. "Oh, I don't like the look of that," he exclaimed. Freddie himself was almost helpless about any kind of manual activity. He didn't drive, he didn't cook, and he certainly didn't change diapers. "I have never been at all good with my hands," he writes in *Part of My Life*. "I am slightly ashamed of this incapacity, but perhaps not as much as I should be. I think that I could have made a greater effort to overcome it. To the extent that it leads other people to do things for me, it convicts me of some self-indulgence."

I don't remember Freddie paying Emily particular attention, though this might have seemed more noteworthy if I had realized she was his first grandchild. Valerie and Julian had married, but both remained childless. A few years later, when we were spending a stretch of time in a rented cottage in Sussex, Freddie, Dee, Gully, and Nicholas all came for a day to visit, and Freddie had the chance to see both Emily, who was now five, and Sean, who was three. Again, I don't remember him showing them much attention, and the visit, altogether, was not a great success. Nicholas and Gully were bored, and Freddie spent much of the afternoon watching a football match on television. Later Dee wrote me a thank-you card that was also a note of apology:

Thanks enormously. We enjoyed ourselves very much and I am only sorry we're such appalling guests—at least *I* can drive but I assure you they're just as bad in the car: Gully reads. Freddie does the x-word puzzle & Nick shouts obscenities at passing Rovers.

Love from Dee

My last encounter with Freddie before losing touch with him was on that same 1975 stay in England. Dee had invited me to lunch but when I arrived at the house seemed to have forgotten that I was coming and excused herself to keep another engagement. This left me with Freddie, just home from his weekly commute to Oxford (since 1959 he had been back at Oxford as Wykeham Professor of Logic, though continuing always to live in London). Dee and Freddie by now both had other lovers and were leading essentially separate lives under the same roof. Their house was one of those tall narrow townhouses with one or two rooms on each floor, and Dee had converted the living-room floor into her own apartment. The walls were painted a deep red and lined with her collection of nineteenth-century portraits of prize bulls. It was here among these stately ruminants that Freddie and I found ourselves, side by side on a sofa, after she had gone out. A cat nestled between us, and we both began stroking it. Neither of us, I think, felt entirely at ease. I was sharply aware of Freddie's physical proximity, and remembering his reputation as a seducer of women, I wondered if he found me attractive. He was sixty-five and I thirty-three. My thought was that he was too old for me, but I certainly felt his appeal. Nothing happened except that we both kept stroking that cat. I have often thought back to this moment since learning Freddie was my father, and in the interplay of my ignorance and his knowledge, I glimpse the prohibitions—what Freddie couldn't say to his grown daughter, who surely ought by now to have known the truth, and what he knew he shouldn't do with her.

After this, I did not see Freddie for a period of twelve years. He retired from Oxford. He and Dee divorced in 1983. Dee moved to New York, where she kept up with my mother, and I saw her at my mother's eightieth birthday party. Freddie married Vanessa Lawson, former wife of Nigel Lawson, chancellor of the exchequer under Mrs. Thatcher, with whom by all accounts he was blissfully if briefly happy. Vanessa fell ill with cancer of the liver and died in 1985, only forty-eight years old. She was, I now realize, only five years older than I.

I can explain the lapse of contact, at least on my part, by my preoccupation in these years with my own family and our more or less staying put in the United States. I was two or three times briefly in England but busy on these trips with other concerns and people. I did think once about phoning Freddie but then didn't have his current phone number. The truth is that Freddie seemed distanced from me, and I was hesitant about intruding into his new life.

We met again, quite by chance, on a Sunday in late September 1987. I was back in New York, working as dean of Brooklyn College. A colleague had invited me to join her for lunch in a restaurant in the Village, the Provençal on MacDougal Street, to help entertain a visiting Italian sociologist. Since I had prior plans to visit and lunch with my mother, I told my friend I might be able to get there later but not to count on me. And then off I went to my mother's apartment.

This was right after my mother had scheduled her second hip-replacement operation and then fled from the hospital the day before surgery. She was still in severe pain from the arthritis but eager to persuade herself that she had done the right thing. At lunch she went on and on, replaying and justifying what had happened, and I was not supportive. I too had geared up for the surgery and felt drained by her not going through with it. I can't remember what I said that triggered the explosion, but suddenly my mother blew up at me—something that still occasionally happened—calling me names, saying she never wanted to see me again, and ordering me out of her home. With studied insouciance I left, upset as always by such scenes but unwilling or unable to fight back other than by refusing to show emotion.

Thus, I found myself at liberty at only one o'clock, and in determined defiance of my mother—she was not going to ruin my day—I decided to join the lunch in the Village. Entering the restaurant, I had sighted my friend's table and was three steps away from joining it when behind me someone uttered my name. I turned and found myself facing a fashionably dressed blond woman with a little girl of about three at her side. "Gully Wells," the woman said. The child was her daughter Rebecca; they were lunching with Freddie and another friend; I was invited to come and say hello. I looked and there he was, slightly older in appearance but, as he rose to greet me, reassuringly the same—dapper and animated and friendly. It was the Freddie of my childhood. I was so happy to see him, and I think he was happy to see me. I later learned that when Gully and I went together to the ladies' room, he announced with pride to the friend at the table, "Those are my two daughters."

Freddie was spending the fall term on a visiting professorship at Bard College in Annadale-on-Hudson, New York, where Nicholas was now a senior. "I'm teaching at a small liberal arts college in upstate New York," he explained in his rapid, plosive speech. "Bard"—the word was pronounced as both an assertion and a query. "I don't know if you've heard of it."

"Oh yes," I said. "I know Bard. My daughter's boyfriend goes to Bard." I think Freddie was a bit embarrassed by the comedown from Oxford, where he had been required by law to retire at age sixty-eight. Bard, however, paid him well; he loved to teach, even if the undergraduates, as he put it, were "appallingly ignorant"; and he liked being close to Nicholas. Urban as always, he came almost weekly to New York, where he stayed with Gully and her husband, Peter. "Freddie," I said, as I got up from his table to join my other friends, "if I were to invite you to dinner in Brooklyn, would you come? I would love you to see my children."

"Oh yes," he replied warmly. "I would love to." He gave me his Bard phone number and carefully explained when he could be reached there.

A week or so later, before I had done anything to follow through on this, Gully phoned me at my office to invite me to Freddie's seventy-seventh-birthday party, to be held at her home on November 1. Freddie would be pleased if I could come, she told me. I was happy to be asked and flattered as well that Gully had gone to the trouble of tracking me down at Brooklyn College. She too, I later learned, had always known that I was Freddie's daughter, but, of course, I had no idea of this at the time. Set to attend the party, I now deferred calling Freddie to invite him to Brooklyn. I could wait and ask him when I saw him—and also think a bit more about whether asking him was such a good idea after all. Donald and I were still together, but we knew our marriage was ending, and having guests was hard.

I mentioned to my mother that I had run into Freddie in a restaurant. I considered telling her about the party and seeing if she would like to come too, but I refrained from doing so. The truth is I didn't want to have her with me.

My mother and I had a set interchange about Freddie—never premeditated but always the same. In the course of expressing how much I liked him, I would comment that I found him nice-looking. My mother would then say that he had grown better-looking as he got older, that when he was young his face was very thin and this made his nose look much bigger. She also, but only once, complained that Freddie looked down on her. How dare he, she said, deign to treat her with that touch of mockery and condescension?

I went to Freddie's seventy-seventh-birthday party and had a very nice time. Freddie greeted me cordially, though I didn't talk much to him after that. He was either being pursued by or pursuing—I didn't get the story straight—an imposing, extremely beautiful brunette, and when not saying hello and goodbye to other guests, seemed happily caught up in this intrigue. Dee was present, and I talked some to her. I also met Nicholas, now twenty-four, an intense young man, dark, quite tall, and very thin, whom I not seen since he was a child. I overheard him talking about being madly in love with a woman in France, and I wondered if he sought to model himself after

Freddie. The party included its share of well-known people. I recognized Mary McCarthy and Arthur Schlesinger and said hello to the elderly Hollywood screenwriter Albert Hackett, who had known both my mother and Fitzgerald in the thirties. I then settled into a conversation with an old acquaintance, Aviva Slesin, about our respective terrors prompted by parties. I confessed to always feeling the way I had when my mother dragged me around as a child to Hollywood functions and I knew no one had any reason to talk to me. Aviva, now a success-ful filmmaker, said that she had come to America at ten as a non-English-speaking immigrant and still imagined she would arrive at a party and not be able to understand a word that anyone said. We laughed at our folly, went on talking to each other, and then to lots of other people.

At the end of his semester at Bard, Freddie returned to England without having been invited to Brooklyn. Later this made me sad, for as things turned out, I missed the one chance I had to bring him together with his grandchildren. The last line of his letter haunted me, "I regret only that I have seen so little of my grandchildren." I had wanted to ask him, but I had lost my nerve. Of course, Freddie could have called me. After all, *he* knew who I and Emily and Sean were. But Freddie was never one to take such initiative. And I was then the one left feeling responsible.

The importance, however, that this "missed opportunity" assumes is only in the perspective of hindsight. I did not con-tact Freddie before he left America, he did not contact me, and once he was gone, I did not think much about it. I did not, as I promised to do on leaving the party, call Gully to get together for lunch. I did not even call Gully or Dee when I heard about Freddie's illness and brush with death of the following summer. Hospitalized in London with pneumonia, Freddie technically "died" for four and a half minutes, the length of time his heart stopped before it was revived. When he returned to conscious-ness, he retained the memory of an "afterlife" experience, which later he wrote a piece about that appeared in the *Sunday Telegraph*. He had seen an exceedingly bright red light and become aware that this light was responsible for the government of the universe. Space seemed out of joint; he felt he could adjust space by adjusting time; and he had gone around showing his wristwatch to the demiurges. Regaining consciousness, he had said to a French friend at his bedside, *"Mes pensées sont devenues des personnes."* This experience left Freddie's atheism unshaken but, as he put it, "slightly weakened my conviction that my genuine death—which is due fairly soon—will be the end of me, though I continue to hope it will be." It weakened, he wrote, "not my belief that there is no life after death but my inflexible attitude towards that belief."

And what would I have felt if instead of hearing of Freddie's return from the dead to tell the tale, I had heard of his dying? My guess is that I would have telephoned Dee or Gully. I would have felt the need for contact with others who had known him and for at least a pause of remembrance. I am sure I would have felt sad at the passing of a person so loved in childhood. But would I have been deeply affected? It is very hard to know. Our past history has been so transfigured by what I know now.

Several people have suggested to me that on some level I must have known the truth, and I realize that I would like to believe this. Can't I say that my feeling for Freddie was strong, and the repression of feeling strong as well?—hence my adoration of him in childhood and my later reserve and inertia, hence my fantasy of a father just like Freddie but never the fantasy that *he* was my father. I like to believe that unconsciously I knew who Freddie was because I then seem less the victim of ignorance, and I qualify the sharpness of the loss.

Nine

THE REVOLVING
PORTRAIT

I FELT A BIT FOOLISH rushing off the way I did that spring of 1989 to visit Freddie in London. Dee had thought I might like to come to the South of France in the summer. Gully even suggested that she and I might go together in July or August, and that this could be fun for us both. I, though, was mindful that Freddie had emphysema. Twice the preceding spring he had been hospitalized with pneumonia; his heart had ceased beating for those four and a half minutes. How could I wait six months and trust that he would stay alive for me? Now that he had acknowledged me, my focus became getting to him before he died. This seemed the essential act of recovery and reparation. Had the news of Freddie's health been any more dire, I probably would have departed on the next plane—still, I am sure, feeling foolish, for what would this hasting to his deathbed have accomplished? Would he really have told me what I hoped to hear, that ever since my birth, or perhaps ever since he first met me and saw how much I was his child, he had cared for me and yearned to acknowledge me? Would he then have folded me in a paternal embrace and, the world set right for us both, died in peace? I mocked my silly sentimental fantasies. Yet getting to Freddie lost none of its urgency.

I understand now better than I did at the time how potent a spell was cast for me by Freddie's stature. Stubbornly unimpressed by the glamour of Hollywood, I succumbed to that of Freddie and his world. My entire background—from my immersion in English literature to the values inculcated by my own education and career to the myths by which I and my family had lived—had fostered my awe. And now, by virtue of a tie of blood, it seemed that I could escape from the mundaneness of my own solid, decent life and ascend into Freddie's rarefied sphere, a transfigured self, the philosopher's daughter.

After I heard that Freddie seemed better, that he and Dee would be returning to England at the end of March and that there was even talk of him coming back to teach at Bard in the fall, I still wanted to visit him soon. I had my spring break at the end of April and decided to go on it to Paris and London. Paris, where I had good friends, was my buffer against the emotional risks of the visit to London. Then too, in writing back to Freddie, I was able to broach my proposed visit as if Paris had already been set and London now became a logical detour. Freddie replied that my "charming letter" had given him great pleasure, thanked me for photos sent of Emily and Sean, explained that I would be receiving a copy of his latest book, a biography of Thomas Paine, and invited me to stay at his house on my visit.

In the remaining weeks before my trip, I was utterly obsessed by the drama of my paternity, swept up ever more intensely in fantasies of what the link with Freddie would bring me despite all my efforts to remember what I had and was without him. I had not forgotten about my mother, but I thought about her almost entirely in connection with the se-

cret she had kept from me, combing her books for clues, trying
to sort out what was true and what wasn't of the things she had
said and written. It was a lie that she had married Trevor Westbrook because she couldn't face the anniversary of Fitzgerald's
death. But it was not a lie, I decided, that the anniversary had
seemed to her unbearable. My guess was she had sought to
blunt its pain by her plunge into casual affairs, hence Trevor
and Freddie and who knows what other passing lovers. I made a
distinction between her lying and what I decided was her essential emotional truthfulness. She was not in love with Trevor,
and she had said so. She was not in love with Freddie, so she
had left him out of her story. I had to admire her. She was a
worldly, independent woman who had scoffed at men's rules.
She had taken that preeminent patriarchal symbol a male philosopher—modern-day descendant of Plato's philosopher
king—used him as a stud, and then had no further use for him.
Minimizing the importance of the lie, I built her into a kind of
feminist heroine: a woman whose lies reflected a virtue of autonomy—she did not need fathers for her children.

Harder to square was my mother's failure to respect what
Freddie might have meant to me, and I wondered what it had
felt like to keep his relation to me secret all those years. "Do
you think she felt guilty?" I asked my daughter, Emily.

"No," said Emily. "Guilt would have sapped her energy,
and she needed her energy for other things."

Perhaps Emily was right. What worried me was not so
much the issue of guilt in itself but my fear that harboring a
guilty secret had set my mother against me. I had been the
person she had wanted to fool. How could I have avoided
seeming her antagonist, or worse still, her victim? I could imagine, if the secret were mine, my own guilt, alienation, and irra-
tional rage at the person I was deceiving. Surely there was evidence that my mother had known such feelings. Shying away,
though, from a painful realization, I told myself that I was not
my mother, that all I was doing was guessing and perhaps I was
guessing wrong.

My best guess was that my mother understood what Freddie had to offer me and that she feared it. She knew how much I liked him and had even done her part to encourage our relationship; however, when it came to sharing me with him more fully—or him with me—she simply couldn't do it. She was afraid of losing me, afraid I might become more attached to Freddie than I was to her, afraid of ways an alliance of philosopher father and Ph.D. daughter might exclude her. If I had to give a single reason why in the ten years after Trevor's death, a time when it seemed to me she had little other reason not to divulge the truth, my mother never said a word to give it away, this would be it—her fear of *her* diminished importance once the truth was known. I realized, however, that this was a theory reflecting *my* valuation of Freddie, and also setting me and her attachment to me at the center of my mother's concerns. I tried to imagine other motives and wondered if I really knew anything at all.

I would have liked a special dispensation to bring my mother back from the dead for just one short clarifying conversation. The best I could do was twice to dream that her ghost returned to visit me. The first dream, containing no reference to Freddie, was set in Florida, where I and my mother's ghost were standing together against the wall of the boardwalk of her Florida condominium, the ocean at our backs. I told her that her being dead was very hard for me—not unbearable but very hard. "Yes, I know," she said. And that was the dream. It was a great consolation to me that I could tell her my feelings and that she seemed to understand so well.

The second dream occurred the first night that I spent at Freddie's house in London. Again my mother was visiting from the dead, and she and I were together, walking out of doors along a winding hillside path where the dry terrain resembled the cliffs leading down to the sea in Southern California. She was a step or two behind me, and I turned to face her. "There's something I need to ask you," I said. For a moment what it was slipped my mind, but then it came back to me. "Oh yes, now

what's all this about Freddie Ayer?" She smiled, about to answer—I could see that she was willing to—and then the dream
was over.

My mother dead, and Freddie, for all my fantasies about
him, an uncertain figure of the future, it seemed to me that
what I possessed more securely than a mother or a father or
even a life was a dramatic and ongoing story. Further chapters
would follow, though like the reader of a serialized nineteenth-
century novel, I had to wait for them; they had not yet even
been written. I was reminded of an anecdote about Dickens,
who went into a bookstore, overheard customers asking for the
next number of *David Copperfield,* and realized not a word of it
yet existed on paper—he must go home and write the whole
installment that night. On the brink of the "unwritten" next
chapter of my life, I had become both reader and recounter of a
story that might very well have been a nineteenth-century fiction. Its themes of the plucky orphan making her way in the
world, the betrayed orphan who is providentially rescued and
transfigured, the concealed sexual secret that becomes a main-
spring to the plot, the discovery of the lost parent, the legacy of
rightful identity, were the themes of Dickens, Thackeray, and
the Brontës. Its drama of deception and perception was supremely the material of Henry James. My life's reading had
prepared me for my life. Now here I was, a kind of Jamesian
narrator-protagonist, recovering the text of my past, then lay-
ing out its intricate plot line to friends and inviting them to join
with me in probing the characters' motives. Why had my
mother concealed the secret? Why had Dee revealed it? "Isn't it
an incredible story?" I would say. One friend countered my
exclamation with her reply, "Isn't it an incredible experience?"
I, however, was experiencing it as a story. This was my way to
order what was happening and move through it, also my only
sure way to have the benefit of the new connection. Freddie
might let me down by dying or not caring, but I controlled the
telling of the story.

As well as people to tell, there were people not to tell or to tell cautiously. Early on I confided in both Emily and Sean, but I held back from speaking to Donald, now living apart from me, and also to my brother, Robert, who was back in California. Sean finally told Donald. "Mom's dad is still alive," he said, and Donald, I gather, at first had visions of Trevor Westbrook resurrected and off in Australia with Carmel. Sean had to explain that the dad he meant was Freddie, and Donald, as he later told me, knew instantly that it was true.

"How was that?" I asked.

"Because," said Donald, "of the physical resemblance. It's really very striking."

With Robert I hesitated because I felt the telling would confirm a distance between us. Despite the rumors about Robert's paternity, I had never thought of him as other than my full brother. We had been close as children and were united by both our common past and an abiding sense of primary connection. One might ask how my new link with Freddie changed this, but I feared that in some subtle way it might. It might allow us to dwell more on our differences and lure each of us away from the orbit of our shared experience. I also worried that Robert would feel left out of my good fortune and that again, as had happened with Trevor, he would see that I was getting more or being preferred. In short, I felt guilty. I was trading up on fathers and leaving Robert out of the deal. Eventually, when not telling began in my mind to create the very distance I sought to avoid, I communicated my news, and my brother was gracious in his expressions of pleasure and support. A few days later, though, when we talked again, he confessed that he couldn't help feeling a little bad that I had a father and he didn't. "You know, Rob," I answered, "I understand. But the truth is that neither of us has a father. It's too late for me to have one now. We both grew up without one."

I believed this as I said it. On the other hand, it was precisely because I hoped the opposite—that it wasn't too late,

that the present could make up for the past, that a new life and
self lay before me—that I was setting off on my pilgrimage to
England.

Making my final plans, I called Dee and Freddie in London.
Freddie answered the phone, and when I said who it was, he
replied with perfect ease and unself-consciousness, "Oh, how
are you, my darling?" I realize that this is a common enough
English form of address. Still, I found it incredibly moving that
Freddie should say to me, "How are you, my darling?" I remembered hearing him say to Nicholas as a child, "Don't be
boring, my darling." Now I was "my darling" too.

What this meant was a link not only to Freddie but also to
his other children and relations. If Robert was now formally my
half brother, I had gained two additional half brothers in Nicholas and Julian as well as a stepsister in Gully. One Sunday in
New York I went to lunch back at the Provençal on MacDougal
Street with Gully and Peter and Rebecca. While Rebecca, wearing a bow in her blond hair, sat happily crayoning the sheets of
paper that Gully had brought along for her, her parents regaled
me with anecdotes about Freddie, and I felt relaxed and happy
to be settling in with them so nicely. Suddenly, though, Gully
startled me. She said that speaking with Freddie on the phone,
she had asked him, "Who is more your daughter? Wendy or I?"
I'm sure she was considering the strength of their whole history: she had lived with him as her stepfather; Rebecca in her
eyes was Freddie's grandchild. And who was I to him? I mum-
bled something about blood not seeming really very important
(a lie) and asked what Freddie had answered. Gully replied that,
charming and diplomatic as always, he had said, "Do you really
think of me as a father? I'm very flattered."

I felt alarmed, not by the answer, which showed the ease
with which Freddie could deflect her anxiety into his own self-
satisfaction, but the question. Here stirred sibling rivalry, yet
without the strength of any past history as siblings. How would
these new "relatives" and I fit together? Sometimes it seemed

fraudulent even to call them my relatives, and I rehearsed the words of connection in order to reinforce their tenuous reality. My stepsister Gully. My brother Nicholas. It was part of the confusion of what was happening that while I felt on the brink of tremendous gain—practically fallen from the sky were a magnificent father and a network of relatives I might truly know and like—it all seemed so precarious. My lifelong fantasies of orphanage intensified with a vengeance, and I braced myself to suffer double deprivation. The new, I feared, would prove a chimera, and meanwhile, I would have lost the securities and connections of the old. Here was Robert now unequivocally a half brother. And my cousin Ann Westbrook—the only cousin I had ever known and liked—no longer related to me by blood at all. Courage failed me, and though I spoke with her on the phone, I didn't tell her about Freddie. It could wait, I thought, until after my trip.

The A1 bus from Heathrow deposited me on the Brompton Road opposite Harrods on a gray and chilly afternoon. The Irish bus driver had asked me if I was touring. "No," I replied, "I'm here to see my father." Now, however, I found myself no more than a hundred yards from my mother's old house on Lancelot Place. Drawn to taking a look at it before I went on by cab to Freddie's house on York Street in W.1, I walked down Lancelot Place with my heavy suitcase bumping against my leg and stood by the door of number 7. Through the gauze curtains on the front windows, I could faintly make out the back window looking out onto the garden, where we used to sit in deck chairs on sunny afternoons. The char, I remembered, was called Mrs. C., and she tended the few pots of flowers. Now the paint on the front window frames was peeling. I stood by the door and felt the great grief of missing my mother that rose up in me in sudden waves. It was hard to move on—I hoped my mother's neighbor might pass by and I could talk to her—but after perhaps ten minutes, I set myself to walking away—the act felt intensely symbolic—back to the Brompton Road and on in a taxi to Freddie's.

Dee opened the front door of the somewhat frayed-looking four-story house at 51 York Street. Paint here was peeling too, and I felt myself sinking into well-remembered gentle English drabness. "Yes, it's Wendy," she said, leading me into the house. And so began the visit that, in the last analysis, would fulfill neither my hopes nor my fears but intensify both at almost every turn. With complex responses to one another, which we failed to express with much directness or frankness, we all behaved strangely, and as I look back on my passage through that front door, it resembles nothing so much as Alice falling through the hole into Wonderland. I would meet the likes of the Red Queen and the Cheshire Cat; I would attend the Mad Hatter's tea party. Everything would seem a little peculiar, but I would accept the terms of the world in which I found myself the way one moves with matter-of-factness through the most surreal of dreams, only later, upon waking, to marvel at its strangeness.

Dee took me up one flight of stairs to the parlor, "the one nice room in the house," she told me. And there was Freddie, seated with his secretary at a round table covered with books. He looked very thin but was correctly dressed as always in jacket and tie with a V-necked wool sweater added for warmth against the damp that always seems to creep into English houses. "So lovely to see you," he said, coming forward to embrace me with a kiss on both cheeks. I noticed that his smile showed a gap in the bottom teeth. We spoke for a few moments, long enough for Freddie to pose a few questions about my journey and then put me through some literary paces, a father's vetting of his daughter, a quiz champ's showing off. He asked me what my subject was. The nineteenth-century novel, I replied. "Ah ha," said Freddie. "What is Mr. Darcy's first name?" My mind raced, and I knew the answer.

"Fitzwilliam," I blurted.

"And where in the novel," he asked, "does it appear?" This, alas, I couldn't remember, so Freddie told me—it is in the signature to the letter that Darcy writes Elizabeth at Rosings.

"And what is Mr. Knightley's first name?" the quiz continued.

"George," I said—I did know my Jane Austen.

"And where in the novel does it appear?"

Yet again, I couldn't remember or didn't know, and Freddie had the pleasure of telling me that it is when Emma says after Mr. Knightley's proposal, "I will promise to call you once by your Christian name. . . ."

I asked Freddie about his health. "Fair," he replied with a wry smile, "But at least I've still got my mind." He then excused himself to continue working with his secretary. The rationale offered later was that she came only once a week, but at the time it was disconcerting to be dispatched so soon. Dee took me up two more flights of stairs. Above the parlor floor was Freddie's bedroom—"Now *that's* all right," said Dee, a judgment later confirmed by Freddie, who referred to having "nabbed the only decent bedroom in the house"—and a good-sized bathroom. The small portrait of Freddie by e.e. cummings hung on his bedroom wall. Later I also noticed that on his dresser Freddie had photographs of all his other children. I looked intently at the one of Valerie, taken I would guess when she was in her early forties, and I thought it showed our resemblance. We had the same eyes—Freddie's eyes—and what Dee called the same "lit-up" quality that Freddie used to have as well. I felt bad that a picture of me wasn't on the bureau, and hoped that if I sent one to Freddie, he would put it with the others.

On the top floor of the house were Dee's small bedroom, a bathroom with only a trickle of running water (the plumber was expected the next day), and a room just vacated by Nicholas (until then with Freddie and Dee but now visiting friends in New York), with the bed unmade and a dish of stale-looking peanuts on the bedside table. This would be my room during my stay. A naked light bulb that didn't work hung from the ceiling; the dirty yellow walls had picture hooks in them but no pictures; curtains were missing from the windows. Freddie had warned me in his invitation to stay at the house that the room was not luxurious.

Dee and I made up my bed and then went into her considerably more cheerful room, where she started swatting at moths one couldn't see and talking about the moth war. The house, I gathered, had been Vanessa's, and whether she had been a bad housekeeper or it had simply been neglected since her death, I couldn't tell. It was now half owned by Freddie and half by Vanessa's three children, one of whom was living in the basement flat. Dee said that she saw herself as a character in *Rebecca* but she couldn't figure out which one. Our conversation was punctuated by sudden aggressive bursts of moth swatting. I felt suddenly forlorn, lonely for the friends I had just left in Paris and panicked in the face of what looked like a dreary ensuing five days. Activities, however, had been planned. We were all going that evening to the opening of Iris Murdoch's new play, a dramatization of her novel *The Black Prince*. "And tomorrow," Dee announced to me, "Freddie and I are getting married again; and it's so nice that you can be here for the wedding."

"Yes, how nice," I echoed, feeling rather like a cornered animal. But I was also intrigued. What did it mean—for her, for me, for Freddie—for me to be there? It seemed strange that I and not Nicholas should be the wedding's attendant child.

The outing that evening to the theater was my first opportunity to gauge the inroads of Freddie's illness. Dee and I were waiting for him in the living room when he came in his black tie down the stairs from his bedroom. "Handsome, do you think?" was his entrance line. But any exertion, I realized, put him out of breath, and he sat doing breathing exercises to recover. It was clear too that he was anxious about the pending excursion, obsessed about punctuality, and worried about the poor weather. "Oh, God, we'll never get a cab," he exclaimed. As we sat for a moment, he gave me a precise account of his two bouts of pneumonia and the four-and-a-half-minute death. The doctors had thought he might not revive or, worse yet, might revive and "be gaga." "But I've still got my mind," he repeated, a truth that became all the more apparent to me in the course of my visit.

I have never been so aware of the difficulties posed by stairs—not even with my mother at her most arthritic. Unlike my mother, Freddie was not a complainer. He would pause before each flight of stairs—of which there were several at the theater—say anxiously but quietly, "Oh God, I'll never do that," but then proceed pretty much without stopping. Winded at the top, he would lean over, hands on his hips, breathing in short exhalations, rather like a runner at the end of the race. All my repressed love for the father he might have been surged in a rush of compassion and admiration. He was old, his hands were gnarled, but for me he had physical grace even in these moments of exhaustion. I found him lithe like a boy in the thinness of his illness.

At intermission and the party we went to afterwards, people accosted Dee and expressed their delight to see her. "Ah, *Dee!* I just heard *yesterday* that you were back!" I was introduced, but not as Freddie's daughter, and I did my best to fight off my old Hollywood-party feelings as Stephen Spender and Iris Murdoch politely shook my hand and looked past me. I felt irrationally happy, however, to be seated next to Freddie during the performance—we whispered a bit together—or to be at his side at the party, the person at hand to fetch him another glass of champagne.

The next morning, Wednesday, April 26, was sunny and crisp. I walked in the morning to Marble Arch and back, a half-hour stroll. Every day of my visit I walked somewhere—one day all the way to Harrods and back, another day to the rose garden in Regent's Park. This was a way to mull over what was happening and also to escape from its intensity. Often I found myself simply concentrating on London: the rows of West End Georgian and Regency houses, the parks, the squares, the soft chill in the air that seemed also to creep into the people, and for all the movement of a great metropolis, that sense of solidity verging on eerie stillness that made me feel both protected and gently sad. This particular day the time for such musings was short. I carefully timed my walk so as not to be late for the 11:30 A.M. appointment at the Marylebone registry.

"Mandrake's" column in the following Saturday's *Daily Telegraph* gave ten inches of coverage to "the remarriage last Wednesday" of Sir Alfred and Lady Ayer. Quoting Dr. Johnson on marriage for the second time to the same person as "the triumph of hope over experience," and chitchatting about the newlyweds, the item was gossip; it could have been written by my mother had she covered the likes of Freddie and Dee. Iris Murdoch and her husband, the literary critic John Bayley, were mentioned as the witnesses (later one of Freddie's obituaries would speak of them as being "the only people present at the wedding"), and I understood why my name had not been given to the press. Nonetheless, my omission from the newspaper accounts had a strange effect on me. So shaky was I in my confidence that I fit in as a member of the wedding that a few printed words in a newspaper almost made me feel as if I hadn't been there.

My role was a strange one, but I played it. I had returned from my morning walk to find Dee dressed in a chic black-and-white-checked suit and Freddie in a gray three-piece suit. I got ready as well, we all donned our coats, and off we set on foot to the nearby registry, where it had been arranged that we would meet up with the rest of our party. Already an admirer of their work, I took an instant liking to both Iris Murdoch and John Bayley. They too had walked to the wedding, but all the way from their flat in Kensington, and they arrived ruddy-cheeked with exertion. I was struck by Iris Murdoch's calm, intelligent face, and also by her extraordinarily functional outfit, which consisted of black walking shoes, blue knee socks, cotton print skirt, white blouse, and green greatcoat. She carried a blue nylon tote bag, which she kept either in her hand or at her side throughout the wedding ceremony and the lunch that followed—I thought it might contain a precious manuscript, then imagined it full of only old clothes. Waiting for Freddie and Dee to go before the registrar, she opened the bag, took out a pair of black Chinese slippers, changed into these from her walking shoes, and slipped the walking shoes into the bag. John Bayley was more conventionally dressed in suit and tie, but with his cherubic face and ring of wild, wispy gray hair fringing his bald pate, he rivaled his wife in benign eccentricity.

Our little party filed into a room where we lined up before the registrar. "Mr. Ayer," the registrar began.

"Sir Alfred, rather," Freddie corrected him. Later Freddie explained to me that he didn't like the title Mister.

The vows were spoken. Augusta Chapman Wells Ayer and Alfred Jules Ayer took each other as lawfully wedded spouses. Iris Murdoch expressed her pleasure to be part of the auspicious occasion. "Dear Freddie, dear Dee, it's such a great honor to be here," she said. John Bayley and I smiled. Our party did not throw rice or confetti, in keeping with the interdiction posted by the front door of the building. We did take some photographs, which Dee later sent to me. The one in which Freddie and I stand flanking Iris and John is the single picture that I have of Freddie and me together.

A bottle of champagne was opened back at the house. Iris Murdoch asked me about my children, and there was some talk of my status as Freddie's newly acknowledged daughter. Dee had told Iris and John about me, and I was grateful to her for having done so. I preferred people meeting me with Freddie to know who I was, and especially on this occasion it seemed to me that I needed to be explained. "Oh, is it public knowledge then?" asked Freddie, joining in the conversation. It was hard to know if this pleased or distressed him.

The party moved on to the White Tower Restaurant on Percy Street, and what for me had been the day's trancelike quality was dispelled as I began to have a better time. We sat clockwise around a table: Freddie, me, John, Dee, and Iris. Greek waiters served us a meal of pâté, duck, and oranges Grand Marnier, and we drank ouzo, white wine, and Greek brandy. The meal was excellent and the conversation even better, talk of literature interweaving with gossip about writers and philosophers. It seemed to me it was the best conversation I had ever heard, but wasn't this what I had imagined Freddie could offer me—a seat at a round table of wisdom and wit? John Bayley was particularly effervescent. He told us a quip he had heard from Isaiah Berlin, *"hic biscuitus disintegrat,* so the cookie crumbles," and held forth very movingly on the moment in *Anna Karenina* when Anna sees a sign in a shop window and realizes that she wants to go home and tell Vronsky about it. "That," said John, "is an example of ordinary happiness." John also referred to failing Freddie's Jane Austen quiz, and I was pleased that my own failure put me in such good company. Freddie joined very exuberantly in the conversation. He seemed to have forgotten about his illness, and I noticed that his breathing was virtually normal. He laughed and told stories. Someone mentioned the character of Mrs. Lammle in *Our Mutual Friend* but couldn't remember her first name. "Hortensia," said Freddie without missing a beat. Turning to me, he observed, "You see what a well-read father you have."

"You're good in literature," I conceded.

"I'm equally good in history," said Freddie. "And you notice that I never even talk about my own subject." Turning back to the group as a whole, he declared that the three best conversationalists he had known were Cyril Connolly, Maurice Bowra, and Isaiah Berlin. John put in a word for David Cecil, but Freddie was of the opinion that David Cecil, good as he was, was no better than the people assembled at our lunch table.

I was very happy at the wedding lunch. Freddie's illness seemed at bay; I admired the people I was with; I felt that they accepted me. I also was pleased that my position at the table next to Freddie gave us the first opportunity of my visit for more intimate conversation. Freddie told me the story of his relationship with my mother, and I also asked him what I thought might be a delicate question. I was curious to know if he had other illegitimate children. Flattered rather then embarrassed by the question, Freddie answered that he had been told there might be one other, but later when he met the child, he was sure it wasn't his. I took note of my gratification in his answer. It meant something to me be reassured that I was unrivaled in my category.

My stay with Freddie and Dee extended for four days after the wedding. I never felt entirely at ease with them but resisted my inclination to stay in my garret room reading *Evelina,* the book I was about to teach in my course on the eighteenth-century novel, in which the heroine discovers and is acknowledged by her unknown nobleman father. My very own new father was at hand, and I knew that the point of my visit was to spend time with him.

He would descend every morning in his dressing gown to the dining room on the ground floor (a rather gloomy room, its walls lined with green-flecked cork) to eat his breakfast and read the paper. Dee would prepare the breakfast, and Freddie would clear the breakfast things away, his one act, as far as I could tell, of helping out with anything domestic. The first morning I had taken a bath when Freddie ate and then eaten when he bathed, but after this we breakfasted together, both at the table reading newspapers. After this, Freddie would dress and then sit for much of the day in a comfortable armchair by the living-room fire with books, chess set, and newspapers at hand. In the afternoons he went for a while to his room to watch a football match on television and to rest. His life was quiet and orderly but also quite sociable. People came over for drinks; once we all went out to a dinner engagement at the Garrick Club; the Sunday before I left we lunched in St. John's Wood at the home of one of Freddie's old girlfriends. Freddie came to life in social gatherings, and perhaps as a consequence, he and I seemed considerably more at ease with each other when also in the company of other people. These were the times we had our more meaningful exchanges.

The other denizen of the house on York Street was Dee, my enigmatic stepmother. If not someone I could relax with—I hardly relaxed on the whole trip—she was at least a person I could talk to more directly than I could to Freddie. It wasn't necessary to pretend, as I felt it was with him, that nothing very special was happening. She seemed to agree that my visit was noteworthy and to be willing to enter with me into its drama. I had a number of talks with her either upstairs on our derelict floor or downstairs in the kitchen, where I would often find her sitting on a stool, cigarette in hand, making phone calls to organize the day, the house, the future. We talked about Freddie; we talked about my mother; we even discussed the review Dee had written of *Beloved Infidel* and the chain of events that ensued from it. I learned that my mother had brought a lawsuit against Dee and the *Sunday Express.* Dee was scared, she told me, but then Max Aitken, Beaverbrook's son, who ran the paper, had taken her aside and said she shouldn't worry, that the paper had received a letter from my mother's brother that told about her family. "What's that got to do with anything?" Dee had asked. And Aitken had said to her, "It shows that the whole book is full of lies."

My mother had backed down from suing the *Sunday Express,* citing consideration for her children as her reason for not proceeding. I had not known about the lawsuit. Nor had I known it was Dee's paper that had received and published my mother's brother's letter. It was this letter that had pushed my mother into telling us about her family and her Jewish back-ground. Oddly, then, Dee Wells had figured in the history of the two secrets that, coming to light thirty years apart, had profoundly and unalterably changed my sense of who I was. She had been involved, although indirectly, in my learning at sixteen that my mother was Jewish; she had been directly re-sponsible for my learning at forty-six that Freddie and not Tre-vor was my father. And this was the woman who had written that outrageous comment about not wanting to touch what she would hand Sheilah Graham ". . . with a ten-foot pole with gloves on" and then been a part of the web of people who knew everything when I knew nothing. I both admired and feared her and never quite pardoned her attack on my mother. Our lives had intersected strangely.

Freddie also spoke to me about Dee's review, but more vaguely. "I don't know why Dee wrote that review," he said. "And I don't know how she and your mother subsequently became friends." It was his recollection that he had never seen my mother again after she walked out of the restaurant in 1959. I don't think that this is correct. I am almost positive that my mother went at least once to Regent's Park Terrace, since I remember her noting Nicholas's striking high forehead and dark curly hair. Still, it was mainly I and not my mother who kept in touch with Freddie, and my mother and Dee who stayed friendly, not my mother and Freddie.

I hoped very much that Freddie could shed light on what my mother had been like in 1941. "Was she very beautiful?" I asked him.

"Yes," he replied. "She was very vibrant. And I remember that she had a lovely nose." He paused for a moment, then shifted to a more detached perspective. "It seemed to me that she thought too much about Hollywood. But that was her job, and I was a great movie fan."

I hoped that Freddie would remember more, and kept very quiet, not wanting to cut off his flow of memory. "I can't remember what we talked about," he continued. "But we got on."

He paused again, then cheerfully and briskly concluded, "Just mutual physical attraction, I suppose."

I gathered that the affair had continued that 1942 winter and spring after my mother returned to New York as Mrs. Trevor Westbrook. "But not later," said Freddie. Not when my mother came to England in the fall of 1943. We touched on the fact of his having taken my mother to the hospital for my birth, and he was at pains to reiterate that it was just an accident that he happened to be dining with her that night. My birth was not expected for another week or so.

"Did you go to see the baby in the hospital?" I asked. Suddenly this seemed a logical question. After all, I was his baby.

"Oh no," said Freddie. "I'm not really very good at babies."

"So you didn't meet me until I was eleven?" I asked.

"That's right," he said.

Freddie suggested to me that I might like to see his portrait that had recently been installed in the National Portrait Gallery. Wanting to please him as well as curious to view the portrait, I made the museum my destination on one of my walks. Entering the twentieth-century section, which is a separate wing from the rest of the collection, I was surprised by its clutter. Portraits are hung close together, and a good many are not even hung, but placed on revolving panels recessed in little alcoves. Three panels, each displaying several portraits, revolve together, each panel to the fore for about two minutes before the revolving mechanism goes on again, the panel in sight recedes, and another comes into view. Freddie had said something about revolving, so not finding him on the walls, I began looking for him in the alcoves. Revolving portraits seemed to be grouped by areas of achievement: Law, Trade and Industry, Sports, Cinema, Music Hall and Revues, Science, Sculptors. I could not find the philosophers and finally consulted a guard to help me out. He directed me to an alcove, but the panels that came round had World War II heroes on them and not philosophers. "They must have been moved," said the guard. "Why don't you stand here"—he pointed to another alcove—"and see who comes round, and I'll look at these panels here."

"What about Bertrand Russell?" I asked, thinking Freddie might be near him.

"Oh, he's up here," was the reply. I saw the large Russell portrait—hung on the wall, not in the alcoves—but he did not seem to be flanked by other philosophers. I explained to the guard that I was seeking a particular philosopher, Sir Alfred Ayer.

"I don't think we have him," said the guard.

"But Sir Alfred himself told me he was here," I insisted.

"Well, the philosophers were over there," confirmed a second guard, pointing to the spot now occupied by the World War II heroes. "But if they're not here, they're on loan or exhibition."

Discouraged by the failure of my mission, I spent a few more moments in the twentieth-century section looking at Vanessa Bell's portraits of Lytton Strachey and Duncan Grant and Grant's of Vanessa Bell (not even thinking of the parallel deception of a daughter). I had no heart, however, for the heroes of earlier centuries and decided to walk back to York Street. My route home took me by way of Wigmore Street, where my mother had lived with Johnny Gillam during her "society period." London, I realized, had become a hard place for me. It entangled me with the ghosts of my mother and Trevor and now the living presence of my father and seemed to leave me little room for myself. Perhaps I would not come here much in future. I far preferred Paris, which I knew more on my own.

Freddie opened the door at 51 York Street. "I went to the National Portrait Gallery," I announced to him, "but I couldn't find you. They said you were on loan or exhibition."

"I was there a month ago," said Freddie, quite concerned.

"I looked on the revolving panels where they said I would find the philosophers. But World War II heroes came round instead."

"Isn't that typical," said Dee, who had just come into the hallway where we were talking.

"Oh no," said Freddie. "I'm not revolving. I *was* revolving, but I objected. Mine is a small picture just under a large picture of Isaiah Berlin."

"You objected to revolving?" queried Dee.

"Yes," said Freddie in his matter-of-fact way. "You're only on for two minutes and then you disappear."

I resisted an impulse to say that I would go back and look for him the next day. I did say that I would ring the museum to ask if Freddie was still up. I understood the matter was of some concern to him.

One of Freddie's obituaries would later sum him up as "kind, clever, funny and vain in about that order." If I have stressed Freddie's vanity, I hope I have not done so in a way that eclipses his other qualities. I would not put "vanity" first in my string of words to describe him, but it was indeed striking to me that a man of Freddie's kindness and cleverness and amiability could also be so unabashedly vain. I had not noticed the vanity so much in our earlier encounters, and undoubtedly it was my own neediness that made me more sensitive to it now. I wanted so much for Freddie to see who I was, and instead I found him fixed on himself. I didn't need him to prove to me that *he* was well read; I hoped that he would find that I was. I wanted him to love me, and he seemed to love only himself. Dee told me that she had invented a game to play with him. It involved trying to devise a subject that in two moves Freddie couldn't bring round to himself. And she failed. It was Dee, however, who also told me at one point when we were alone together, "It has cheered Freddie up immensely to have you here."

"You mean I pass muster?" I asked.

"Definitely," said Dee.

It occurs to me, but only now, that Freddie's expressions of vanity were also a part of his battle against the pain and constrictions of illness and age. A sick old man with emphysema, he had his mind, he had his wit. He could stump me and John Bayley with his wicked quiz on Jane Austen. He could take pleasure in such conundrums as the one he posed to me and Dee after the wedding: "I've been married four times, had three wives, and two divorces." He could see himself as only just behind Connolly, Bowra, and Berlin as a conversationalist and Wittgenstein and Russell as a philosopher. There was a revealing moment when Freddie and I watched a tape a friend had made of him doing a BBC interview about his afterlife experience. "I'm pretty good, don't you think?" he said, turning to me as we watched. But then a few minutes more into the show, not to me but to himself, he exclaimed with marked distaste and some anguish, "The voice of an old man!"

Whatever my worries about my standing in his affections, I admired Freddie as I encountered him that April two months before his death. Although in constant physical discomfort, he was uncomplaining and essentially undaunted, extremely courteous to other people, a lover still of social gatherings, of good conversation, and, above all, of work. Freddie explained to me that he had stopped doing philosophy about ten years earlier because he had stopped getting new ideas. But since he knew he was a good writer, he thought he could write other things. Hence followed not only the autobiographies but also his intellectual biographies of Voltaire and, most recently, Thomas Paine. Before I left, Freddie gave me copies of all his books that were in paperback, writing an inscription in each. On the dedication page of *Part of My Life,* which reads *"To my children,"* he added in his tiny script, "Including Wendy, with much love, Freddie."

Freddie's current writing project was a response to a festschrift of commentaries on his philosophical writings. He was also planning an upcoming trip to Spain to give a lecture in Spanish at the University of Madrid. I was reminded of my mother, arthritic and touring the country at eighty to publicize her latest book on Hollywood. She and Freddie were alike in their undiminished zeal in old age to keep on working, this being for both of them, I think, the central way to express and affirm who they were.

I cannot say of Freddie as I can of my mother that I know he loved me. I do think that he was genuinely fond of me, and there were moments, too, when he expressed this to me directly. My last afternoon in London, we had returned to York Street from our luncheon engagement and were gathered in the living room. A young American architecture student whom Dee knew had come over with his girlfriend for a drink. I was sitting on the floor next to Freddie's armchair and talking about my return to America when Freddie turned to me and said, "I'm very proud of you." Startled, I replied immediately, "I'm proud of you too." I wanted to ask why he was proud of me—I really didn't know—but this seemed a gauche response to his compliment, and so reticence prevailed. There was some talk of my coming back in August with the children and visiting in the South of France. "We can fit you in anytime," said Dee. For at least that evanescent moment, I felt like "one of the family."

The next morning my plane departed early. Dee was up when I came downstairs at six-thirty, writing a letter to Nicholas. I ate my breakfast and then went to bring down my suitcases from the top floor. As I passed Freddie's door, he emerged from his room in his bathrobe. "I loved having you," he said and gave me a big hug.

When I got back to America, the strain of my visit caught up with me and I experienced a reaction both against Freddie and against my own overheated emotions. "I'm too old to be a new daughter," I found myself saying when friends inquired about the trip. All the impulses stirred by the visit—of anxiously seeking approval, of yearning for parental protection that wasn't realistically available, of loving the parent yet feeling so angry with him for his shortcomings—were reminiscent of my feelings for my mother. She, however, was dead, and I now had a chance to be something other than a daughter. I had been so overwhelmingly a daughter all my life.

I must also admit that I had found Freddie disappointing. How could I not have? My expectations had been so high. I had looked to him to make up for ways that my mother had failed me and found him to have some of the same failings. He was just as self-involved as she—and she, at least, had taken care of me. I was not sure that I would go to see him in the summer. Better to wait and see how I felt in a couple of months. In any case, Freddie was definitely planning to spend the fall 1989 term back at Bard. He and Dee would be renting a house near the college, and there would be plenty of opportunity to see them then. I imagined that we could all have Thanksgiving together in the kind of family gathering I had always wanted to be part of—Freddie and Dee and Gully and Peter and Rebecca and Nicholas, if he was still in New York, and Emily and Sean and me. This would bring Freddie together with my children, and I found myself displacing my hopes onto them. If it was too late for me to make sense of Freddie as my father, it was not too late for Emily and Sean to get to know and enjoy him as their grandfather. I remembered how wonderful Freddie was with young people. I was sure they would like him and he them. Emily even passed the Jane Austen quiz when I tried it out on her, and my guess was that she would beat Freddie in any quiz about ancient Greek literature or history. Then too, maybe it wasn't altogether too late for me. What the project needed was patience and time.

On May 23, Dee telephoned me from London to tell me that Freddie, just back from successfully delivering his lecture in Madrid, had been rushed to the hospital with a collapsed lung and had been placed on a respirator in an intensive care unit. She reassured me that she thought he would get better, but I nonetheless felt all the fear and pain of what his death would mean to me. I broke down after our conversation. "Don't die, Freddie. Please don't die," was the plea I kept crying aloud.

A good friend of mine challenged my anguish. "You got five percent and you want a hundred percent," she said to me. "And you'll never get it."

"No, I don't expect a hundred percent," I answered her. "But I had a kind of settlement in mind—that Freddie would live a couple of years, that I would get to spend some time with him, that the children would get to know him and, when he did die, they would know who he was and could remember him with me."

Emily was home, having finished her first year at Swarthmore. As always, she expressed her clearsighted opinion as we discussed what it would mean for Freddie to die. "It's like a nasty trick is being played on you," she said. "It's ironic. And it's hard. But it's not really an awful loss. It's just that it could have been such a gain."

But to imagine the gain and then not to have it, I argued, can also bring a very awful sense of loss.

Dee's phone call marked the beginning of a vigil that lasted more than a month. So as not to intrude upon Dee with too many inquiries of concern and also to have direct contact with Freddie and his situation, I got into the habit every few days of phoning the intensive care unit of University College Hospital. A nurse would answer, I would identify myself as Sir Alfred Ayer's daughter phoning from New York, and I would ask how he was doing. I always felt a bit strange presenting myself as Freddie's daughter, but the nurses in the ward were all very nice about giving me information, and no one questioned my legitimacy. Freddie himself couldn't speak. Aside from being on the respirator, he almost immediately underwent a tracheotomy to drain the fluid from his lungs and thereafter communicated with the world by writing notes on a little pad he kept at his side. At first the situation was pronounced critical, but more optimistic reports followed, and Freddie seemed slowly to be getting better. A report I received twelve days before his death had him up and sitting outside and listening to the cricket on the radio. "He sends you his love and says he's doing okay," said the nurse.

Then on Monday, June 19, not having talked to the hospital for close to a week, I phoned and was told that Freddie was "a bit poorly" and "not so well as last week." He was back full-time on the respirator after "a turn for the worse"—later I learned this was a chest infection—over the weekend. The nurse felt it would be advisable for me to check daily.

Suddenly I felt a powerful surge of fear commingled with resentment. Of course I would check daily. I had checked daily on my mother, one day hopeful, the next distraught, in response to all the finally insignificant slight improvements and deteriorations. I would do the same with Freddie, but I felt that he had not earned my concern. I had not been involved in much of his living. Why should I have the burden of such involvement in his dying?

Tuesday's news was worse. By Wednesday there were kidney complications. Dee's sister was visiting Freddie when I made my call, and she came to the phone to speak with me. "This is Wendy," I said. "Do you know who I am?"

"Oh, Wendy, come right away. He's conscious and would recognize you," she responded.

I explained that I was phoning from New York and felt embarrassed to have to say that this was where I was.

"Oh, I thought you were in London," she said.

"No," I replied but did not explain that my reason for not being there was that no one had asked me to come—not Freddie, not Dee, not Freddie's doctors. The last word from the doctor, the sister told me; was that there was a fifty-fifty chance the kidneys could be set right, but she nonetheless sounded very sad. Dee and Nick, who was back in London, had just left the hospital.

Later in the day I reached Dee at home. She explained that the low blood pressure was affecting the kidneys and that there really wasn't much hope. Suddenly I realized how hard on her the situation must be. She spoke of having a nice time again with Freddie after so many rotten years. He had passed her a little note in his quavering handwriting saying "I love you," and I gather that on his deathbed Freddie fell in love with her again. I don't pretend to understand Dee's emotions, but it struck me that she sought Freddie's love just as much as I did.

Thursday and Friday, Freddie slipped further towards death and was put on dialysis. Then Saturday he was markedly better. Nick, I learned, had hooked up a television set in Freddie's room, and Freddie was able to sit up and watch the cricket. I spoke with a doctor, who explained that this amazing rebound from death's door was due to the dialysis helping the kidneys. "So there's hope?" I asked.

"What you must remember," he cautioned, "is that the major problem remains. The lungs. And they cannot improve." I decided that I would write Freddie a letter and send it by ordinary mail as an expression of my hope that he would be alive in five days' time to receive it. What I said in it now strikes me as sentimental about both Freddie and myself. Perhaps I was putting on record that I was what I wished I was—my father's loved and loving daughter. At the time, however, I meant every word I wrote:

Dear Freddie,

I am writing this in the hope that you will be well enough to read it when it arrives. I know that your illness is very hard. I wish I could be with you, and I certainly am in my thoughts. I have been calling the hospital quite often to see how you are and trust that the nurses have passed on my messages of love and concern.

One of the nurses referred to you as "Freddie"—I had asked for news of Sir Alfred—and I could tell that she liked you very much. Also I spoke with a doctor who said he was impressed by your "strong character." This made me very proud. You are clearly a courageous and gracious patient.

It means a great deal to me that you are my father, and I have been thinking about the important and positive influence that you had on me in childhood, even though I did not know our relationship. I want you to know that I love you. I am hoping you will soon get stronger, and I look forward to coming to see you later this summer.

Emily and Sean join me in sending great love.

Wendy

Freddie did not receive this letter. When I spoke to Dee on Monday morning, she told me that Freddie was dying. "As Lady Bracknell says in *The Importance of Being Ernest,*" I then heard her saying to me, " 'To lose one parent, Mr. Worthing, can be considered a misfortune. To lose both smacks of carelessness.' "

Dee's joke intensified my sense of her remoteness. I am sure she was exhausted, and I think she found it difficult to deal with the pressure of my anxiety. Nonetheless, I felt cut off from her. My father was dying and his wife was taunting me with the wit of Oscar Wilde. Freddie's improvement on Saturday had been a temporary rebound, after which he deteriorated quickly. He died around 2:00 A.M. London time on Tuesday, June 29. I found out by phoning Gully. Dee did not get in touch with me, although later when I wrote her a letter of condolence, she in due course wrote a nice letter back, saying how sorry she felt for me, how hard it is when "what appears to be the future suddenly becomes the past without ever having had much innings as the present," and how lucky that I had visited when I had.

So there it was. Better for Freddie, I guess, to be dead quickly like that than to suffer the progressive constriction and deterioration of emphysema. As for me, I agreed it was lucky I had visited, but basically I felt awful—yanked about and bruised and left as a memento of my extraordinary hopes with the memory of a few stray phrases of affection. "I am happy and proud to own you as a daughter." "I'm very proud of you." "I loved having you." "How are you, my darling?" "He sends his love and says he's doing okay." It was a help, though, that Freddie had died, as the saying goes, so well. I understood his contentment in his own powers of concentration. When I heard about him watching cricket that final Saturday on television, I could imagine him sitting up in his bed, his little writing pad at his side, totally immersed in watching the game, a completely happy person. My mother in her last few months had been so angry and frightened, such an impossible invalid, so hard on everyone around her. Freddie affirmed both his courage and fundamental contentment by the grace with which he died. I could take pride in having such a father.

At the very end, though, it occurred to me to wonder, how did he feel? Gully said she couldn't bear to think of him in such a reduced condition. I felt, more primitively, a sense of awe at the extinction of a such a vibrant intelligence, at the dying of a philosopher. In the last hours of his life he couldn't talk; he couldn't hear; he couldn't breathe; he couldn't defecate. Did he, I wonder, still have his admirable mind?

Ten

THE TWELVE
BOOKS

FIVE WEEKS after my visit to him, Freddie was in the hospital; eight weeks after my visit he was dead. The night that he died, I sat alone at home by the shuttered living-room window, hands gripping the upholstered armrests of my chair, and, in my desolation, eager perhaps for someone to blame, felt as angry with my mother as I had that February afternoon five months earlier when a photograph had confirmed Freddie was my father. Then, almost immediately, the whole complex of feelings shifted. I set Freddie aside—he seemed to fade almost as quickly as he had loomed—and it was my mother, not my father, whose loss I mourned. As I look back to that extraordinary 1989 year, from the memorial service for my mother, which took place in New York in January, to the memorial for Freddie, which was held in London in December, I see its strange emotional pattern. In the first half of the year, beginning with the memorial for my mother, I moved so rashly, so expectantly, towards Freddie; in the second half, beginning with the shock and disappointment of Freddie's death and ending with his memorial, I turned again to my mother. The resonance of my history with her was so much stronger than that of my history with Freddie. She seemed to draw me back in and make Freddie unimportant. As men had always done, he paled beside her. Stubbornly, soothingly undiminished, my fallback and refuge at a time of pain, she seemed again the only parent I had ever had.

I am sure I was atoning for my temporary desertion. Throughout the preceding months, I had missed my mother and been susceptible to moments of sudden and overwhelming grief. I would be fine, and then some thought of her, or not even directly of her, perhaps just the sight of some old lady on a park bench, would bring on a great flood of tears, a great wave of realization that she was gone and that I was unutterably sad. But when these waves subsided, there I was again with so much else to think about. I was a person who had suffered a loss but then been given an extraordinary compensation. It was like my mother "being given" children in compensation for the death of F. Scott Fitzgerald. My mother had died, and I was then given my father. Freddie died, and it was her death that came into focus, hers that seemed the only death that mattered.

And thoughts of my mother could still comfort me too. It was as I remembered coming back from boarding school to 607 North Maple Drive, back to the soothing securities of home after knocking and getting knocked about in the world. Of course, those securities didn't exist as I imagined them, but something real did. "I love you very much," my mother had said to me the last time I saw her, in Florida two months before her death. We sat together on her terrace in Palm Beach, my mother so thin by then, an etherealized sparrow about to die, but telling me with intense, quite somber finality that she loved me. This, it now seemed to me, was what she had wanted to leave me with—the assurance that she loved me and another declaration from one of our last phone conversations that I also found haunting and consoling: "You and I, Wendy, we understand one another." These utterances were not casual. Here was someone who had loved me, who had identified her life with mine. I wasn't sure we understood one another. But what did this matter? My mother hadn't really been talking about insight but about affinity, about loyalty. Whatever she had done, however misguided she had been, this much had been true.

I speak of a period of mourning, but my awareness was almost more of my mother's abiding presence than of her absence. I had rented a house for the summer of 1989 on Fire Island, and on long solitary walks along the beach I would look out at the ocean and find it almost inconceivable that my mother no longer existed in the world. It seemed to me that if I concentrated long and hard enough, I could call up her spirit. It would rise up out of the sea at a point just short of the horizon. It hovered just out of reach, and if only I could dig deep enough within myself to evoke it, I was sure it would be at my side. Again and again I had this peculiar feeling of our proximity. Sometimes it would seem as if I were crossing over to the land of the dead; at other times that I was about to pull my mother back to the land of the living.

On a brief trip to a North Sea resort in Holland, I realized, looking across that body of water, that England was on the other side—England, the English seaside, the ghost of Lily Shiel. I imagined fifteen-year-old Lily working as a skivvy in Brighton and going down to the boardwalk on her day off to stroll along it and breathe in the sea air and the freedom. I remembered my mother many years later on our visits to her sisters standing with me on that same boardwalk and inhaling that same glorious air. *"Ah, die Luft, die Luft."* Where had such vitality gone? Surely it wasn't extinguished. For the first time in my life I understood why people go to seances and believe in the possibilities of communion with the dead. I didn't harbor such beliefs, and yet day after day I felt the undertow of my mother's sorcery and the strangely soothing captivity of bereavement.

Freddie in the context of this almost mystical involvement with my mother was less than a ghost. He hardly existed in memory, let alone in the neurons of the air about me. I was glad to know he was my father. If nothing else, the knowledge gave me a new sense of my physiognomy. I had been aware of changes in my looks as I grew older that I had not been able to explain; whereas at twenty I looked very much like my mother, I now looked much less so, and I had found this vaguely disturbing. What in fact had been happening was that I was looking not only less and less like my beautiful mother but more and more like Freddie. Since I had found Freddie handsome, even in old age, I now gained a different model of beauty on which to chart my own aging: the longer nose and face, the eyes, the smile. So this was something. I had Freddie's looks. I had his genes. But basically I had given up on him meaning much more to me. When I lunched in New York with Gully (we seemed on a brink not quite yet crossed of being friends), we talked about Freddie, and I could see that she missed him acutely. As I dispassionately noted to myself, *I* didn't. How could I? I didn't have the history to miss him. Or to put this another way, I might have missed him more if I hadn't known I was his daughter. I didn't have the history to miss him as a father.

I had not gone to Freddie's cremation service, which was held at Golders Green and attended by a few immediate family members and friends. No one assumed I should be part of this, neither others nor I myself. Had I expressed the wish to be included, even though it meant traveling all the way from New York, I am sure that no one would have told me not to come. It was not clear to me, however, that I belonged among Freddie's more intimate mourners. I was not close enough either to him or to them to have this standing.

"Don't bother about the funeral," Gully had said to me over the phone before she herself left for London, the purpose of her trip less to attend the perfunctory ceremony than to be with her mother at this stressful time. "What you should come to is the memorial."

The memorial was taking shape as a large public event—in Hollywood terms one would call it a gala—at which Freddie would be honored in keeping with his public stature and importance. To the memorial I had been cordially invited, and despite my general numbness about this father's place in my life, it seemed not only appropriate but essential to me that I should attend it. Throughout the summer and into the fall, through everything else I was doing—staying at the beach, thinking about my mother, going back to teaching—I waited for the memorial to be organized, knowing that whenever it occurred, however convenient or inconvenient the date, I would travel to England to sit in a large public space—at one point Westminster Abbey was under consideration but was then rejected because of Freddie's atheism—to listen to important people eulogize A. J. Ayer. I would go because I had decided that whatever the discomfort of going, the alternative of not going would be worse: an overt expression of my alienation and a choice to miss out on even more than I had missed already. I could imagine myself brooding in future years about my perverse, self-defeating decision. That I had not gone to Freddie's memorial would linger as a lifelong regret. Still, I did not imagine that in going I would have a good or comfortable time. In my mind there were two scenarios: the first in which people would know who I was and gossip about me in whispers behind my back, the other in which they would not know and I would sit like the unbidden guest at the wedding feast. And known or not known, how could I avoid the sting of this last and most bitter irony? The daughter who has missed out on her father's life comes to hear him praised in death.

The invitation arrived, a rather austere white card bearing the logo of University College, London, and making the formal announcement of occasion, time, and place:

A Meeting in Honour of
Professor Sir Alfred Jules Ayer
will be held in
The Logan Hall, Institute of Education
20 Bedford Way, London WC1H OAL
on Tuesday 12 December 1989 at 11:30 A.M.

I sent back my reply card saying that Professor Wendy Fairey would be pleased to attend the meeting. Then to bolster my courage, I went out and bought an expensive black silk suit, a cream-colored silk blouse, and an antique silver pin to wear on the jacket. Adding my mother's double-strand pearls for good measure, I modeled the outfit before my bedroom mirror and imagined how the guests at the memorial would be impressed by Freddie's daughter. Or if no one paid me much heed (scenario 2), I could all the better hold my own as the elegant woman in the black silk suit.

My next step was to call Dee, with whom my contact had been slight since Freddie's death, to make sure that she knew I was coming. She did indeed and invited me to stay at the house on York Street, an invitation I gratefully accepted. It was getting hard to cast myself as the outsider, particularly when Dee said I should be sure to keep free the evening of December 11 for the "family" gathering on the eve of the more formal event. So there I was—set to stay at the house and included as a member of the family. I felt relieved but still uneasy.

Arriving in London on the evening of Friday, December 8, I waited in vain to reclaim the larger of my two suitcases, the one that contained most of my clothes, including the black silk suit and cream silk blouse. It never appeared on the baggage carousel, because, as I was able to ascertain before leaving the airport, it had gone by mistake to Santo Domingo. I was assured that it would arrive the next day, or the day after at the latest, still in good time for the memorial. As bad luck would have it, it didn't. Although not lost forever, my suitcase arrived in London only in time for me to pick it up at Heathrow on my way home to New York. I was fortunate to have most of my shoes in the small bag that had not been lost. As for clothes, Dee lent me a few skirts and blouses; I bought a maroon pleated skirt at Liberty's that matched with a sweater still in my possession to give me an outfit for the family party; and a friend of my mother's lent me a decently elegant black-and-red wool suit to wear to the memorial. Everyone said I looked just fine. To me, nonetheless, to whom everything was loaded and portentous, it seemed a telling irony that I should end up at Freddie's memorial in borrowed clothes. I took pride in my ability to improvise and cope, but the symbolism of disarray was stronger than that of survival.

Equally resonant with implications of both losing and finding was my return to the National Portrait Gallery on the Sunday before the memorial, where this time I found Freddie's portrait. Entering the now familiar twentieth-century wing, I searched for the portrait of Isaiah Berlin that Freddie had said his was under. Locating Sir Isaiah (himself beneath a biochemist), I felt a sensation of rising panic when Freddie was not on the same wall. But then I saw him. He was unsmiling and not very prominent—the portrait, as he had accurately described it to me, was a small one—but there it was. I remembered Freddie telling me he liked the portrait, which other people had criticized as too somber. I don't think I can say whether I liked it or not. The triumph was to have found it. Nothing else much mattered to me. I only wished that I could have now gone back to York Street and reported my success to Freddie himself.

But mightn't he, although not revolving, have still objected to his placement? Above him hung a large picture of Marcus Joseph Sieff, Baron Sieff of Brompton, who had joined the family firm of Marks & Spencer; to his right was a bust of Sir

Philip Harris, a businessman in the carpet and furniture trade; to his left a small painting of Gerald Maurice Ronson, property developer and service station magnate who introduced the first self-service pumps to Britain. And there among these favorite sons of a nation of shopkeepers was Freddie. I read the wall label: "Sir Alfred Jules Ayer 1910–1989, Professor of Logic at Oxford University 1959–78, author of *Language, Truth, and Logic,* the leading British statement of Logical Positivism, by Humphrey Ocean, 1985."

There was no Freddie to go back to at York Street. I had spent a week at Freddie's house in April and he was there; I spent a second week at the same house seven months later and he was dead. Everything about the house that was the same brought home to me this painful difference—as did everything about it that had changed. Perhaps the identical rearrangements and renovations would have occurred, or at least most of them, if Freddie were still sitting in the living room reading his books and playing chess—it had been Dee's express intention to take the house in hand. The fact, though, that he wasn't made the changes so much more telling. On the upper floors it was mostly a matter of the shifting around of bedrooms. I now had Dee's old room; she had moved downstairs to Freddie's; and Nicholas, who introduced me to friends as his "sister," was back in the room that had been mine on my visit in April. This was still in a derelict condition, though the upstairs bathroom had been renovated and the house, all in all, was in better trim.

Serious redecoration had begun on the ground floor, where the dreary cork-and-green wall covering in the dining room was gone and the room was now painted the deep red color that I remembered from Dee's floor of the house at Regent's Park Terrace. A large oil portrait of Dee hung prominently on one wall. It showed her seated on a cushion on the floor, one arm around the shoulder of a German shepherd, with an expression on her intelligent face that struck me as both weary and benign. I locked gazes with this life-sized representation and sensed how complex were my feelings towards my father's widow and survivor. We seemed alternately wary friends and polite antagonists. She was Lady Ayer. And I, gloomy victim and beneficiary of her intervention, who was I? A guest. An interloper. The illegitimate daughter in borrowed clothes.

Pictures of Freddie that on the earlier visit might have seemed a reflection of his vanity now served to memorialize him. In the downstairs hallway was a caricature drawing by someone named "Springs" and a photograph titled "The Thinkers" depicting a middle-aged Freddie in the midst of five little boys, the group gathered closely together on a London park bench. Four of the boys had typically English faces and straight blond hair, while the fifth little boy, with a longer face and dark curly hair, was Nicholas. Upstairs in the drawing room now hung the portrait of Freddie by e.e. cummings as well as a second portrait, the work of a friend and former lover, which depicted a delicate-featured fortyish Freddie with a markedly high forehead and narrow face. The other portraits in the room were Dee's collection of bulls and other animals, now displayed around the fireplace. Sitting morosely one evening on the living-room sofa when everyone else was out, I consumed several glasses of sherry and gazed at the paintings of the five bulls, one cow, one dray horse, and one Indian princess in chains.

My one respite from the turmoil of my bad feelings was at Dee's family party on the eve of the memorial. Held in the drawing room at York Street, amid the portraits of Freddie and the bulls, the party offered me the experience I had always imagined for myself of being part of a large warm family. Here were Gully and Peter and Rebecca, who had arrived from New York and were staying not at the house but in a flat in South Kensington. Peter, a great talker, held forth sweepingly about differences between England and America, while five-year-old Rebecca wended her way sweetly among the guests in the same black velvet party dress (the hem now let down) that she had

worn that previous December evening on which Dee had first
talked to me about Freddie. I met Dee's sister Priscilla, whom I
had spoken to on the phone before Freddie died and who now
expanded on her love for Freddie and her pleasure in taking
care of him, here at the party with her husband and son. I met
Dee's brother Woody, who lived in Massachusetts and owned
restaurants. And finally, "family" included the regular occu-
pants of 51 York Street: Dee and my brother Nicholas. It was
Nicholas who kept repeating, "Is this my family? I look about
me and everybody is family." My God, I thought, he means me
too.

The party also assembled a number of old family friends,
one of whom, a large handsome woman named Amanda, close
to me in age, had worked for Freddie and Dee as an au pair in
the South of France. Now married and with children of her
own, she ran a small nursery school in London. I found her
easy to talk to, and she explained to me how Freddie and Dee
had changed her life. She had been eighteen, a county girl from
Bedfordshire, when she had answered the ad for an au pair to
go to France and take care of Nicholas. Suddenly she found
herself with these bizarre and exciting people. Dee would com-
plain, "That bloody Amanda. God damn it, Amanda. She can't
do anything." And Freddie would say, "Charming girl, charming girl." And then Freddie would take long walks with her and
listen to her and, as Amanda put it, "sort her out."

Amanda told me that I had Freddie's hands. "I loved Freddie's hands," she said. "And you have Freddie's hands, particularly the forefinger."

Hearing this made me want to cry. I had missed all the fun
in the South of France, but I had Freddie's hands. I remembered my awareness of his hands on my visit in April. They were
gnarled, and they seemed large, as old people's hands often do,
in relation to his frail forearms and body. Hadn't my mother
told me that I had her hands, though in a smaller version? The
day after Freddie's memorial, his old girlfriend Jocelyn Ric-

kards, the painter of the delicate portrait in the living room, invited me to lunch, and she as well observed that I had Freddie's hands. To have this noticed independently by two different people moved me deeply. They saw so immediately and absolutely that I had Freddie's hands. Yet I had had these hands all my life, unaware of the connection.

I felt happy at the party and expansively well disposed towards everyone there. I talked to Francette, the old family friend who had a house in Paris on the Ile St. Louis and had been the person at Freddie's bedside when he woke up from his afterlife experience and said, *"Mes pensées sont devenues des personnes."* I talked to Dee's friend from Barcelona, who invited me to come and visit her there "anytime." I talked to Gully and Peter. I talked to Dee and Nicholas. And everyone was speaking with great animation and telling stories about Freddie. "He was always laughing, talking, drinking," said Francette. "Or else being silent with himself, in which case he was inside himself. And he was never pompous." Then people had their memories of his incapacities and of his charm. He couldn't open a can of cat food. He couldn't change a light bulb. He was so marvelous with children. He took so to Rebecca. Amanda said she had cried because now her children would not know him. And Priscilla told how the nurses in the hospital had wept when Freddie died. And I, content in the role of a listener, felt integrated and connected and a part of the fun going on now even if I hadn't been part of it then. And then suddenly in the middle of all this gaiety and celebration, I was overcome by a wave of terrible fatigue. It all seemed too much, being part of this new family. I'd had enough.

Still, the family party had drawn me in and united me with this group of people. I am pleased that I had this experience, particularly since the actual memorial, which occurred the next day in an austere cinder-block auditorium at University College, was such a flop for me. I had anticipated being miserable at Freddie's memorial, but I had not anticipated the precise quality of the misery. It was nothing so simple as being either gossiped about or ignored. I was not the subject of gossip. I was not ignored. I was simply confronted with the unimportance of my existence in the larger context of Freddie's life and achievement. I have seldom in my life felt so isolated and lonely.

My worry about not being acknowledged proved completely ungrounded. On the list of "Acceptances for Ayer Family Meeting"—the list that was later reproduced in the newspaper accounts of the event—there I was under "family attending," second only to "Lady Ayer (widow)" and "Mr. Julian Ayer and Mr. Nicholas Ayer (sons)," although wonderfully transfigured as "Professor Wendy Ayer (daughter)." The error was so replete with irony that it was hard to imagine it as unintentional. It seemed perhaps a way both to display me and to hide me, though I accepted Dee's assurances that it was simply a mistake. At any rate, there was Professor Wendy Ayer, daughter, listed after the widow and sons, and before stepdaughters, stepsons, stepson-in-law, stepdaughter-in-law, and stepgranddaughter. The precision in the duly noted relations to Freddie contrasted oddly with the liberty taken with my name. Not that I minded my moment of legitimization. Why not Wendy Ayer? Was Ayer any less "true" a name for me than Westbrook or Fairey? I toyed with the notion of an official name change. Or at least I had a moment of regret that here was a name that might have been mine but never had been.

Following the listing of family members came the names of the four hundred or so guests, most of them eminent—intellectuals, politicians, publishers, journalists—who had accepted the invitation to Freddie's memorial. With titles ranging from the "Mister" that Freddie so disliked to a strong showing of "Sirs," "Professors," and "Doctors" to a scattering of "Right Honorables" and "Lords" and "Ladies," they represented a turnout of the British liberal establishment. I recognized some of the names—Isaiah Berlin, Alan Bennett, V. S. Pritchett,

Stephen Spender, George Weidenfeld, among others—but in fact knew almost no one aside from people from the previous evening's family party. Peter Foges and I walked together into the stark auditorium. "I know everyone here," said Peter.

"I don't know anyone," said I. He was complaining. And I was too.

I took my seat in the row reserved for family and observed the speakers now assembling in a row of chairs on the stage. I had watched Dee at the house that morning putting on a quilted red-and-purple dress and thought it a strange choice for a memorial. Now there she was, an effective splash of color in the midst of five gray-suited men. To the far left was Roy Jenkins, now the Right Honorable Lord Jenkins of Hillhead, Chancellor of the University of Oxford; to his right Professor Sir Peter Strawson FBA, Waynflete Professor of Metaphysical Philosophy at Oxford; next to him Professor Ted Honderick, Grote Professor of the Philosophy of Mind and Logic at University College, and as such the current occupant of Freddie's old chair. Next came Dee, to whose right sat Dr. Jonathan Miller CBE, and Mr. Peter O'Toole. Whether from their placement on the high stage or simply from their size as individuals—Honderick, Miller, and O'Toole were extremely tall, Roy Jenkins quite ample, and neither Dee nor Peter Strawson someone to call small—the group created an impression of people slightly larger than life. Freddie had been small, the shortest boy in group pictures taken at Eton, and I by British standards was certainly smaller than average. My perception of the speakers as oversized served to distance them from me. I noted in myself both the fear of my own insignificance and an intensified sense of detachment.

Lord Jenkins began the service, coming to the podium, starting with a joke, and then, as the next few speakers would do as well, launching into the prepared text that aimed to be both portrait and assessment of the eminent deceased. Lord Jenkins's Freddie, the politician's Freddie, was the clear-sighted atheist and engaged philosopher-citizen. If there was a stark secularism to the occasion, an absence of the softening influence of the church, how well, asserted the speaker, such an ambiance accorded with Freddie's honesty and "incomparable lucidity." Next came the notation of Freddie's "quiet insolence," which had "altered the terms of the argument," and of the fact that Freddie's "obituary impact" equaled that of Bertrand Russell (how fitting, it struck me, that this particular speaker should be mindful of the validating power of the media). Freddie, Roy Jenkins concluded, had been "kind, tolerant, and generous" and, as in his support of the reform of laws governing homosexual conduct, "a fine ally with which to go into a fight."

It fell to the two philosophers who followed to convey more fully Freddie's philosophical achievement and his place of honor in the British empirical tradition. Peter Strawson, as angular and soft-spoken as Roy Jenkins was rotund and booming, seemed almost to be delivering a mini-lecture on the key philosophical tenets of A. J. Ayer. Defining Freddie's "group" as Locke, Berkeley, Hume, Mill, and Russell, he compared Freddie's treatment of the subjective impressions of sense with that of Hume and reviewed some of the key points of Freddie's theory of knowledge. At first I found him dry, but I liked his final statement that "no one was ever less in danger of imprisonment in a purely private world" and his praise of Freddie as "gallant and profoundly liberal." Ted Honderick's Freddie, ever a voice of "pellucid empiricism," was also more of a philosophical buccaneer, a "hussar against nonsense," a "logical elf," philosophy's *enfant terrible,* who began his first book with a chapter on "The Elimination of Metaphysics" and ended it with one on "Solutions of Outstanding Philosophical Disputes." Ted, whom I had met on my earlier visit, had been Freddie's friend and protégé, and from this privileged position he also recollected Freddie's vanity, his loyalty to friends, and "a bet about whether Jane Austen gives the very words in which

Mr. Darcy proposes for the second time."

I had found the first two portraits of Freddie inspiring but somewhat impersonal. Ted's was warmer, a more intimate sketch. Yet its polish and cleverness, as indeed I had felt of the speeches that preceded it, served to call attention as much to the skill of the eulogist as to the qualities of the deceased. Yes, everyone spoke with such eloquence. Why did Freddie seem to me so strangely absent? Was it the hall? The essential reserve and decorum of the speeches? My state of mind? I awaited the concluding speakers, who might prove less formal, to see if they would right the balance.

Jonathan Miller, doctor, satirist, playwright, and director, had been Dee and Freddie's neighbor at Regent's Park Terrace, and I hoped he might do better than the others in evoking Freddie's spirit to keep us company in the stark cinder-block hall. Now we had Freddie as popularizer—the figure who had made philosophy "clear, exciting, and accessible"—and also Freddie as "social merrymaking Freddie" as well as "the exacting logician": the man with something "inextinguishably festive about his character," "an appealing streak of vanity" and a habit of twirling his key chain. The portrait was apt. Yet Freddie still seemed muted and veiled. Did Jonathan Miller love Freddie? Perhaps that was the problem. The speakers had all liked and admired Freddie. But I suspect they hadn't loved him. I would have preferred to listen to the au pair Amanda rather than all the important people who were finding such well-chosen words to fulfill the assignment of the hour.

Peter O'Toole had been enlisted as a professional actor to read, as he put it, "one of Sir Freddie's favorite poems." Tall and gaunt with his wonderful ravaged face, he stood at the podium in his light-gray suit and white tie—a subtle parody of the male dress code—put on his reading glasses, and began to recite Tennyson's "Ulysses" in a beautiful, languorous drawl. I loved his reading, I loved listening to one of *my* favorite poems, but what did this poem have to do with Freddie? His favorite authors, as far as I knew, were Jane Austen and Trollope and Proust and Thomas Love Peacock. I had never heard him talk about poetry. I had never heard him burst into verse the way my mother liked to do. Freddie was vivid but he wasn't lyrical. "I cannot rest from travel: I will drink/Life to the lees." The poem's expression of yearning, restlessness, and emotional hunger for experience reminded me of my adventurous mother, not of my philosophic father. Again Freddie eluded me. I couldn't situate him in relation to the poem.

When Peter O'Toole had finished, it was now the turn of the final speaker. The one woman on the stage, the only speaker without a prepared text, Dee Wells, Lady Ayer, came forward to the podium and began very quietly. "I should have prepared," she said, "but I thought I would simply say how it was recently." She spoke about getting back together with Freddie, reconciling differences, coming full circle. She spoke of being with him in France with the almond trees in bloom in February and Freddie doing his breathing exercises. He was well still in April, "swanning around" in a black tie and playing endless games of chess with Nick. Freddie died, she said, on June 27 (I took note that her tone was shifting), and on June 30 he was attacked. Dee did not mention the attacker by name—it was a part of her thetorical strategy to refer to him only as "that minister man." This, I learned later, was Mrs. Thatcher's minister of higher education, Robert Jackson, who had written a critical letter to the *Independent* in response to Richard Wollheim's obituary in that paper. "Anger is a very restorative thing," said Dee. She described the letter that she in turn had composed—"had the Himalayan she-bear ever learned to write a letter, this is the letter she would have written"—and the minister's ensuing explanation that his attack was really on Wollheim (who evidently had used the obituary as a vehicle to attack the government), not on Freddie. "Well, you could have fooled me," said Dee, at which the whole audience laughed and applauded. She then announced that as a gesture of protest against the government's attitude towards higher education and as a "permanent avenging of Freddie," she intended to establish the A. J. Ayer Memorial Scholarship.

I had liked the first part of Dee's speech, in which she so movingly described Freddie's final months, then felt uneasy when she went on at such length about the minister. I didn't understand the agenda, and it worried me that the focus seemed again to be shifting away from Freddie. It was Dee's attack on the minister that got coverage in the next day's papers. "Ayer's Wife Attacks Minister," read the headline for the *Evening Standard*'s "Londoner's Diary." In the *Daily Telegraph* "Sir Peregrene Worthorne's Diary" covered the memorial in a general way and then focused on Dee's "fiery eloquence," which was matched, noted the writer, "by a blazing patchwork dress of red and purple—no widow's weeds for her." "Hers was a performance Freddie would have enjoyed enormously," the piece concluded. "What sweeter words could be found to send the liberal establishment cheerfully on its way?"

In retrospect, I more fully understood and savored the skill of Dee's performance, but not on that depressing morning. What I understood then was that Freddie belonged to the tradition of British empiricism, to the liberal intellectual establishment, to Dee and Nicholas, and not to me. Filing out of the auditorium to join the mass of people in the large bare room adjoining Logan Hall that had been designated for the reception, I felt only lost and miserable. A pianist at one end of the room was playing Freddie's favorite Cole Porter tunes. I hovered near the piano. I hovered near the hors d'oeuvres. Intermittently I attached myself to the few people I knew, but feeling such a burden to myself, I was sure I must also be one to others and quickly disengaged from conversations. Occasionally I would be introduced as Freddie's daughter, and no one seemed to respond to this as strange. Rather compulsively, I found myself explaining my equivocal status first to Roy Jenkins and then to Peter O'Toole. Each expressed a proper degree of polite amazement and then moved on to talk to other people.

Finally, I encountered Dee and Gully, both in tears from the emotion of the morning. The next thing I knew I had my arms around Dee's neck and was sobbing that I missed my mother. This was absolutely true, but it also struck me as the last thing Dee wanted or needed to hear. Here she had gone to such trouble to involve me with herself and Freddie, and I was bawling for my mother. I apologized and moved away from her. Ted Honderick was organizing a group of people to go to lunch and asked if I wanted to join them. I didn't really, but it seemed I should do something. We ended up, a party of about a dozen people, at an Italian restaurant, where I drank too much red wine, ate pasta on top of the greasy hors d'oeuvres I had consumed at the reception, and accomplished nothing but to feel ill and depressed as I walked in the 4:00-P.M. winter twilight back to York Street.

All in all, the week of my visit was disjointed. I spent a lot of time talking on the telephone with the staff of Pan American Baggage Services and felt far more intimate with Maureen and Norman and Marilore and the other Pan Am employees, who thanked me for my patience and kept assuring me that my bag would turn up any day now, than I did with anyone at 51 York Street. Conversations at the house were guarded and cursory. I saw other friends who lived in London, and as on my previous visit, I took my solitary walks. One of these brought me to Upper Grosvenor Street, where I noted that the International Sportsman's Club, my mother's old club, was now designated by a brass plaque on its front door as the London Arab Investment Bank Ltd. This seemed to me such poignantly visible evidence of the eclipse of the past that although I knew the club had been gone for many years, I stood on the spot and wept.

I was melancholy, and I was angry. Out one evening with a friend, I found myself over an after-theater pint of bitter in a pub giving voice to a sweeping denunciation. "I feel violated," I said. "By my mother who lied to me. By Freddie who was too passive to counteract the lie."

"Are you a better parent?" challenged my friend. I thought for a moment, not wanting to be self-deluding or unfair. The key point was not my loving or providing for my children or even giving them a father; it was respecting them as people who existed apart from me. Gathering courage, I answered her. "Yes."

And then there was my legacy. It was on my second day at 51 York Street that Dee told me how Freddie had said to her, "I must do something for Wendy." I held my breath, waiting to learn what that something could be. When friends in America had asked me whether Freddie had left me any money, I had consistently treated the inquiry as rather crass. "Oh no, I don't think so," I had said. "Nor did I expect him to."

"And soooo"—Dee drew out the word—"he has left you the choice from his library of twelve books of English literature."

Later when I got back to New York, I tried to analyze what was so awful about Freddie's bequest. I would have felt better, I think, to have nothing. Or if Freddie had left me *all* his books of English literature, or if he himself had chosen the twelve books, or if he himself had chosen even one. Typically, however, he was passive. And I was left to comb through his library—with its thousands of books of philosophy and history and biography and the literature of different countries—to pick out my precisely defined dozen. Dee thought I might like to take a six-volume set of the novels of Jane Austen, and to this I quickly assented. Jane Austen had been important to Freddie and had figured in our history. Then, too, the selection half completed my task. Six books down. Only six to go.

It was on my last day at the house that I set about choosing the remaining books. Dee, who had fallen victim to the flu epidemic then raging in London, was sick in bed and not available for consultation. I considered deferring the project to another time, but driven on by the desire to claim my due and then be done with the whole anxiety-ridden business, I took courage and ranged Freddie's bookshelves, looking for volumes of English literature that I might consider apt or special. There was Trollope's *Can You Forgive Her?*—a germane enough title. It came, however, in two volumes, and aside from my worry that I was adding too much weight to my baggage, my indecision as to whether to count this as one book or two perplexed me to the point of paralysis. Finally, I settled on a 1901 edition of Oscar Wilde's *Intentions,* which included his essay "The Decay of Lying"; a leather-bound edition of Tennyson's *In Memoriam;* an 1865 leather-bound edition of Dickens's *A Christmas Carol;* a Hogarth Press first edition of Virginia Woolf's *The Moment and Other Essays;* and an e.e. cummings, *95 poems,* in which the author had scribbled a few words to his friend Freddie. Some of the other cummings books in Freddie's library had inscriptions addressed to both Freddie and Dee, and these I was careful to pass over.

And there I stopped—with eleven books chosen. I kept worrying about weight, but what would have been the added weight of one more title—even if in two volumes—particularly since I was still without my big suitcase? My thought in retrospect is that I deferred my twelfth choice because this saved me from reaching the limits of the legacy. With eleven books chosen and one to go, any of the multitudinous books of English literature in Freddie's library was still potentially mine. I think too that I was making a statement to Dee and to myself that I was not a person who would snatch up every last crumb that was thrown to her. Later Dee wrote to ask me to give back the cummings, saying that the whole collection of cummings had been left to Nick and offering me another choice. I gave back the cummings but did not replace it. It felt even better to have stopped at ten books than at eleven.

And so ended my year as the daughter of Freddie Ayer. I had departed from 51 York Street to catch my plane back to New York, creeping out of the house on a dark rainy morning before anyone was awake, slipping the key through the mail slot, and walking away with my books in a plastic bag. It was a depressing end. And yet I almost welcomed my release from a strange stretch of fantasy, from a spell, from an illness, as if having Freddie as a father was a disease and the pain of the memorial the strong dose of medicine that cured me.

Freud writes about the "family romance," the child's fantasy of having different, more aristocratic parents to replace given ones who seem too ordinary. The family romance is not supposed to come true. It ends—or at least normally ends—with a relinquishment of illusion and a coming to terms with the real, with accepting the ordinariness of parents and self, yet seeing that ordinariness has its own dignity. But suppose what seemed intractably "real" proves the illusion? Suppose the "family romance" appears truly to be realized?

Throughout my life, I had struggled with the issue of fathers, real and imagined. I thought I was a person who could make do without a father, to whom having a father simply hadn't been very important. Yet look at my history.

The only father who ever actually lived with us was Bow Wow, the stepfather I totally rejected. I offset him in my mind not with Trevor but with the dead F. Scott Fitzgerald. Fair, fine-boned, delicate, intelligent, Fitzgerald was as etherealized as Bow Wow was corporeal, as literary as Bow Wow was unlettered, as charming as Bow Wow was crass. I dubbed him my spiritual father and can say that he also, in a sense, lived with us at 607 North Maple Drive, helping to shape my education and ambitions, offering me, in his relationship with my mother, an image of love between a man and a woman, and in what I knew of his relationship with his daughter, Scottie, of a father's concern for a daughter. His influence on my life was important. I think he served me well.

Then, of course, there was the man I always thought was my father, the father who was not a "monster" but whom we cast in our family as the father manqué: the engineer who could build and fix things but could not build a bridge to his children, the man of property who disinherited us in his will, the inarticulate father who could not tell us that he cared, the anti-Semite who *we* knew didn't know we were Jewish, the father whose tangible but remote existence served above everything else to make us feel fatherless.

And I, who had borne the burden of such failure of love and connection, was suddenly rescued from the shame of it, the shame of having failed to stir a father's love, and given both an explanation and a second chance. No wonder Trevor hadn't loved me; he hadn't after all been my true father. So now I had a better father. I was the philosopher's daughter, the daughter of festive Freddie Ayer. The family romance had come true.

But of course it hadn't. The philosopher was ordinary too. He was indisputably attractive—handsome and brilliant and amusing, and kind as well. But he was weak; he was self-centered; he himself needed to be taken care of; he was not much good at looking out for other people. I realized all this, but hope died hard. I reduced my demands. All I wanted, I told myself, was a little time—time to figure things out, to live with Freddie and the idea of him more calmly. He died, however, before I could even catch my breath, leaving me with my scattered, confusing memories of his presence in my life and my ten books from his library of English literature.

George Eliot, having lost her faith in God, pronounced in her most austere and hortatory manner that "we must do without opium and live through all our pain with conscious clear-eyed endurance." I think I knew Freddie; I think I loved him. I know I am his daughter and thus know better who I am. Yet he too, in the last analysis, was a father manqué, joining with the famous dead writer and the respected English engineer as figures who hovered on the edge of my life, shadowy fathers, fathers of air, fathers who evaporated, more symbol than substance. It is an irony that the only person who ever really sought to be my father, the only person who ever truly played the role, was my mother, Sheilah Graham.

Eleven

ORPHAN AND DAUGHTER AGAIN

*I*T WAS ODD how the speakers at my mother's memorial kept stressing her candor and her innocence. Odder still, I did not think them wrong about her, not then in early January 1989 or even later when I knew more conclusively that she had lied to me about Trevor and Freddie. Can there be candor that does not depend on telling the truth? Or innocence that survives a lifetime of conniving and duplicity?

The speakers at the memorial did not dwell on my mother's celebrity. They did not strive to fix her in a canon. (What would it have been—Hedda, Louella, and Sheilah? Or perhaps the mistress-muses of famous writers.) They did not discuss the importance of her column, which helped to create the myth of Hollywood, or of her books, which fostered the myth of herself as a twentieth-century heroine. Rather, they expressed their feelings—love, admiration, affection—for a person who had charmed them, who had entered their lives with her great zest and warmth and invited them, if they would go along with her, to be part of the fun. I, who had suffered so much conflict about going along with her, was the proud architect of this occasion, and it pleased me very deeply. A few days after the memorial, I would learn that my mother had misrepresented to her children the date of her marriage to Trevor. A month later, I would receive Freddie's letter telling me he was my father. Even on that day, the presence of Dee and Gully among the guests was a reminder of the questions that had been raised and not yet answered. But I think you could have told me at the memorial that I was the daughter of Zeus or Yahweh and not deflected me from my purpose: to give this day to my mother, to make her this offering. I had not "come right away" to Florida, but the memorial was my important chance to be my mother's good daughter, to show that I could be trusted to honor her and not to lose her, to take charge finally of us both. So much seemed at stake. If I did this right, might she not be propitiated, tamed, placated? Might I not lay her frightful ghost to rest and be free at last to claim my own scope? More than to escape her, I had the idea that I could somehow absorb and dissolve her within me—as in a kind of birth process backwards. This seemed the way to feel at once less orphaned and less guilty for surviving her as I struggled with the meaning of her death.

To plan the memorial, I lunched at the Russian Tea Room with eighty-six-year-old Jean Dalrymple. I sat with her at the very table where my mother had looked happily past me into the mirror, and I listened to Jean's pronouncement that the memorial should be simple. She and my mother had decided, she told me, that it should be an informal gathering of family and good friends, with Jean leading off and other people then called upon to speak. This seemed fine, I said (concealing my little wave of depression that my mother had talked to Jean and not to me), though I was less sure I agreed with Jean's sugges-tion of the Russian Tea Room or "21" as the setting. Certainly I wanted something secular. Although my mother had not been

as insistent an atheist as Freddie—I remembered how she loved
the music at the occasional Christmas or Easter or funeral service she attended—a church or chapel of any Christian persua-
sion felt too connected with the sham of my Episcopalian past,
and even to think, however unseriously, of a synagogue seemed
dragging my mother back to the origins she had so decisively
rejected. The problem was solved when another of my mother's
close friends, the devoted Kathleen Flanagan, offered the use of
the Irish American Historical Society, of which she was vice-
president. At first this seemed a bizarre option, since, aside
from my mother's romance with Fitzgerald and her friendship
with Kathleen, what possibly could link her with the Irish?
Nonetheless, when I went with Kathleen to check out the
handsome building on Fifth Avenue at Eightieth Street and
saw the three oak-paneled rooms of the parlor floor, which,
connected by French doors, could be opened up to create a
capacious but still warm public space, I was persuaded that we
had the perfect setting. The director hovered over us, recount-
ing how my mother through her friendship with Kathleen had
attended some of the society's functions and how happy everyone had been to welcome her. Why not the Irish American
Historical Society? I found myself thinking. I even began to
take a certain pleasure in the incongruity. Since my mother had
been an outsider to any group, there really was no organization
to which she more obviously belonged.

Going through my mother's telephone book, making lists
and then phone calls, I ended with a prospective gathering of
forty to fifty people, all friends, many connected with show
business but none especially famous. I also decided, in consultation with Jean and Kathleen, against putting an announcement
of the memorial in the paper. I did not want to attract fans, the
press, the merely curious. This was to be a private, not a public
affair; it was to be intimate, not impersonal; genuine, not ostentatious. I felt as if I were rescuing my mother from the
people who did not really care for her. I was serving as her
protector, the way I had tried, for example, as a child to protect

her from the rudeness of Errol Flynn. I suppose in truth it was I who needed protection. Sharing my mother with a world where I didn't count had always been painful. The friends invited to the memorial knew me too.

Meanwhile, Robert, my logical ally and partner in these plans, was still off on a remote Greek island without his own telephone. It occurs to me, but only now, that if his counsel and help had seemed more important, I might have waited for his return before proceeding. I didn't wait, and by the time my brother reached New York in mid-December, an event had been arranged that he did not feel a part of. It was in Florida, where we went to clean out the apartment, talk with lawyers and realtors, divide up photographs and silver, that he told me he would not be coming. He was headed back to California and did not wish to travel east again. Also he was angry. "There's a direct line," he said to me, "that runs from Mom to you to Emily. Men to Mom were either fools or drunks, and I'm not coming to the memorial." Adding for good measure that the memorial was my way of mourning our mother, not his, he wished me well and that was that.

I felt angry and abandoned, but then I got used to his not coming, and on some level I liked it. It simplified the focus. More than ever, I could be the important child, my mother's caretaker and descendant. When people at the memorial kept saying how much Sheilah had loved Wendy and Robbie, the mention of my brother's name jolted me into remembering that he existed, and I hastened to make his excuses for not being there.

If Robert was not at my side in those oak-paneled rooms of the Irish American Historical Society, I was able to muster two children and one estranged husband as "family." And then there were the forty family friends. The old ones arrived with that anxious punctuality of the aged well before the announced time of 4:00 P.M. The children and I helped them into seats in the circle of sofas, armchairs, and folding chairs that we had formed around the two front rooms, and I felt such tenderness towards them in their frailty, such a release of my power both to feel and to take care of things, that it seemed almost as if I could absorb their pain and constriction and infuse them with my strength and health. Younger guests milled about. Two flute players, graduate students from Brooklyn College, played Baroque duets in a corner of the room.

At a signal from me the flutists ceased their playing. I stood in the archway between the two rooms, and I spoke, I could tell, very well. I said a few words about my mother's last months, about "hip, hip, not hurray" and the obituary, about *"Je suis mon ancêtre"* and my pride in being her daughter. I expressed how helpful it was to me to feel the support of the people now gathered in these rooms. My mother, I said, had always suffered from feeling orphaned and abandoned. But here were all these people who had cared for her. I did not think about my own fears of abandonment. Too much else was on my mind.

Opposite me in a seat of honor sat Jean Dalrymple, the friend whose beauty, more prim than my mother's, had inspired my mother to joke as they grew older that Jean reminded her of "Queen Victoria in her middle years." I noted that this beauty had deepened with age; it had acquired an otherworldly translucence. Neat as always in a black skirt and white blouse, her hair pulled back under her black-brimmed hat, Jean rose when I introduced her and took the speaker's position in the archway.

She spoke of knowing my mother for fifty years. They had lived to be among the "old olds," she said, and she knew exactly what to say on this occasion because she and Sheilah had discussed it. She then told the story of how she and my mother had met in the thirties. Jean was then a press agent—José Iturbi and Igor Stravinsky were among her clients—and she was always trying, though without much luck, to get items about them into my mother's column. One day, out the blue, my mother had phoned to ask if Jean could get her some concert tickets. Jean had obliged, and after the concert my mother had called to suggest they have lunch.

"When?" had asked Jean.

"Today," had said my mother.

"And she was so beautiful," said eighty-six-year-old Jean Dalrymple, her words obliterating the intervening half-century. "She had the most beautiful peaches-and-cream complexion. And"—here Jean slowed her words in awed remembrance—"gen-u-ine golden hair."

Jean's voice broke. "You must forgive me," she said, dabbing a handkerchief to her eyes. "I am so moved remembering her. You see, she was so beautiful, and I loved her very much."

Watching and listening to Jean Dalrymple, I felt moved by a vision I had always believed in though I had glimpsed it for myself only through the medium of a few black-and-white photographs. Jean had evoked my mother at the height of her beauty, golden and radiant. That beauty was my mother's trump card—along with her wit. It enchanted people. It had enchanted me. Beauty and wit. Jean had them too. I yearned for my mother; I admired her surviving friend who stood there bearing witness to another's power and her own, sincere yet consummately artful.

Jean continued with a survey of some of the "little adventures" that she and my mother had shared over the years. There was a man they had competed for. He had slipped away from them both and been nabbed by his secretary. "And then," said Jean, "we could get on with being friends." Jean concluded, never afraid to state an opinion, that she had been against the hip operation. "We're too old," she had told my mother. But my mother had replied, "We're so old it doesn't matter."

Other speakers followed. Ninety-four-year-old Jimmy O'-Toole stood leaning on his cane and recited an Irish prayer. Dee Wells spoke of my mother's endearing quality of "simplicity." My friend Helen Dimos broke down after her first sentence about knowing my mother since she and I were college freshmen but then pulled herself together to tell how my mother had always encouraged and inspired her. Gerold Frank read a prepared text that described his 1957 experience of driving with my mother to the top of Laurel Canyon, his purpose to stir her memory of Fitzgerald's vow, made on that very spot, never to drink again if only she would come back to him. Judy Hallet, my friend since our years at Bel Air Town and Country, said how much my mother had valued education and what care she had taken to educate her children. Speaker after speaker, both my mother's friends and mine, stressed how much my mother had loved us. "Clark Gable's ears or Liz Taylor's latest amours could never compete for her attention with an unexpected sneeze from daughter Wendy or son Robbie," said one old friend who later I was to learn had also been an old lover. Gerold Frank remembered how patient my mother had been when we children bounded in to interrupt their work sessions. Even Helen and Judy, who it seemed to me should have known better, cited Sheilah's great unstinting love of her children. I listened with some incredulity. The statements were too simple. What about "No hungry generations tread me down"? Still, I could not help but find it reassuring that all these people had such a strong impression of our importance in our mother's life.

Altogether about a dozen people spoke, with me, though I hadn't planned it, calling on them one by one. Throughout the ceremony I felt extraordinarily responsible for everything that was happening. When Helen Dimos broke down, I felt like a director of a play helplessly watching an actress blow her lines on opening night. "Get on with it," I silently urged her. The speakers, I felt, should not be dreary. When Jean spoke so poignantly of my mother's beauty or Jimmy O'Toole recited his Irish blessing, not only did I feel personally moved, touched, surprised, but I exulted that this offering of mine to my mother was shaping itself so well. I did not feel particularly sad, since I was far too busy and elated in my role as impresario. Perhaps Helen's tears were a reproach to me. I am sure also that they frightened me as the intrusive face of desolation.

Before the ceremony began, I had asked my children if they would like to be among the speakers, and both had said no. But then, as we were nearing the end of the program as I had planned it, Emily signaled to me that she would like to be called on. I saved her for last, aware of my own eagerness to hear what she would say. Emily had loved my mother, but in an unawed kind of way, and I trusted in her ability to see and say the uncompromised truth. Moving into the archway between the two rooms, unsmiling and thoughtful, eighteen-year-old Emily Fairey, my daughter and Sheilah Graham's granddaughter, the descendant on whom my mother had fixed, far more than on me, as a continuation of herself, began to speak. "My grandmother wasn't an easy person," she told the gathering,

and I had my difficult times with her as well as good times. But she was my grandmother, and she was important in my life. When she died, my mother brought home a box full of her photographs. I looked through these, and there were lots of glamorous ones. Of my grandmother being presented at court. Or standing with Marilyn Monroe and looking herself like a movie star. And many others. But the picture that struck me most wasn't any of these. It was a picture of a little girl, around eight or ten years old, with all her hair cropped off and these incredibly sad, haunting eyes. This was my grandmother in her orphanage. And as I thought about the life my grandmother had led, about all the things she had gone on to do, I kept going back in my mind to that picture. It just seemed so amazing to me that the little girl in the picture could have done the things that my grandmother did. That is what I keep thinking about. That is what stays with me.

Emily spoke as if she were working something out in her own mind, quietly and seriously. Rather than addressing her listeners, she pulled them into her reflection. I was pleased she had said that my mother was difficult. That was a part of the person we had known, and it needed to be said. Good for Emily. Then I, of course, was familiar with the photograph from the orphanage. The childhood image of my mother floated alongside that of the daughter who stood before me. They resembled each other—in the shape of the face, the high cheekbones, the dark-blond hair and peaches-and-cream complexion. I wondered if Emily, hardly more than a child herself, was thinking about herself as well as about my mother—she seemed to understand so well both vulnerability and aspiration. I was moved by her eloquence and felt immensely proud of her. When Emily finished, the group slowly abandoned the circle of chairs to move towards the refreshments set up in the back room. "Emily, you were wonderful," said Sean and Donald and I, gathering around her. "Oh yes?" said Emily, in the flush of her triumph. "Did you like what I said or how I said it?" "Both, both," we answered.

I thought how pleased my mother would have been with Emily's speech—she would not even have minded being called difficult. In the end we did not have poetry at the memorial. Not Swinburne. Not even Keats. But my daughter, Emily, had talked about her grandmother in a way that cut to the heart of things. And Emily would not forget her. Alienated from her past, my mother had touched and linked with the future. Perhaps Robert was right, that there was a direct line from Mom to me to Emily. If so, I felt at that moment in good company. My mother was dead, and Emily and I were alive to remember and survive her. But surely Robert and our sons would remember and feel linked with her too.

I was not concerned at the memorial with my mother's lie to me. To cope with that day, I set it aside. Later, my problem became how to cope while taking the lie into account, though certainly a part of me just wanted to forget it. The lie seemed to me to have a fearsomely disruptive potential. I was afraid it could make me so angry with my mother that I would lose my whole past. How does one fight with a person who is dead? I didn't know whether to be angry or forgiving, to see the lie as pivotal or dismiss it as inconsequential. It was the turmoil of my confusion that stirred me to my subsequent effort. I wanted to understand my mother better, at least to the extent that research and empathy made this possible. In a way the lie had turned her into a stranger, and I found this very hard. I wanted to repossess her; I also wanted to know our differences, the point where we parted ways and our interests diverged. To know more, of course, might turn out to be even more upsetting. It was when reading *A State of Heat,* the autobiographical novel that I could largely decode, though names were omitted or veiled, that I realized, truly realized, how many men my mother had slept with. I felt surfeited and entangled, too close to her pleasure and her need. My quest led me in the end beyond my mother as beloved infidel to an encounter with that little girl in the orphanage. But there were many intermediate stops before I got to that child.

One was the Russian Tea Room, where on September 15, 1989, my mother's birthday, I was shown by the maître d' to "Miss Dalrymple's table." Jean had always lunched with my mother on her birthday, and this year, nine months after the memorial, she was lunching with me. I had been especially eager for the lunch because it had occurred to me that if there was anyone alive whom my mother might have told about Freddie, it would be Jean Dalrymple. They had been friends for so long. They had been independent professional women and girls together on the town, sharing, so I had come to understand, the same sense of the game. Both had played with men and used them, less for gain, though perhaps for that too, than to feel desired and desirable. It seemed likely to me that they would also have shared sexual secrets.

Jean was not feeling well. She was suffering, she said, from a loss of interest in life, and the little cough she then gave into her handkerchief seemed intended to dramatize this extraordinary assertion. Shortly, she was telling me about the play she had seen the night before and a friend she had rescued in the forties from the doldrums. The coughing ceased; interest in life seemed to revive; I waited to choose my moment. It came after the waiter had set before us our grilled tuna with beurre blanc. There was a lull in conversation, and I jumped in.

"Jean, were you in New York in the 1940s during the war?"

"Of course," she said. "That was the time of my greatest success."

"And you knew my mother then?"

"Certainly."

I tried to ease into my question. "I've found out something rather startling about my life," I told her. "Did she ever say anything to you about Trevor Westbrook not being my father?"

"Yes," Jean answered. She looked braced but not surprised. "I think she did."

"Well, that's what I've learned. He wasn't."

"And have you learned who your father is?"

"Yes, it was Freddie Ayer."

Jean nodded. I had given the right answer. So she knew. I then presented the story as Freddie had told it to me, and Jean said this was pretty much what my mother had told her. It was not in the forties that my mother had confided in Jean, but later, Jean said, when I was already a teenager.

"We were sitting right here," she explained, "talking about all the crazy things we'd done in sex."

I listened quietly. You mustn't crowd people with questions. Give them time to remember.

"She was complaining about you," Jean continued. "And I said, 'She doesn't look anything like you. She's so absolutely different from you.' And that's how it came up."

Jean's words stung me. I could well imagine my mother complaining about me and then telling her secret, almost as an attack on me, an act of disavowal. But could it really make me seem less her daughter to be also Freddie's daughter and not Trevor's? I guess it could since Trevor as a father had for her absolutely no reality.

"I don't understand," I said, "why she never said anything to me."

"There was a lot your mother didn't tell her children," answered Jean. It struck me that she rather liked saying this. She liked the advantage of her greater knowledge.

Jean didn't think my mother had looked back much or felt guilty, but she did think my mother had been afraid of me and that not telling had seemed better both for me and for a relationship that Jean characterized as "already difficult enough." My mother had told Jean that I "already had enough against her."

"Oh really?" was all I could think to say, but I felt hurt and depressed.

"Yes," said Jean. "She was terrified that you'd walk away from her. Basically she was terrified of you."

"She should have had more confidence in the connection," I replied. In my mind I was struggling to fight back against Jean's words. What my mother would have said to Jean Dalrymple would not have been the whole of what she thought and felt. It was a partial truth and as such a distortion. It left out love.

"She had no confidence at all," said Jean. "Always she was back in that orphanage."

Telling Jean what had happened with Freddie, I found myself on the verge of tears. Jean did not ask any questions, but she acknowledged that it must have been hard to have found my father and then lost him like that. Nine months earlier when we had met at the Russian Tea Room to plan my mother's memorial, she had told me about her own father, a charming rake, who seemed doting but had essentially neglected her. Now she continued her life story from the point when she, like my mother, had gone out on her own while really still a child. With a $100 bill, a present from an uncle killed on the last day of World War I, she had enrolled in a typing course rather than in high school. And on then she went—to two jobs on Wall Street, then her vaudeville act with the young Jimmy Cagney. We had reached 1928, and the hour of our lunch was over. "I want to hear more next time," I said.

"I hope you don't feel too bitter," said Jean.

"Oh no," I reassured her.

What I did feel as I made my way home was intensified anxiety and confusion. I had hoped that Jean would know about Freddie. Then in many ways it was hard for me that she did. Her knowledge added little to my own (she said she didn't know who Robert's father was); all it did was make me feel bad. "To think that she would tell Jean Dalrymple rather than telling you," said Emily, echoing more closely than I found comfortable my own amazement and discomfort. Jean also troubled me in her resemblance to my mother. Denied much family, love, or education, these women had nourished themselves, believed in themselves, and triumphed. Yet I could see the cost to them of their toughness. It ended in a kind of isolation. Jean told me that she had never had the experience of great love. At least my mother had loved us, I told myself. And Scott Fitzgerald. I had asked Jean about Fitzgerald—was he really so important?—and she was fervent in affirming that he was. "Just think," she said, "of that College of One. What a marvelous thing to do for another person. I wish someone had made a high school of one for me."

The more I talked to people about my mother, the more persuaded I became that the key to deeper understanding lay in knowing more about the orphanage. "She came out of an orphanage," said our old friend Mike Kaplan, my mother's editor at *Daily Variety*, "and bluffed her way into being a newspaperwoman. Sheilah Graham was her own creation, and she did a helluva job."

"She was not sure of herself emotionally," said Ted Berkman, writer and old family friend. Ted was the person who had startled me by revealing his involvement, after Bow Wow, as my mother's lover.

"But where were we?" I had asked him. "Did this really go on in our house?"

"I guess you kids were asleep," he chuckled.

It was Ted's theory, which he had discussed with several psychiatrists, that anyone who grows up in an orphanage is scarred beyond redemption. He saw the role of fear in my mother's life and remembered how people could intimidate her. One minute she'd be the frightened little girl; the next she'd be lashing out, or as she put it, "fighting for her life," the orphan alone against the world.

I was astonished to learn that my first cousin Ruby, a daughter of my mother's sister Sally, had been sent when her father died in 1930 to, in her words, "the same school as your mum." Her telling me this over the phone—it took me a moment to translate "school" into "orphanage"—then led to my request that she see and talk to me. It was June 1990, and I was back in England. I wanted to visit Ruby, a nice woman in her mid-sixties, at her home in Brighton, but she seemed reluctant to have me come. She explained that I would be disappointed. She did not have much to say. The orphanage, she said, was pretty much as my mother had described it, and being in the orphanage had cut her off from the family, so she knew very little about them. "I'm sure you know more than I do," I answered. And indeed I was right.

The Shiel family, I learned over Ruby's Sunday pot roast, had been prosperous before our grandfather's 1905 death from TB. He had kept his own tailor shop in Leeds, where Ruby's mother had helped out with the buttonholes. I do not know if it was before or after the father's death that the family came to London, but my mother was very little at the time. She had, however, been born in Leeds, and her first interweaving of lies and truth that I have found in print clings to this origin while obliterating her subsequent London history. A 1927 clipping from the *Star* recounts that Miss Sheilah Graham, the chorus girl understudy who had gone on for Mimi Crawford in *One Dam Thing After Another*, "told a . . . reporter that she was born in Leeds and came to London only two years ago." A more detailed story in the *Yorkshire Observer* further elaborates: "I am a native of Headingley [my mother is quoted as saying] where my father, the late Mr. L. Graham, lived in retirement. I never had any schooling but stayed at home to nurse my mother who was an invalid. At seventeen I was an orphan and found myself looking out for something to do."

Calling herself an orphan, my mother suppressed both the orphanage that had provided her schooling and her actual family: the father and mother (Ruby was as ignorant as I of their names), the siblings—Esther, Sally, Henry, Meyer, and Morris. It was the siblings, particularly the three brothers about whom I knew so little, whom Ruby now brought alive for me. Our Uncle Henry, the brother known to me only as the one who had beaten my mother senseless after she hit her mother, became a successful tailor with his own shop in London and "the odd bit of property" here and there before eventually emigrating to South Africa. Uncle Morris, the youngest brother, held positions as a buyer in the tailoring departments of Simpson's of Piccadilly and Lillywhites and finally had his own ladies' dress shop in Southend. Uncle Morris, Ruby assured me, was a gentleman. He spoke so well. You'd imagine he had gone to the best schools. He sounded like an Oxford-educated gentleman.

Both Henry and Morris had died in the fifties, survived by the renegade brother, Meyer, the one who had betrayed my mother to the *Sunday Express.* He had sent to the paper a photo of the family on the beach at Brighton. It got blown up and then you could recognize my mother. I recalled that he was the brother who had taken my mother with him on thieving expeditions when they were children.

I was especially interested in Morris. He and my mother had been together in the orphanage. Was it a coincidence that these were the two members of that family who learned best how to "pass" in the world? What had been the role of the orphanage in the forming of their aspirations? I tried to think about the intersection of the orphanage, the Jewishness, and also the historical time and place of their childhood—England during World War I. It seemed reductive to explain their behavior in these terms. But what else did I have to go on? Ruby, speaking of her own six miserable years in the orphanage, stressed that you didn't trust people or feel too connected with them once you had been in such a place, and I felt that she had told me something about my mother. The Englishness, the Jewishness, the orphanage, the shame and aspirations, the lying that had begun so early—these were the pieces of my puzzle, the strands of yarn that I sought to weave into a fabric of adequate understanding.

My cousin also confirmed what I had already deduced through my own sleuthing, that the legendary "orphanage"— why had I never thought to ask my mother its name?—was the Jews Hospital and Orphan Asylum in the southeast section of London known as Norwood. Looking under the heading of "orphanages" in the Jewish Yearbook of 1910 (which I consulted in a local history library in the East End of London), I had eliminated the other entries: The Spanish and Portuguese Jews Hospital and Orphan Asylum in Mile End Road, the Jews Temporary Shelter in Leman Street, the Jewish Home in Shepherd's Bush (too far west). That left Norwood, and I was excited to learn that in the Mocatta Library, an Anglo-Jewish collection at University College, London, a number of this institution's records had been preserved.

Thus, on a sunny but blustery June day, six months after I had attended the meeting to honor Professor Sir Alfred Ayer in the auditorium directly across the street, I found myself making my way to a back room of University College's main library. I had an appointment with Mr. Munk, the Mocatta Library archivist, who soon had placed before me a reassuringly substantial pile of documents.

Norwood, I gathered, had been an important institution.

The Jews Hospital and the Jews Orphan Asylum, founded respectively in 1807 and 1831, had moved to the Norwood location in 1863 (the main building was a landmark for miles around) and merged in 1876. At the time my mother entered it in 1910, Norwood was the largest Anglo-Jewish institution in the country. In 1918, the year that she left, Captain de Rothschild was elected its president. Of the Norwood documents listed in the Mocatta Library catalogue, I now had the following before me:

> List of Applicants, 1901–1903
> Sulking and Punishment Book—girls punished
>   for sulking, 1913–1915
> Monthly Register of Girls' Conduct,
>   1905–1915
> List of English and Hebrew Prizewinners,
>   1898–1910
> Headmaster's Scrapbook, 1910–1918

What could seem more unexceptional than this expression of interest in family history? I explained in a matter-of-fact way to Mr. Munk that I was looking for my mother's name in the records of her orphanage. I did not explain that for the first thirteen years of my life I knew nothing about this orphanage, and that subsequently it assumed for me such mythic proportions that any concrete facts about it, even its name, seemed quite irrelevant. It occurred to me to wonder what my mother would have thought if she had seen me there in the archives of the Mocatta Library, the documents of the Norwood orphanage spread before me, using the skills of my academic training to learn about her past, to fill in the facts and names and dates. It's possible that she might have felt exposed, but I don't think so. I think she would have liked the attention. Then too, she was always so enthusiastic about "research." It was something she admired, and then hired other people to do for her. But I was not trying to please or impress my mother. I needed something for myself, even if I wasn't quite sure what it was. Information. Insight. Perhaps just the knowledge that I had carried my search as far as possible before admitting its essential failure.

Of the documents before me, it seemed sensible to begin with the List of Applicants, 1901–1903. My mother's name would not be on this, but I hoped to learn something about applicants of her era. Children were "elected" to the orphanage, the same word, strangely, that was used in connection with Freddie's admission to Eton. The records gave particulars for each candidate and then the outcome—admission or rejection. Eight-year-old Barnet Abrahams, for example, had been rejected. Despite an invalid father who was unable to work, five children, aged ten, eight, six, four, and three, dependent on a mother with no occupation, the family receiving an allowance from the Jewish Board of Governors, his case was deemed "less urgent than so many others." Davis Bloom, with father dead, seven children dependent on mother, mother taking in lodgers, one brother a tailor's, another a cabinetmaker's apprentice, had gained admission. As had Louisa Rosenthal: father insane, six children dependent on needlewoman mother. The pattern repeatedly was the large family, the father dead or invalided or mad, the mother unemployed or working as a laundress, a hawker, a needlewoman, a charwoman. Very few of the children seemed to lack both parents, so it would seem that my mother had not been unusual in having a living mother. When children were rejected, it was because their cases were judged relatively unurgent or because medical grounds existed on which to turn them down: tuberculosis, a slight curvature of the spine, a defective heart, "a remarkable condition of venous obstructions in both thighs," rickets, or squinting. Thank God my mother had not been a squinter. I began to feel positively elated that her application had been successful.

Eager to look for her name, I turned to the Sulking and Punishment Book, 1913–15. My mother would have been nine to eleven in these years. I wondered if I would find her. Sulkers were listed alphabetically, and I looked under S. Here was Annie Spiegel, age twelve, who had sulked when corrected in class and as a punishment lost monitor's privileges for a week and been ordered to bed with the little girls "since she behaves like one." And Lily Symmonds, a two-entry offender, branded "sulky, lazy and incurable" and deprived of all forthcoming treats. Worse still was Rebecca Summer, sulking whenever spoken to, showing a "horrid temper," and banned from taking part in any of the arrangements for the forthcoming holidays. And Fanny Shapiro, who had sulked in class "for no reason whatsoever." But there was no Lily Shiel. My mother had not been a sulker. I might perhaps have known that without even opening the book.

It interested me that sulking, above all else, should be the crime. Minnie Fox, coming into line late and told that she would have to write an imposition, "immediately sulked." Hilda Bluestone, reprimanded for repeatedly breaking her glasses, "sulked for a week." The punishments then were ones of deprivation and humiliation: mealtime or bedtime with the little girls; no treats during Purim; cancellation of holidays. Most disturbing to me was the sadistic energy that seemed to go into the description of each child's depravity, a zeal I also sensed in reading the Monthly Register of Girls' Conduct, 1905–15. Here children, identified by number rather than name, gained a monthly mark against them for such lapses as Fighting, Rudeness, Disobedience, Neglect of Duty, Laziness, Untidiness, and Deceit. Occasionally the monotony of these recurring words would be broken by the appearance, often in a new hand, of a new word—Slyness, Greediness, Shrieking, Untruthfulness—or a less generic offense—breaking sister's spectacles, spoiling dress. The register had columns marked "Very Sat.," "Sat.," "Unsat.," "Very Unsat.," but these were ignored in the obsession with misconduct alone.

It occurred to me to wonder whether children were treated differently at Eton. Wasn't I encountering a notion of "discipline" that was culturally pervasive, a widespread late-Victorian voyeuristic zeal in sniffing out the badness of the young? To suggest, however, that Eton was in respects no better than

Norwood seemed too denying of the social gulf between them. For one thing, at Eton they did not shave the children's heads for lice.

I still had not found my mother when I turned to the Head-master's Scrapbook, 1910–1918. Now truly the differences be-tween the Jews Hospital and Orphan Asylum and the most self-congratulatory public school in the land began to blur. The scrapbook was a fascinating compilation of items: of grateful letters from alumni looking back with thanks and praise and nostalgia to "my dear old Norwood" as they moved into jobs as tailor's or milliner's apprentices or clerks or workers in facto-ries; of concerts and prize day programs; of descriptions of the Norwood meal plan and the best means of introducing por-ridge for breakfast; of plans to organize a 1914 "reunion for Old Boys" or summer holidays at Margate; of the questions on the Hebrew exam conducted by the headmaster (write a brief life of Maimonides; give an account of the expulsion of the Jews from England); of the English literature read by "boys of the top class" *(David Copperfield,* a biography of Napoleon, *The Last Days of Pompeii,* Lamb's *Tales from Shakespeare, The Cricket on the Hearth, From Log Cabin to White House).*

What struck me most forcibly was that Norwood indeed took the public school as its model, and also that its Jewishness did not pervade the whole institution. Certainly the Jewishness was there. The students studied Hebrew and observed the holi-days. But so consistently it seemed set apart, I would say almost forgotten, in the equally strong thrust towards assimilation. One 1912 "Election Day" program, which serves to illustrate this point, began with a unison song, "Oh Peaceful England," followed by "Farmer's Autumn Song," in which the children acted "the harvest of oats and wheat and barley," and then a recitation, "Fairies to the Rescue." Occasionally such programs would include a Jewish song, but not always. Predominantly their emphasis was bucolic, fanciful, and patriotic (the British Grenadiers or the defeat of the Spanish Armada time and time again). And every program, whether it was for a prize day, election day, sports day, or simply a "gramophone concert," ended with "God Save the King."

I began to have a sense, almost as if I were living it myself, of how a bright child, betrayed by family and circumstance and cast into this orphanage, might form an idea of the English world she wanted to be part of, that it would seem possible to be part of. But she would know that in order to join it, she needed to leave poverty and Jewishness behind.

Still, after five hours of reading through the documents, I had not yet glimpsed my mother directly. She was not a sulker. She was not yet in the years covered by the Headmaster's Scrapbook an alumna, and I doubt in any case if she would have written one of those letters about Norwood being "such a splendid home." In 1918, the year the scrapbook ended, my mother would have been fourteen and in her last year in the orphanage. She had always boasted that she was top of the school. If I were to find her, it seemed to me it would be as a student leader mentioned in connection with some of the programs.

I started looking at names more carefully. And there she was. The year that Meyer Fogel, Norwood's first "Holt Scholar," accepted a scholarship to go on from the orphanage to a public school, from which he wrote back to the headmaster, Mr. Kaiser, how he had "dropped into [his] place with great ease and met fine fellows," there several times was my mother's name, though confusingly spelt Shael, not Shiel. The program for a cricket tournament listed Lily Shael as one of the team captains. On the list of 1917–18 Lectures, while M. Fogel spoke on the Wonders of Transport, L. Shael's topic was Elizabeth Barrett Browning. In the cast of characters for "A Ladden and Out, 1918," L. Shael, future West End chorus girl, played the character of So Shy. And there she was again in one of the concert programs, singing "The Pigtail and the Fan." Finally, I found her name, this time spelt Shiel not Shael, in a letter sent to Mr. Kaiser by Gertrude E. Spielmann, a member of the

Governing Board, to thank "you and Mrs. Kaiser, Miss Good-
win, Miss Blond, and Jack Diamond and Lily Shiel" for the
get-well letters that had moved her so deeply.

I had found her. Lily Shael. Lily Shiel. Was she playing with
her name even then, changing a vowel for a more refined and Ger-
manic effect? Orphanage programs printed Shael, but she had
written to Mrs. Spielmann as Shiel. As always, she eluded me.

Still, I had passed those hours reading through the Norwood archives, and the experience felt like my own rite of passage. I had been an applicant for admission, hoping to pass the
medical exam and not to be rejected as a squinter; I had been a
child eluding the labels of sulking and deceit, a Hebrew
scholar, a reciter of poems about the Spanish armada, a taster of
the nearly inedible morning porridge, a head girl named Lily
preparing a talk on Elizabeth Barrett Browning or being chosen as student representative to write a letter to a convalescent
member of the Governing Board. Gerold Frank, in working
with my mother on *Beloved Infidel,* had made a note: "We need
characters, anecdotes, people—adults, children—for your
childhood. Otherwise you grow up in a vacuum." Yes, hadn't
the world around my mother always been a kind of vacuum?
Even when we knew the other players, her mythic figure muted
and obscured them. Time and place and other people were
always just the backdrop to her extraordinary act of self-creation. But I now had filled in the vacuum, at least a little. I had
gone looking for my mother in her orphanage, eager to know
what I could about her, to have factual, specific, unmediated
knowledge, to track her and to pin her down. I had gone looking for the child who grew up to do the things she did, to lead
her life and be my mother, to create Sheilah Graham and her
daughter, Wendy, to care for me and to betray me. And I had
found the figure I was looking for. I had glimpsed her as she
existed at the outset of the story, before there even was a story,
though I'm sure it was forming in her mind. I had touched and
been touched by something real. It seemed an act of recovery.

ENVOI

I WENT BACK RECENTLY to Southern California, where I had not been for twenty-two years. As my plane crossed the starkly brown San Gabriel mountains and began a twilight descent into that vast Los Angeles valley, I thought of the passage in the first chapter of *The Last Tycoon* where Fitzgerald describes how his movie tycoon hero Stahr had flown up "very high to see," and "beating his wings tenaciously . . . had stayed up there longer than most of us" before "settling to earth" with the memory of his vision. The chapter ends as the airplane Stahr is now traveling on, returning from the East, comes down into the warm California darkness. I imagined how my mother must have felt, arriving here for the first time in 1936, her whole career as a Hollywood columnist still before her, looking down at the mountains and the valley and wondering what adventures lay ahead. But above all, I had my own memories. I had flown back here from our family trips abroad, from boarding school, later occasionally from college, returning to my California, to my mother's house, to the vistas that always surprised me after the dense greenness of the East: the arid sweep of desert and mountains and sea, a scenery of palm trees and dusky eucalyptuses. This was where I came from, though it took being back here to remember the connection, to know that the curve of a stretch of coastline or the feel of the cool, high-skied, cricket-filled nights was more achingly familiar than any place known since.

I wanted to see our old house, and I decided to drive there from where I was staying in Santa Monica. I would go not the short way along Wiltshire, but the way our family always liked best when traveling between the beach and home, the winding scenic route along Sunset. I drove north on the Pacific Coast Highway to the spot, just south of Wylie's Bait Shop, where Sunset intersects with it. Here I turned right, leaving the coast. So much was as I remembered it: Will Rogers State Park on the left, the housing development on the right that way back had been a polo field, every twist and turn of the eucalyptus-lined road. I saw the sign for Mandeville Canyon, a name I hadn't thought of since last I passed this spot, yet so sharply, so resonantly familiar. Hadn't Don Defoe, Ozzie's neighbor on *The Ozzie and Harriet Show,* lived down Mandeville Canyon?—I had played at his house with a daughter named Penny.

Soon I was approaching the Bel Air West gate, where we used to turn to mount the hill to Bel Air Town and Country. I considered detouring but decided against it. On I went, through Brentwood and Westwood, past UCLA and the signs for Beverly Glen. Blue signs with yellow lettering announced the roadside sale of maps of star homes. Weren't these the same signs (though the maps must have changed) that I had passed on the daily drive home from school? Now I was curving into Beverly Hills, reading, almost chanting to myself, the familiar litany of street names: Whittier, Rodeo, Crescent, Rexford, Alpine, Foothill, Elm. Elm with its palm trees was the street before Maple. I made the right turn onto Maple, driving beneath the familiar arch of gnarled trees—whatever they were, they weren't maples—down the 700 block and into the 600s.

Robert, who set his detective novels in Beverly Hills and

had come here to do research, had warned me what to expect. Our house, he told me, was so altered he was sure I would drive right by it if I didn't pay careful attention to the numbers. True, the new circular driveway and cluttered landscaping (a row of ficus trees distracting from the lines of the old magnolia) as well as the house's current beige color did a lot to camouflage the 607 North Maple Drive I had known. But the house was recognizable. Or so I decided, as I backed up my car, having indeed driven by, and parked along the curb. It was then that I noticed the open windows and doors and all the workmen. 607 North Maple Drive was under complete renovation. Getting out of the car, I walked up to two Hispanic workmen seated in the open front doorway and explained why I would like to take a look inside. I'm not sure that they understood me, but since no one objected, I proceeded past them, past the familiar heavy carved oak door and into the house that had haunted me ever since I left it as my life's central symbol of substance and ephemerality, of paradise and paradise lost.

The house had been enlarged and greatly altered since we lived there, but its features that remained the same had far stronger resonance for me than the changes. The sunken living room (slightly expanded on one side) still existed as a wing off the main two-story structure. Its four French doors had been replaced by newer French doors, but the room retained the same basic design. Upstairs my bedroom seemed about two-and-a-half times its former size, but one wall and window were in their former location, and as I had so often done in childhood, I could look out the window onto the red tile roof of the living room. I could also see the annex over the garage that my mother had built as Bow Wow's office. Crossing the upstairs hallway into my mother's bedroom, I noted that this was the least-changed room in the house—it even had the old window frames. It was such a little thing, but I was very pleased to see those window frames unaltered.

After about half an hour of wandering through the house

and backyard (which now had a swimming pool), it seemed time to leave, or rather I had the sense that it would be time to leave if I weren't so loathe to lose the access by walking out the door. The house cast a kind of spell on me. It was astir with the workmen yet at the same time preternaturally still. Reluctantly, I bent my steps towards the front doorway. I walked past the two men, now plastering in the marble-floored front hall—in my day this had been red tile—out the doorway, down the circular driveway, and back to my car. Then just as I was about to get in and drive away, a Mercedes pulled up behind me and the driver got out, a well-dressed middle-aged man. We were standing a few feet apart in the road.

"Is this your house?" I asked him. The answer was yes. This was Mr. Abrishami, who had just bought the house, he told me, from the Abelsons and was renovating it from top to bottom. I explained to him what I was doing there, and he assured me that he had heard of Sheilah Graham, though I half suspected that he hadn't and was only being polite. We talked a few minutes, and then I left.

I was very happy to have met Mr. Abrishami. The encounter seemed to rescue my house, to rescue me from the realm of dreams, from the ahistoricity of myth, and to give me a link with the future. Mr. Abrishami would live at 607 North Maple Drive with his wife and three small children, just as we had lived there thirty years earlier with our mother. This had been my house, and now it was his. Perhaps his children would go to the Hawthorne School on Rexford. I drove by that too and saw the large number of Arab and Persian children in the playground. I had a reassuring feeling of continuities, of my own place in a larger whole.

"I'm proud of you for surviving your mother," said Emily to me recently.

"What do you mean?" I asked, struck by the starkness of her vision.

"Well, it wasn't easy. Your mother was very hard on you. And you survived her."

I wondered what qualities Emily saw in me when she said this. Was it simply that I had held things together and shown the studied equilibrium in which anger was so well repressed that Dee had counted on when she told me about Freddie? Or was it better than that—some strength and achievement of self in the face of another's powerful effort to make me a piece of her story?

Reclaiming myself from my mother's fictions—that has been my ongoing struggle; that is what finding Freddie has enabled me to do so dramatically. I am still my mother's daughter, but my birth now seems less an act of parthenogenesis. It may sound fanciful, but I can feel Freddie's genes in me in a way I never did Trevor's, and I have a new sense—you might call it *my* new fiction—of being the daughter of a mother *and* a father, hence a person with two strands of heritage reaffirming a separate self. I am not my own ancestor, but now I have a pair of ancestors. I am the daughter of Sheilah Graham and Freddie Ayer. To know this, to have discovered it as I did, makes me somehow more securely myself.

I like in my mind to mate them, my complicated, vital progenitors. Both philanderers, if the word can be extended to women, both Jewish yet alienated from their Jewish heritage, they were the most charming of egotists and ebullient of survivors. I have used the word "ordinary" in my summing-up of Freddie, but truly neither of them seems to me very ordinary. Their talents aside, they believed in themselves in a way that was extraordinary, that you could say was quite monstrous. It was at other people's expense; it was certainly at my expense. Yet it still heartens me to be their daughter. And I admire them both.

Neither accomplished all that seemed possible. My mother wanted to be a serious writer, thought perhaps she could be, but never even tried. Freddie too had his regrets. "Do you think that Freddie was disappointed?' asked the philosopher Ronald Dworkin.

"Why?" I countered.

"He fell out of fashion," Dworkin replied.

I recall Freddie's wistful statement to me that he would be remembered for a book he had written at twenty-five. I remember my mother so often talking about what she might have done if only she had had a proper education. Yet whatever their disappointments, they both kept going, with exuberance, with élan, with success, without self-pity.

It was Emily, even before I did, who knew that I would write this story. I had just told her and Sean about Freddie rather than Trevor being my father, but the person who was central in our thoughts was neither my old father nor the new one. "You'll get back at her," said Emily.

"I'm not sure that's what I need to do," I replied. "But what do you have in mind?"

"You'll write about it," said Emily. "Don't you see? That's your legacy. She wrote all those books about herself. But this is the story she didn't tell. She left it for you."